W9-AOP-696

HISPANICS IN THE MORMON ZION, 1912–1999

Number Twenty-two:
Elma Dill Russell Spencer Series
in the West and Southwest

HISPANICS IN THE
MORMON ZION

1912–1999

Jorge Iber

TEXAS A&M UNIVERSITY PRESS

College Station

Library of Congress Cataloging-in-Publication Data

Iber, Jorge, 1961–
      Hispanics in the Mormon Zion, 1912–1999 / Jorge Iber.
          p.   cm.—(Elma Dill Russell Spencer series in the West and
      Southwest; no. 22)
      Includes bibliographical references and index.
      ISBN 0-89096-933-7 (cloth)
          1. Hispanic Americans—Cultural assimilation—Utah.   2. Hispanic
      Americans—Utah—Religion.   3. Utah—Ethnic relations.   I. Title.
      II. Series.
      F835.S75 I24   2000
      305.8680792—dc21
      99-054608

CONTENTS

ILLUSTRATIONS

PREFACE

In March of 1998, after I had presented a paper entitled "Los Nuevos Pioneros: The Genesis of a Hispanic Community in Salt Lake City, Utah, 1912–1939," several colleagues approached me and expressed utter amazement that a cluster of Spanish speakers existed in one of the "whitest" states in the union.[1] I assured my astonished peers that not only did northern Utah have such communities, but they were growing, vibrant, and diverse. A recent article in the state's most important newspaper, the *Salt Lake Tribune*, noted that in 1997 Hispanics[2] accounted for almost 117,000 (or about 6 percent) of Utah's inhabitants and pumped almost $1.4 billion (after taxes) into the state's economy.[3]

By the middle 1990s Spanish-speaking men and women lived in all of Utah's major cities and towns, working in tourist, industrial, and service-related occupations. John Medina, head of the Utah Coalition of La Raza, recently noted that the owner of a Chinese restaurant in Ogden told him, "I have nearly all Hispanic employees—they are the best damn workers." Doug Jex, research director for the Utah Department of Community and Economic Development, asserted that the state's vibrant economy during the 1990s provided a partial explanation for the dramatic growth of this population. "The tight labor market . . . and the depressed economy in California have contributed to the growth of the Hispanic population. And there has been an increase in wages in jobs where many Hispanics work." In addition to laborers filling lower skilled and service sector jobs, many Spanish-surnamed professionals were moving into the area. In response, national retailing chains such as Sears and the more upscale Nordstrom now advertise in the pages of *La Prensa* and *Mundo Hispano,* Spanish-language newspapers in Salt Lake City.[4]

Although these *comunidades* (communities) are growing and prospering to a certain extent, this does not mean that northern Utah is devoid of ethnic and racial tensions. At a recent town meeting in fashionable Park City, Shelley Weiss, founder of a group called Conexión Amigo (Friendly Connection), noted that many white parents in this wealthy town are disturbed and irritated by the presence of "Mexican" children in "their" schools. "Angry parents said,

'Our schools are going to hell. Our kids' education is being compromised. That's why we left Southern California.'"[5]

While some wealthy whites may not want their children mixing and sharing classroom space with the sons and daughters of those who wait on them at restaurants; clean their toilets, homes, and cars; and cook their food, affluent Hispanics are also susceptible to racism, bigotry, and stereotyping. The case of Ronald Molina is instructive in this regard. Molina, a certified public accountant from Miami, moved into a quarter-million-dollar residence in an upscale development of Heber City (Wasatch County) in 1991.[6] Molina had specifically sought a locale where he could get away from the hectic activities of business life in southern Florida and enjoy a more peaceful and laid-back lifestyle. He soon realized that the size of his bank account and his connections to the corporate elite back in Miami did not immunize him from scrutiny and suspicion. "Molina quickly noticed that he was . . . being watched by strangers. At one point he approached an unknown observer parked at the bottom of the hill in his circle, looking through binoculars at the house. Then, over the next year, Molina's garbage was frequently removed from his property; obviously shuffled through leaving ripped garbage bags on the street. Additionally, UPS packages had holes poked in them on delivery. Molina also claims that on several occasions he noticed someone looking in the windows of his house."[7]

On September 6, 1994, members of the Wasatch Area Drug Enforcement Network (WADEN) and other agencies (the Wasatch County sheriffs and Heber City police) executed a search warrant at the Molina household. They ransacked the house and accused the owner of being a drug dealer. While officials did discover drug paraphernalia and "a small amount of green substance" in his son's room, they did not uncover evidence that warranted Molina's apparent classification as the "Scarface" of Heber Valley. The Molina family's attorney claimed that his client's ethnic background was the principal reason for the initial suspicions by police. Since he was "Hispanic, from Miami, and had money, the police considered him a 'drug dealer' and . . . therefore undesirable."[8]

As the brief anecdote reveals, by the late 1990s the Spanish speakers of northern Utah faced both obstacles (such as racism and stereotyping) and opportunities (a growing number of service-sector jobs) similar to those encountered by their counterparts in other parts of the American West and Southwest. But while in many ways similar, the historical and social milieu of the Beehive State is not identical to other locations. In the heart of the Mormon Zion religious faith and denominational affiliation have played a crucial role in the genesis, development, and expansion of this comunidad. Scholars of Mexican American/Chicano/Latino history have not examined this facet of *colonia*[9] life in great detail. In his seminal work, *Becoming Mexican American: Ethnicity, Culture and Identity in Chicano Los Angeles, 1900–1945,* George J. Sánchez noted that "the relationship between ethnicity and religion is still a relatively unexplored area for historical research, particularly in Chicano history."[10] This book will help fill in part of this lacuna in historical knowledge.

The late 1970s and early 1980s witnessed the rise to prominence of Chicano scholars such as Albert Camarillo, Richard Griswold del Castillo, Ricardo Romo, and Mario T. García.[11] These scholars marked the beginning of a new era in Chicano historiography, one that moved beyond the internal colonialism model of Chicano-Anglo relations.[12] Instead of presenting this history in overly simplistic terms, such as Rodolfo Acuña did in his 1972 edition of *Occupied America: The Chicano's Struggle Toward Liberation,* this new generation of historians "showed the variation and nuances in the larger context of inequality that marked relations between Anglos and people of Mexican origin."[13]

These studies detail the discrimination, segregation, and labor segmentation that limited social and economic mobility of colonia members. Richard Griswold del Castillo and Albert Camarillo, in particular, effectively demonstrate how the replacement of pastoralism by North America's market-driven economy after the Mexican American War led to a sharp decline in the social and economic standing of many California Chicanos.[14] The organizations and mechanisms used for survival in the Anglo-dominated world were also examined in these manuscripts.[15] The segregated neighborhoods that these men, women, and children inhabited were not simply open-air warehouses of human misery, want, and despair. The barrios of Los Angeles, Santa Barbara, Santa Ana, and El Paso birthed and nurtured mutual aid societies, churches and religious groups, and other organizations that helped reinforce identity, community spirit, and cultural traditions of these individuals.[16]

These histories also detail internal differences that existed among the Spanish-surnamed population. Whereas some previous scholars viewed Chicano history as "a collective experience," the works published by Camarillo and others focused on intragroup differences in class, cultural continuity, group size, location, density, and responses to American economic domination.[17] In sum, the history of this population in the conquered territory (and elsewhere) is not monolithic; "class differences have been compounded by generational change, cultural variations, attitudinal diversity, and differing notions of ethnic ideology."[18]

Although in many ways pathbreaking, these histories tell only part of the story of colonia life in the United States. In the final pages of his important 1990 essay, "Recent Chicano Historiography: An Interpretive Essay," Alex M. Saragoza points out several facets of Chicano history that future generations of writers in the field would need to address. Among these Saragoza cited the necessity of detailing the impact of "American culture and ideology" on barrio inhabitants. "On this point, the current discussion among historians of the influence of advertising, the mass media, fashion, consumerism, and related issues holds important possibilities for examining the sources, as well as the consequences, of the ideological variation among Chicanos, particularly after 1940."[19] Since the publication of Saragoza's essay, several works have addressed some of these issues. Most notable among the scholars mining this vein of the Chicano experience are George J. Sánchez, Vicki L. Ruiz, Manuel P. Peña, and David Reyes and Tom Waldman.[20]

In addition to examining cultural and ideological influences, Saragoza suggested that Chicano scholars transcend geographic lines. There are colonias in almost every part of the United States; the barrios of California and Texas do not make up the totality of Mexicano and Mexican American experience. How have the lives of Spanish speakers been affected by "the specific texture of American society" in various sections of the nation?[21] Erasmo Gamboa, Zaragosa Vargas, Juan R. García, and Félix Padilla, among others, have pointed toward an examination of cities such as Detroit, Chicago, Milwaukee, and Saint Louis and regions such as the Midwest and the Pacific Northwest with newer and smaller colonias.[22]

A significant step toward a more thorough and complete understanding of the various aspects of colonia life was taken in 1989 with the publication of Arnoldo De León's *Ethnicity in the Sunbelt: A History of Mexican Americans in Houston.* De León does not contradict the major conclusions drawn by previous historians. Patterns of labor segmentation, discrimination, and limited social and economic mobility are clearly evident in Houston. However, by presenting various divisions within the community, as well as locating his study in a city with a "newer" colonia, De León effectively argues for a shift in Chicano historiography. De León's work demonstrates the value of portraying barrio life as far more complex than a simple "homogenous Mexican community ('us') versus white society ('them, the Anglos') dichotomy."[23]

Although Saragoza outlined an ample and ambitious agenda for new research, one topic seemingly overlooked as worthy of study was religion—in particular, the impact of conversion upon the lives of Spanish-surnamed people. Since the late 1960s a growing body of scholarly work has scrutinized the social and personal significance of devotional transformation among millions of *creyentes* (believers) in Mexico, Guatemala, El Salvador, Ecuador, and Brazil.[24] While the list of works on this topic by scholars of Latin America is multiplying, the subject has generated little interest and enthusiasm among historians of the Mexicano and Mexican American experience.

One of the few historians examining linkages between religious belief and ethnic identity among Spanish speakers in the United States is Timothy M. Matovina. In his 1995 work, *Tejano Religion and Ethnicity: San Antonio, 1821–1860,* Matovina asserts that religion and religious celebrations are an "essential component of ethnic identity" and that Tejanos used Catholic rituals as a tool of resistance against Anglo domination in pre–Civil War San Antonio. While local elites created what David Montejano terms a "peace structure" with Anglos in Bexar (through intermarriage and other social and commercial linkages), this did not mean that large numbers of Spanish speakers surrendered important aspects of their culture (such as religious affiliation) under new social and commercial realities.[25] One of the most significant contributions of Matovina's study lies in his examination of the important roles played by priests in these patterns of resistance. Matovina's monograph details that some Tejanos did convert to Protestantism, but the overwhelming majority of Hispanic men and women used their Catholicity as a "cultural and religious mechanism to express their own ethnic legitimation."[26] Social scientists Ana María Díaz-Stevens and Anthony M. Stevens-Arroyo reaffirm this conclusion (within a twentieth-century context) in their 1998 work *Recognizing the Latino Resurgence in U.S. Religion: The Emmaus Paradigm* by stating, "we view religious tradition as a constituent element of Latino identity because it has provided the organization and the institution upon which a sense of peoplehood was built."[27]

Another vital source for understanding the use of Catholic ritual and belief as a tool in contesting Anglo domination is the three-volume series *The Notre Dame History of Hispanic Catholics in the United States.*[28] In the first manuscript of this collection Gilbert Hinojosa examines twentieth-century manifestations of issues raised by Matovina. Hinojosa contends that it is impossible to understand the relationship between the Mexican American community and the Catholic Church without examining the "faith of the community and their popular ritual expressions . . . and their response to and participation in official ecclesial initiative and worship."[29] The work also focuses on the legacies of individual priests and their service and ties to various barrios, examines relations between Catholic Spanish speakers and Protestant missionaries, and spotlights the role of the church in seeking greater social justice for Mexican Americans (especially after the start of the *cursillo* [little course] movement in the United States in the late 1950s).[30]

Over the past eight decades colonia members in northern Utah have encountered a peculiar "texture of American society," and this, in turn, has impacted on the community's development. These Spanish-surnamed individuals comprise a small percentage of the area's population and, more significantly, live in a location where Catholics are a distinct minority. The Spanish-speaking cluster in northern Utah has assumed patterns different from counterparts in other parts of the American West and Southwest. Rather than being compacted, the community is fairly well dispersed: there are no heavy concentrations in large and distinct barrios. In addition, the comunidad is relatively new, with the majority of the American-born Spanish speakers arriving (from New Mexico and Colorado) after 1940 and substantial numbers of Latin Americans migrating since the 1960s. This means that the Spanish-surnamed populace of northern Utah in certain ways does not fit the generational model described by Richard A. Garcia in his important 1991 work, *Rise of the Mexican American Middle Class: San Antonio, 1929–1941*.[31]

Garcia's study describes a community that, during the first three decades of the twentieth century, had a great deal of economic and philosophical diversity (with the presence of exiled *ricos,* a developing middle class and a large working class). Between 1912 and 1930 there were occupational differences extant within the northern Utah Spanish-speaking group, but the titanic struggle between the ideological positions of *lo mexicano* (embraced by the ricos) and *lo americano* (supported by the emerging middle class) that took place in San Antonio did not exist in northern Utah. In some ways this led to a degree of unity: most Spanish speakers were poor, lived in the same parts of Salt Lake City and Ogden, and worked at low-skilled, low-paying occupations. But, as stated earlier, the issue of denominational affiliation is of vital importance in telling the history of this comunidad. In this cluster religious difference is the primary fault line. Missionary efforts by the Church of Jesus Christ of Latter-day Saints (the LDS Church) have created a sizable number of converts among Spanish speakers, and those who convert live a different history than do those Spanish-surnamed men, women, and children who retain their ties to the Catholic Church.[32]

This study will consider the years 1912–99 with particular emphasis on the post–World War II period. It will survey the process of community formation and development and trace the changes that have occurred over the past eight decades. Specifically, the following issues will be addressed: 1) social, cultural, and economic diversity among Spanish speakers and changes in the colonia's structure over time; 2) differentiation of assimilation and acculturation patterns among cluster members; and 3) the relationships of various Spanish-surnamed groups to each other and to the wider society. This work will examine the most unique feature of this community: the presence of a large number of LDS Hispanics. With the creation of a Mexican branch (called the Rama Mexicana) in the 1920s, the LDS Church has made a concerted effort to be a presence in the community. This has led to a colonia that, by the 1990s, is highly diversified in its religious and other beliefs.

The sources relating to Utah's Hispanics can be attributed primarily to one individual, Vicente Mayer.[33] During the early 1970s Mayer, and a few graduate students at the University of Utah, produced short, empirical works that broadly frame the history of the state's largest minority group. Their most important contribution, however, is a collection of approximately one hundred interviews with Spanish speakers from all sectors of society. These oral histories provide a crucial starting point.[34]

Supplementing these interviews will be information from organizations such as the American G.I. Forum, SOCIO (Spanish-Speaking Organization for Community, Integrity, and Opportunity), Centro de la Familia, Centro Cívico Mexicano, the State Office of Hispanic Affairs, the Utah Hispanic Chamber of Commerce, the Utah Hispanic Yellow Pages, the Utah Coalition of La Raza, records of the Salt Lake Catholic Diocese and the Church of Jesus Christ of Latter-day Saints, unpublished documents, as well as newspapers and journals. There is a paucity of primary materials on this community outside of Utah. The Paul Schuster Taylor Papers at the Bancroft Library at the University of California, Berkeley, contains a few items which describe the circumstances faced by *betabeleros* (beet workers), *mineros* (miners), and *traqueros* (track gang workers) in Utah during the late 1920s. The Chicano Studies Collection at Berkeley also holds some materials from the magazine *La Luz* that briefly examine the history of comunidades in Weber and Carbon Counties. The Mary and Jeff Bell Library at Texas A&M, Corpus Christi, which houses the Dr. Hector P. García Papers, contains information relating to the existence of American G.I. Forum branches in Salt Lake City and Ogden during the middle 1950s.

In sum, this work will use available materials to spotlight successes, failures, trials, tribulations, contributions, and divisions of Hispanics in the Beehive State. The text adds another fragment to the expanding mosaic that is the history of the Spanish-speaking people of the United States.

As with all book-length projects, there are many people who have shared in the completion of this long and arduous task. I would like to thank the individuals who guided this manuscript through the dissertation stage and helped me complete my doctoral work at the University of Utah: Dean L. May, Rebecca Horn, Edward J. Davies, and William Carlisle. Thank you for your commitment, advice, patience, and friendship. To the head of my doctoral committee, Robert Alan Goldberg, thank you for your good humor and encouragement. You went above and beyond the call of duty and were a sincere friend as well as an academic mentor. I treasure your opinion and friendship and hope to be worthy of your trust.

To the various librarians throughout the country who selflessly searched for materials without complaint, my thanks go to Walter Jones, Special Collections at the University of Utah's Marriott Library; Gordon Irving, Church Archives, Historical Department, Church of Jesus Christ of Latter-day Saints; Bernice M. Mooney, archivist for the Salt Lake Catholic Diocese; Lillian Castillo-Speed, head librarian at the Chicano Studies Collection at the University of California, Berkeley; David Kessler and Walter Brem of the Paul S. Taylor Collection at the Bancroft Library, University of California, Berkeley; Grace Charles at the Mary and Jeff Bell Library, Department of Special Collections and Archives, Texas A&M, Corpus Christi; the staff of the State Office of Hispanic Affairs, especially former director Lorena Riffo; and the staff of the Utah State Historical Society, especially *Utah Historical Quarterly* editor Stan Layton.

Several individuals have read parts of this manuscript and provided guidance and criticism. Thanks to: Dean L. May, Robert Alan Goldberg, and Armando Solórzano (all of the University of Utah); Ignacio García of Brigham Young University; Stan Layton; Arnoldo De León of Angelo State University; and Joseph A. Rodríguez of the University of Wisconsin, Milwaukee. Thanks also go to several of my colleagues and friends at Texas Tech University for making my transition from graduate student to assistant professor of history smooth and relatively painless: Alan Kuethe, Jim Reckner, Don Walker, Paul Carlson, Alwyn Barr, Otto Nelson, Les Cullen, Monte Monroe, and the Idaho-bound Mark Barringer.

There are several persons who did not live to see the completion of this manuscript, but without their help and support this work would not have been possible. My mother, Bertha Iber; my grandmother Encarnacion Rodriguez; and my aunt Georgina Lopez all contributed to my personal, spiritual, and professional life. All that is good in me I owe to them; the faults are mine exclusively. All three were women of courage, dignity, and faith who helped my family forge a new life in a new land after being forced out of our native Cuba. Without their love, understanding, and encouragement my life would not be the same.

The final acknowledgment is the most meaningful and heartfelt of all. To my wife, Raquel, who gave up a comfortable professional life in Miami to help me pursue my degree and academic career: I will never be able to repay you for your love, kindness, and patience. I am truly a fortunate man to have such a spouse and partner in my life; thank you for everything.

HISPANICS IN THE MORMON ZION,
1912–1999

1

The Birth of a Colonia

1900–30

The potential of the land that would become the state of Utah has been viewed in different ways by various peoples. The first Europeans to visit the area, Spanish explorers, hoped that this land would prove of value to a dying empire. Later, Mormon settlers envisioned the possibility of building up God's kingdom on earth. Still later, mineral developers saw the opportunity to establish kingdoms of a more worldly nature. The lands of Utah have held great promise, regardless of the observer. The Mexicano and Mexican American laborers who arrived in northern Utah during the early years of the twentieth century were, in this manner, not unlike those who came before. For them Utah, with its mines, railroads, and beet fields, held the hope of economic possibilities. This chapter will explain the economic and other forces that attracted a variety of people to northern Utah and how they shaped the land to their needs. The following questions will be considered: What were the results of Spanish explorations? How did Mormon settlement patterns and Utah's economic development (and its ties to the rest of the United States) impact the area and its people? After these foundations had been laid, how did the Hispanics in this area adapt? What was life like for those Spanish-surnamed men, women, and children who "pioneered" into an area beyond the established line of Spanish/Mexican settlement?

On September 18, 1776, Father Sylvestre Velez de Escalante (who was joined in his travels by Father Francisco Atanasio Domínguez) wrote these glowing terms to describe the area around present-day Jensen, Utah, in the state's northeastern corner: "In the vicinity of these rivers which we crossed today there is good land, and sufficient for planting, and easily irrigated. There are beautiful poplar groves, good pasturage, lumber and timber for three good sized towns."[1] The journal entry detailed a hospitable land seemingly ripe for Spanish colonial expansion. However, the empire lacked the will, ability, and personnel to fulfill the potential these explorers saw. In the same year that these

3

Franciscans traversed these parts, "Juan Bautista de Anza led an expedition from Sonora across the Colorado near Yuma to found the new mission which became San Francisco. . . . With this as a beginning, the dream of a Utah mission weakened and then dissolved in the changing political climate which saw Spanish Louisiana retaken by Napoleon through the secret Treaty of San Idelfonso in 1801 and then sold to the independent nation rising to the east in 1803."[2] The first Spanish-speaking people to enter the lands of what would become Utah merely passed through as travelers.[3] After 1776 Catholic interest in this region would not resurface for almost one hundred years. Anglo settlement would wait until the late 1840s and the blessings of another holy man.

Although Spanish settlement did not follow the Velez-Domínguez expedition, trade with the native peoples of the area did. Initial contacts led to exchanges of slaves, horses, and firearms during the eighteenth and nineteenth centuries. Spanish/Mexican traders and the native people continued a slave trade even after Mormon settlement.[4] As the Mormon pioneers established and then extended their bridgehead in the Salt Lake Valley, the influence of these traders lessened until it completely disappeared.[5]

The Mormon pioneers traveled to the Salt Lake Valley in search of a religious sanctuary. The settlers soon realized that their oasis had limited land, water, and timber. Expansion, therefore, became crucial to support their growing flock. The Saints' communities expanded along two different tracks: the gradual augmentation of settlements both north and south of the Salt Lake Valley; and the creation of colonies, such as Cedar City and Saint George, well beyond the settlement line for production of specific goods.[6] The LDS faithful quickly claimed a growing land base and proposed the creation of the state of Deseret. The colonizers also began construction of what has been labeled a "bootstrap economy." The isolated towns faced two crucial needs, food and transportation, but Brigham Young was determined to limit "trade and commerce with the gentile world."[7] Young and the church hierarchy moved to remedy these problems through the founding of more settlements, the establishment of church organizations that shuttled members to and from Salt Lake City (to improve communication between outposts), and cooperative economic endeavors. These self-help efforts established the agricultural and transportation foundations of Utah. The church's encouragement of local industry, thrift, and "group maneuvers" also served to limit contact with Gentiles.[8]

LDS activity in Utah virtually eliminated the Spanish/Mexican trade, but contacts between the groups did not completely disappear. During the last quarter of the nineteenth century Spanish-surnamed individuals played an important role in the livestock operations of private individuals and LDS Church flocks in southern Utah (as well as tending some of their own sheep).[9]

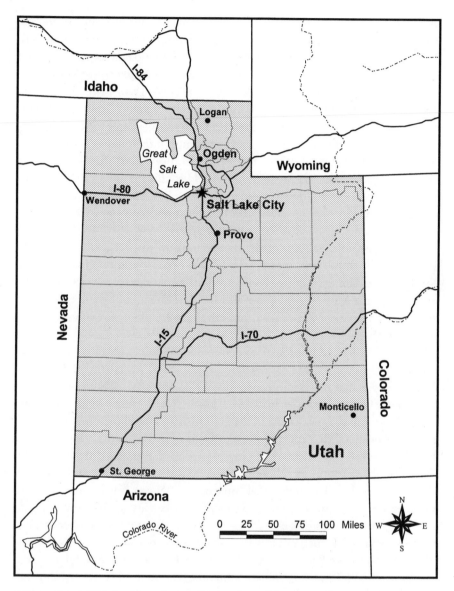

Map 1. State of Utah with major east/west and north/south arteries. *Map by Kevin R. Mulligan*

A small community of northern New Mexicans developed in and around the town of Monticello, and by 1920 their "population was substantial enough to have created several distinct neighborhoods. . . . These newcomers occupied themselves by working their homesteads while also hiring themselves out as cowboys and sheepherders on surrounding ranches in San Juan County. Because of this early presence . . . in Monticello, the town became a gateway for the entrance of hundreds more Hispanos to Utah. As people crossed the border into the state they found . . . warm greetings in their native tongue."[10]

During the last years of the nineteenth century and the first two decades of the twentieth, then, the small number of Hispanics in this area managed to carve out a viable, if not overly prosperous, niche in Utah's rural economy. The community of Spanish speakers grew to a few hundred people by the 1920s, and this settlement served as a gateway for *Nuevo Mexicanos* (New Mexicans) heading to the northern part of the state to look for work. Clearly Monticello represents an important aspect of Utah's Hispanic history; these families brought their "life-cycle customs and liturgical observances" into the southern expanses of the Mormon Zion, but it is the development of the state's industrial base that sparked the creation and development of larger communities to the north.[11]

"The finding and mining of coal, iron ore, and other readily usable materials was stressed from the earliest days of Mormon settlement in the Great Basin, but precious metal mining was usually discouraged. Wealth, specifically gold and silver, was looked upon as a hindrance to progression. Although many Mormons did participate in the gold rush and the church found uses for the precious metal that trickled in from California, the Saints were happy to have the wicked influences of the mining camps far removed from Zion."[12] While Brigham Young and church leaders struggled to keep the influences of the gentile world at bay, individuals such as Col. Patrick Edward Connor and his California Volunteers (who arrived in Salt Lake City in 1862) quickly recognized that opportunities existed for mining in Utah. By September of 1863 Connor reported to his superiors that deposits of gold, silver, and copper existed near Salt Lake City. Between the time of Connor's correspondence and Utah's statehood, Bingham Canyon (and other claims in Big Cottonwood and Little Cottonwood Canyons, Park City, and Tooele County) generated millions of dollars worth of precious metals for investors and attracted thousands of Chinese, Irish, Greek, and Italian miners to the area.[13]

Even before statehood in 1896, events in northern Utah laid the groundwork for the arrival of these and other immigrants. By the 1880s the territorial capital was well connected to the larger national economy. The mining/mineral industry was the linchpin around which Salt Lake City built its position as the preeminent settlement of the territory.[14] Leonard J. Arrington summarized the economic history of early statehood by noting the emergence of commercialized farming, the arrival of national industrial corporations, and the creation of specialized businesses.[15] These enterprises were producing not only for local markets but also for regional and national ones. No longer would the state depend, almost exclusively, upon small-scale agriculture and manufacturing located in Mormon towns. The other sector of Utah's economy, based upon "jerry-built, non-Mormon mining districts," began to take center stage.[16] Utah's location also made it an ideal railroad center between California, the Midwest, and the East Coast. Both Salt Lake City and Ogden would become sites of railroad activities. By the 1910s ties existed with San Francisco, Portland, and Los Angeles, and there were transcontinental links with Chicago, Minneapolis, and Saint Paul.[17]

Rapid development of key sectors before 1910 created an increased demand for unskilled laborers, and many immigrants, including some Spanish speakers, responded. In this regard, northern Utah was little different from other parts of the Southwest and West; Spanish-surnamed people primarily found employment in commercial agriculture, transportation, and mining. A brief examination of the census records shows how this population increased in response to these demands. In 1900 the federal census counted 40 people of Mexican birth in Utah, and by 1910 the number had increased to only 166. The 1920 census reported 1,666 persons of Mexican birth in Utah. Most of these individuals (by a ratio of 2.7 to 1), lived in rural areas, but the state's industrial hubs were beginning to stimulate conditions necessary to foster colonias.[18]

The early *pioneros* (pioneers) to the northern regions of Utah left few written documents relating their daily lives and experiences. Fortunately, during the early 1970s a group of graduate students at the University of Utah set out to record the reminiscences of some of these men and women (this was followed by a second series of interviews conducted by Leslie Kelen during the 1980s).[19] One of these trailblazers was a man named Rafael Torres from Rancho Guerrero, Michoacán, Mexico. Rafael was born in 1901, the son of farmers. His parents, Celso and María, raised corn and a few animals to support their family. Rafael recalled that his early years were filled with hard work helping his father operate the farm. Because of his chores, Rafael did not have the time or the inclination to attend school and so remained illiterate while in Mexico. The coming of the Mexican Revolution in 1910 drastically altered the young boy's life. The family was forced to sell its tools, horses, and livestock in order to flee the fighting. Making matters worse, María became ill and was unable to help Celso make ends meet. Eventually he returned to Rancho Guerrero to attempt the resumption of farming. Unfortunately, all he had left was a small parcel of land; the other implements of his trade were gone. When the fighting resumed in the area the Torres clan left for good.

María died in 1916, and the children were sent to Morelia to be with Celso's extended kin. Both Rafael and his father worked in the nearby mines. It was at this time that Rafael heard about opportunities in the United States. Along with his uncle and seven other men he headed north to El Paso, Texas, in April of 1919. In Juárez they contacted a recruiter, who hired them for the Utah-Idaho Sugar Company. The men labored in the sugar-beet fields of southern Idaho where the pay was meager and the work hard. Rafael recalled that his earnings were only sufficient to keep him alive and that he could not afford to return to Mexico. He and his comrades continued working in agriculture until 1922, when they found work as part of a railroad gang in Kemmerer, Wyoming. These jobs lasted only a brief time, but as part of their severance from the railroad the men were offered passage to their next destination. On the suggestion of one of the group members, they headed for Salt Lake City.[20]

Rafael's endeavors and travels brought him in contact with two of the three industries that would employ the majority of Spanish-surnamed labor in Utah. One of these sectors, the sugar beet industry, began as a result of an LDS Church and private business partnership during the late 1880s.[21] Once the practicability of beet production in this part of Utah was determined, construction began on a four-hundred-thousand-dollar facility in Lehi in late 1890.[22] During the first two decades of the twentieth century the Utah Sugar Company (and later other firms located in the Cache Valley) expanded and established new factories in Utah (as well as in Idaho and Washington state).[23] Beet production dominated Utah agriculture during the 1910s; by 1916 the Beehive State ranked third in the nation in sugar output.[24] In other beet-producing areas of the United States this crop generated a call for stoop labor to block and thin the plants. Utah's experience, however, differed from that of other states. From the earliest days of the industry farmers and their families (Utah's "Mormon boys and young men") performed these backbreaking tasks.[25]

The entire decade of the 1910s was prosperous for the beet processors, but the years of World War I were especially so. The number of acres planted for the Utah-Idaho Sugar Company (the new incarnation of the older Utah Sugar Company) expanded from forty-six hundred to more than fifty-nine hundred. Local labor was in short supply during this period, and corporate management imported "about 2000 people, mostly Mexicans to secure their labor for beet field work."[26] For the first time in the company's history the pool of Mormon boys was not sufficient to meet corporate demands.

As a result of this increased demand (in the Cache Valley and elsewhere), a small community of Mexicanos sprouted in the Box Elder County town of Garland. In June, 1920, the *Salt Lake Tribune* reported on the size, employment, and conditions of these *familias* (families). Evidently, the existent circumstances met with the reporter's approval, for he entitled the article "Mexican Workers Find Utah Paradise."[27] The nirvana of these Spanish-speaking workers consisted of railroad track gang labor during the summer and thinning and topping beets during the spring and fall. Although the locals expressed some concerns about the presence of these individuals (after all, they were foreigners and Catholics!), these Mexicanos were considered "useful members of society outside of the beet fields."[28]

Rafael Torres's oral history provides a less idealized picture of beet production in Utah. Rafael was only eighteen when he answered the call of the Utah-Idaho Sugar Company and began toiling in the fields of Grace, Idaho. Interviewed when he was eighty-three, Rafael remembered how harsh a task it had been to thin and top the crop: "Of course [I] was tired—you get awful tired. Especially when you cultivate beets. See, you have hoe . . . [and you] bend over all day. It wasn't very easy." Living conditions were grim; even cooking and heating were difficult because there was "no running water. No water sometimes. And no stoves. We used kerosene, oil stoves. Or just wood."[29]

Frances Yánez and her family worked the sugar beet crop during the late 1920s. Born in October of 1919 in Amarillo, Texas, Frances was brought to Salt Lake City when she was three months old. Her parents suffered discrimination in Texas and decided to go north in hope of a better life. Once in Utah, Frances and her kin traveled in gypsylike caravans from Salt Lake City to Idaho in order to work the fields. When the season ended, the family returned to the capital city to hunker down for winter. There was seldom any work for members of the Yánez clan during these months; consequently, much of the autumn season was spent hoarding money to ward off the winter's cold and hunger.[30]

While conditions proved difficult for most Spanish speakers in Utah agriculture during the late 1910s and 1920s, not all associated with this industry worked in unskilled positions. Oral histories and city directories revealed some occupational differences among colonia members. Between the years 1919 and 1922 the Salt Lake City Polk Directory listed more than one hundred individuals with Spanish surnames. The majority were classified as "laborers," but some worked as foremen, barbers, and porters.[31] Some managed to create a fairly prosperous life for themselves and their families; a few worked as labor agents for the sugar companies. Ellen Córdova's husband, Alfred, was just such an individual. Ellen's British father and German mother were both LDS converts who moved to Salt Lake City to be near their church's base. Alfred was from Taos, New Mexico, and had gravitated to Utah in 1921 to seek better employment opportunities than could be found in his hometown. The couple married in 1924.

In Salt Lake City, Alfred teamed up with Jeff Pino, a Mexicano, who ran a labor recruitment office (located on 462 West 200 South) and had contacts within the various sugar companies (a second Spanish-surnamed recruiter, N. J. González, operated a similar business called Apex Employment Agency on 470 West 200 South). Córdova acted as Pino's agent, sometimes traveling as far as California to find workers. Córdova also produced and sold custom-made shirts and suits to his *clientes* (clients). Pino died in the late 1920s, and Alfred took over the entire business. He and his family eventually moved into the food business, becoming suppliers of Mexican food products and restaurateurs.[32]

A second area of employment concentration for Spanish-speaking labor was in mining/mineral processing. By 1884 Salt Lake City and its hinterlands boasted seven smelters, two mills, and two sampling works. The key event in this industry's history, and a circumstance crucial to the development of a *comunidad* (community), occurred in 1903 when D. C. Jackling became general manager of Utah Copper.[33] Corporate expansion was rapid, and by 1907 the company was operating a concentrator in the Salt Lake City suburb of Magna, a smelter in nearby Garfield, and full open pit mining in Bingham Canyon. By 1910 Utah Copper stood poised to play the central role in the development of what John D. Rockefeller called "the greatest industrial sight in the world."[34]

Jackling's mining operations required a large number of laborers, and thousands of immigrants heeded the call. During the 1890s most men who worked in Bingham hailed from the British Isles. However, as the technology used by mining companies improved, the call for skilled miners decreased and drastically altered the ethnic composition of Bingham Canyon. Where Cornish and Irish miners had predominated in the later nineteenth century, by 1912 Bingham was a polyglot society of different nationalities numerically dominated by Greeks and Italians.[35]

With better capitalization and a booming demand for copper during World War I, the companies operating in Bingham improved their mining technologies. This changeover to a more mechanized and less skilled workplace proved both a boon and a liability to the various nationalities in the canyon.[36] Some groups, the Swedes for example, were able to achieve relatively secure, skilled machine-tender positions. Other groups, such as the Greeks, Italians, and eventually the Spanish-speakers, would be relegated almost exclusively to performing fatiguing tasks, such as laying down track for giant steam shovels.[37] The town of Bingham was ethnically diverse, but the

Spanish-surnamed presence was negligible before 1912. An examination of Utah Copper Company employee identification cards for the years 1909–19 revealed that only twelve Spanish-speaking individuals, six Mexicanos and six Spaniards, toiled for the company before 1912.[38]

It was not until the strike of 1912 that more than a handful of Spanish-speakers appeared on the company's payroll. On September 17, 1912, approximately one thousand men struck against the mines. Reports indicated that the work stoppage was brought about by the announcement of a 25¢-per-day wage increase. The pay scale that prevailed before the strike was $2.00 per day for surface employees, $2.50 per day for muckers, and $3.00 per day for miners. The employees rejected this offer and demanded a 50¢-per-day increase.[39] To replace these employees the companies hired thousands of strikebreakers, many of them Mexicans. The Salt Lake City papers noted the arrival of these *mineros* (miners): "A party of 150 Mexicans arrived at Bingham. . . . They were guarded by armed deputies . . . they were taken to the Utah Copper Company's works where they began work this afternoon. Most of the strikebreakers are former mining men of Arizona and Old Mexico."[40] Of the 635 Mexicano, Spanish, and Mexican American workers identified in Utah Copper's records between 1909 and 1919, more than half (330) signed up to toil during the fall of 1912 and early 1913.

As had been the case with the Italians and Greeks before them, these men worked the most demanding and difficult jobs. Of the 563 individuals for whom an occupational classification was listed, 409 worked laying down track, the least skilled and lowest paying job. The difficult working conditions are reflected by the transitory nature of Spanish-surnamed employment at Utah Copper. On average, the employees hired between 1912 and 1919 did not remain with the company for more than a few months. The mean number of days in Utah Copper's employ for the Spaniards was 138 days; the Mexicanos and Mexican Americans, who likely had other options available in other parts of the West and Southwest, stayed on for only 43 days.

As was the case with many immigrant laborers, most of these men arrived in Utah without their families. In the first quarter of the twentieth century Utah's Hispanic society was overwhelmingly composed of young, single men.[41] The records of Utah Copper support this contention. Of the 276 Mexican employees for whom location of family members was listed, only sixteen claimed to have relatives with them in Utah. Just one Mexicano brought his wife to live with him in the state. If a Hispanic man did travel with a relative, it was most likely a brother or a cousin so as to double earnings and share living expenses. It is not an understatement to suggest that Mexican women were a rare and wondrous sight in the streets of northern Utah during the 1910s and early 1920s. They were so scarce that an early Mexican resident of the city stated that, "when you saw a Mexican woman it was like seeing your mother."[42] The situation for the Spaniards was similar. Of the 268 individuals for whom information on location of relatives was garnered, only forty-three had family members in Utah. Once again, the most common relative in the Beehive State was a brother; only five of the men claimed to have their wives living with them.

Of the several thousand Hispanics estimated to have been brought to break the 1912 strike, most left northern Utah after industrial peace returned. However, a small number did remain and eventually brought their familias. The importance of the strike to the colonias of northern Utah was not necessarily in the number of those who remained. Rather, the impressions of these men of Utah spread and spurred future migrations.

Filomeno Ochoa followed the first wave of workers to Bingham, arriving in 1923. Born in Mexico in 1899, Filomeno arrived in the United States not knowing a word of English but hoping to find better conditions than those in Mexico. As was the case for the overwhelming majority of Mexicans who traveled to the United States during the early 1920s, Utah was not Filomeno's first choice for a place to live.[43] He eventually found his way to Utah and found a job in Bingham. The Mexicano had the two principal qualifications mining employers required, youth and strength. While he asserted that he "was treated all right" in Bingham, Filomeno still felt that his bosses made him "work like a mule." In most instances the most difficult tasks were reserved for Spanish-surnamed workers, and other employees complained if the "Mexicans" were assigned "white" jobs. Filomeno recalled that other ethnic groups often circulated petitions demanding the removal of all Mexicans from the work site.[44]

The third major sector of employment for Spanish-speakers in Utah was the transportation industry. The development of mining/mineral processing (and other industries) in the American West and Southwest would not have been possible without the labor of Mexicano and Mexican American *traqueros* (track laborers). Railroad labor historian Jeffrey M. Garcilazo briefly describes the impact of these industries on Utah's economy in his dissertation, "Traqueros: Mexican Railroad Workers in the United States, 1870–1930": "When railroads finally arrived, the cost of transportation dropped low enough for operators profitably to extract lower grades of ore. The open-cut mining method represents one such technique first perfected at the Bingham Canyon mine in Utah. . . . like other parts of the Southwest, railroads and mining companies imported thousands of Mexican (from southern Colorado and northern New Mexico) origin workers along with European and Asian immigrants to insure a profitable return on the ore."[45] As early as 1923, Union Pacific payroll records showed that 40 percent of the track labor between Salt Lake City and Milford, Utah, was Hispanic. During the busy summer months when "extra gangs" were used, the percentage of Spanish-surnamed individuals in some of the teams went as high as 70 percent. Until the early years of the Great Depression these laborers represented 25 to 30 percent of the permanent track force and nearly 35 percent of the summer labor force for the railroads operating in Utah.[46]

One employee who helped keep the Union Pacific Railroad (UP) running in the Beehive State was Vicente Mayer, Sr. Born in the state of Jalisco in February of 1906, Mayer's attempts to find work in the United States eventually led him to Los Angeles. In 1924 a friend of Vicente was hired by the UP and assigned to Salt Lake City. Vicente accompanied him to Utah where he remained and spent forty-six years working for the company. In a 1970 oral history interview, the retired railroad foreman claimed that the company treated him fairly, although he did remember certain abusive practices. During a period of financial uncertainty for the corporation in the 1920s employees were asked to "give back" ten cents per hour but were promised that the wages would be repaid at some future date. They never were. Vicente also stated that Hispanics did heavy labor but seldom, if ever, were given the opportunity to move into even low level supervisory positions. He recalled only one Mexican who was promoted to foreman before 1940. Vicente toiled as a traquero for almost two decades before advancing to section foreman after World War II.[47]

Another veteran of Utah track labor was José Méndel. José was born in Mexico in February, 1907. He moved to the United States and worked picking lemons in the San Fernando Valley of California. Méndel followed the harvests for a few months until he procured employment with a railroad company. Ultimately he was transferred to Woods Cross City, just north of Salt Lake City. When interviewed in 1970 José could still vividly describe the difficult process involved in laying down rails. "We [did] everything by hand, pulling the spikes, and driving the spikes and putting in new steel; no machines then, just by hand." During several years José worked for the railroad for six months and then traveled to California to find winter work.[48]

Ogden was also an important transportation hub for northern Utah. Lucy Chávez-Hernández's father was one of many Spanish-speaking men who worked on the railroad. Lucy was born in Mexico in 1910, but her family fled to the United States in 1917 to escape the revolutionary turmoil. Lucy recalled that her father also "wanted to see how it was, and you know. He [wanted] to find a job." Lucy's father worked in agriculture topping beets and picking lettuce for four years before bringing his family to Ogden. Once in the city, they fell into a routine that was familiar to many Spanish-speakers in the West and

Southwest. The father would toil for the railroad, the mother would help to improve the family's finances by providing room and board for other workers in the area, and the entire family would work the beet fields during the fall. Lucy described her family's life as one in which, "there was always work . . . they'd get done with one thing and then there was something else."[49]

Paul Schuster Taylor's research notes from his 1927 visit to Salt Lake City provide supporting evidence regarding the conditions described by the *betabeleros* (beet workers), *mineros*, and *traqueros* interviewed by Mayer and Kelen in the 1970s and 1980s. Taylor consulted labor recruiters, field supervisors, and Mexican consulate C. M. Gaxiola to gather detailed information regarding the working conditions, daily life, and various domicile locations of Utah's Mexicanos and Mexican Americans.

Labor contractor E. D. Hashimoto informed Taylor that Mexicanos had worked as *traqueros* in the intermountain region since the first decade of the 1900s. In Utah these Spanish-speaking laborers at first worked alongside Japanese, Greeks, and Italians. Hashimoto proudly stated that the other groups (especially the Japanese) had long since moved on to better-paying work (such as mining and farming). He believed that it was the "Mexican" culture and lifestyle that had, in part, held the Spanish-speakers back. Taylor quoted Hashimoto as stating that "Mexicans [are] content to remain laborers, [because they] are floaters and don't make a permanent place by acquiring property." F. D. Brown, a recruitment agent for some of the coal companies, seconded this opinion. The mining corporations (except those in Bingham) had typecast the Mexicanos and Mexican Americans as "undesirables [with] low output [and as a] bad influence on American youths for they got bad work habits." Although some employers held low opinions of these individuals, they were hired because they were willing to work cheaply and move from location to location in order to satisfy labor demands. Consulate Gaxiola estimated that about three thousand Mexicans traveled throughout Utah, Idaho, and Montana in order to work the sugar beet crops (as well as perform other types of menial labor). Many of these workers eventually moved to California in search of winter work. Others, according to Hashimoto, returned to the villages of southern Colorado to live among "the descendants of old 'Spanish stock.'"[50]

Around 1920 steady, if not necessarily well-paying, work in one or more of Utah's principal economic sectors encouraged Spanish-speakers to coalesce into compact urban settlements near smelters, railroad tracks, and depots. The line of demarcation between the immigrant community and the rest of Salt Lake City society was State Street, which divides the metropolis's eastern and western sections. The west side was the wrong side of the tracks, and almost all Spanish-surnamed persons in the city lived in an area bounded by North Temple Street on the north and 1000 South on the south. Conditions in Ogden were similar. Almost all of Ogden's comunidad resided near the railroad depot and track in an area bounded by Wall Avenue on the east and Washington Avenue on the west, between Twenty-third and Twenty-seventh Streets.

While this description makes the west side and Wall Avenue areas seem typical barrios of the American West and Southwest, not all of the traits of barrio existence were present. Albert Camarillo and other historians have characterized barrios as sectors that are usually located near places of industrial employment, where persons of Mexican origin predominate. These locales, Camarillo asserts, provide residents with a feeling of home and security in the midst of economic and social uncertainty.[51]

This definition only partially described the circumstances existent in northern Utah. While the Spanish-speaking population did cluster near work sites, other elements of barrio life were not yet in place. Before the middle 1920s there were few Mexicanas and children in the area. Baptismal records for the Salt Lake Catholic Diocese (which encompasses the entire state) revealed only fifty-three *bautismos* (baptisms) during the entire decade of the 1910s.[52] Additionally, the limited financial resources of the diocese meant that the Roman Catholic Church did not have the wherewithal to fund or staff facilities designed to meet the needs of these Spanish-speakers.[53] Finally, even in the areas of heaviest concentration, the Mexicanos and Mexican Americans did not constitute the majority population of the west side or Wall Avenue areas. These people shared their living spaces with large numbers of Italians, Greeks, Japanese, Syrians, and Koreans.[54]

Although many areas of the United States enjoyed economic prosperity during the 1920s, Utah endured a severe post–World War I recession. Decreased demand for metals and a return to full production by European farmers were damaging blows to key state industries. Reductions in these areas also touched rail transportation, causing layoffs and cutbacks that further slowed commercial activity.[55] Although Utah's economy did not boom during the Jazz Age, it still drew an increasing number of Spanish-speakers. By 1930 the northern Utah Hispanic clusters had evolved and resembled a more complete community. The number of native-born Mexicans in the state increased from 1,666 to more than 4,000. An imbalance persisted between the sexes (with men outnumbering women by about 2:1), but the number of families increased dramatically (more than 1,000 of these persons were children under the age of ten).[56]

While the presence of *mujeres* (women) and children may have helped create a more stable and normal social environment for these mineros, traqueros, and betabeleros, it also fostered new problems. The increased number of children presented the group with a new concern. What kind of education, if any, would these children receive? What circumstances would they face in public scholastic institutions? As part of his 1927 Utah work Paul S. Taylor conducted a survey of the state's various school districts to ascertain the number of "Mexican" children in local schools (the final tally was 389 pupils). Not surprisingly, most (46 percent) attended schools in the Salt Lake City, Jordan (a suburb of the capital), and Ogden districts. Unfortunately, this aspect of life mirrored many of the problems encountered in the workplace.[57]

Catholic schools operated in the area, but they were expensive and primarily served the needs of the sons and daughters of families from the nearby mining towns (primarily Irish and Italian).[58] Once enrolled in area schools many of these children suffered indignities and discrimination. The experiences of María Dolores García provide a glimpse into these conditions. María Dolores, a native-born Mexicana, was the daughter of a traquero. Her father worked for a company in the Northeast for six years before arriving in Salt Lake City. María Dolores recalls being derided by her peers because of the food she ate and for not using utensils. Because of this "a lot of kids . . . didn't want to sit by you or play with you." In addition, many of the children made fun of María Dolores because of her skin color. The Spanish-speaking children who were lighter skinned, it seemed to this child, were more readily accepted by their playmates.[59]

Ramón García, another student, proved to be less patient than María Dolores. Although born in Salt Lake City in June of 1926, he was targeted for abuse because of his appearance and ethnic background. In frustration he slapped a teacher. Ramón was promptly arrested and taken to juvenile court. In the sixth grade he decided to drop out of school. This Hispanic child eventually became a common laborer earning minimal pay at a local factory; unfortunately, this scenario would be repeated time and again during the years covered by this study.[60]

Life in northern Utah not only created problems for Spanish-surnamed children but also produced changes for the women of the burgeoning community. The increasing number of familias meant that there would be more mouths to feed, and that led many colonia women to seek remunerative employment either inside or outside their homes. Edith Meléndez's mother provides an example of the type of work performed to help make ends meet. Edith was born in Sargintine, Colorado, in 1925. Her parents moved to Colorado from Mexico in the hope that they could provide their child with a better life. The family arrived in Bingham Canyon when Edith was about two months old. Her father worked as a leaser—he would mine an area and receive a percentage of the value of the mineral output. Edith's mother helped her family by running a boardinghouse for Mexican mineros. These services were crucial both to the provider and to the customer. The money earned by Edith's mother helped solidify the clan's financial stability. For the mineros a bit of food, prepared in the traditional style, helped make life a bit more bearable. The steaming plates of chorizo, tamales, and tortillas helped nourish both their bodies and their souls.[61] As the communities in Bingham and other areas expanded and developed, some of these women took up other occupations. By the middle of the 1930s some even operated small businesses such as bars, restaurants, and pool halls.

By the onset of the Great Depression, Hispanics represented the largest minority group in the state. They lived in urban colonies clustered on the west side of Salt Lake City and in the Wall Avenue (near the railroad depot) of Ogden. Although their numbers had increased, they did not constitute the majority population in these areas. These laborers worked in low skilled, poorly paying jobs in the agriculture, mining/mineral processing, and transportation industries. By 1930 families were more prevalent than they had been in previous years, and the society of Spanish-speakers was changing from the earlier one which had been dominated by young, unmarried, male immigrants.

Still, the institutions where northern Utah Hispanics worked, studied, and prayed did not yet reflect their cultural inheritance. If social and cultural needs were to be addressed in a place lacking Spanish traditions, the people would have to create their own community organizations. During the 1910s and early 1920s the foundations for such entities were built. After 1925, and especially during the 1930s, Utah's Spanish-surnamed population took the next step. They began creating organizations and institutions which would reflect and nurture that which they considered to be *lo nuestro* (our own).

2

"Lo Nuestro"
The Creation of Hispanic Organizations in Northern Utah, 1920–35

During the 1920s northern Utah's Spanish-speaking population underwent a rapid numerical increase and other significant changes. Between 1920 and the start of the Great Depression the rural/urban ratio of the Spanish-surnamed in the state declined from 2.7:1 to 2.1:1. The decade also saw an increasing number of Mexican Americans moving to Utah (the percentage of foreign born in this population declined from 79.1 percent in 1910 to 55.3 percent). Finally, where once young, single immigrant males predominated, now familias and children became more prevalent.[1] While the cluster's composition changed during the decade, working and residential conditions did not. Most of these families and individuals lived on "the wrong side of the tracks" in neighborhoods located near Salt Lake City and Ogden's industrial areas and railroad depots. The vast majority of laborers toiled in low skill, low wage occupations. Fortunately, the existence of more family groups made it possible for needy individuals to connect to an "ethnic network" for assistance. From these associations, "they drew strength from . . . family members and fellow countrymen who lived nearby. Through the daily struggle to survive in an oftentimes hostile environment, these newcomers constructed a world for themselves, shaped by their memories of past lives and the reality of their present situation."[2] As Timothy M. Matovina, Ana María Díaz-Stevens, and Anthony M. Stevens-Arroyo have demonstrated in their recent works, religious institutions and affiliations played important roles in this constructed reality.[3] This league of vecinos (neighbors) also functioned as a means to celebrate and enjoy traditions and customs of a faraway homeland.[4]

Neighborly ties were valuable but limited. As a result, during the 1920s and into the years of the Great Depression northern Utah's growing colonia took the first steps toward creating permanent organizations to address some of their social, religious, and economic necessities. This chapter will postulate a framework for understanding the genesis of and differences among these groups, explore the creation and social results of those entities, and provide a sketch of northern Utah's early Hispanic associations, their goals and efficacy.

George J. Sánchez's seminal 1993 work, *Becoming Mexican American: Ethnicity, Culture, and Identity in Chicano Los Angeles, 1900–1945,* provides an effective scaffold from which to understand the reasons for creation and diversity among these groups. Sánchez describes the existence of "ethnic networks" among colonia constituents in the Los Angeles area. Low social and economic mobility caused many Spanish-surnamed individuals to emphasize ethnic ties as a coping mechanism against the varied stresses of daily life. But this "connectedness," Sánchez argues, was not necessarily to a fixed set of customs. Rather, it meant the establishment of a collective identity that would provide physical and psychological support.[5] The groups that northern Utah Hispanics established would become the organizational arms of preexisting neighborly ties. The various assemblies would provide different types of social services to the colonia's constituents, while at the same time fostering a psychic link to ethnic identity and traditions.

Although an overarching collective identity based upon residential, occupational, and cultural patterns took shape during the 1920s, this did not mean that all persons would be subsumed under this identity or seek the same things from it. Sánchez acknowledges the existence of a "continuum of experience"; individuals need not maintain all traits and customs to consider themselves part of the comunidad.[6] In addition to consideration of personal decisions involved in the retention or discarding of specific cultural traits, the texture of American society in which these Hispanics lived and worked should be taken into account.

The most significant factor in the case of northern Utah is the social impact of religious conversion and affiliation upon the lives of Spanish-speaking men, women, and children. Richard A. Garcia notes the existence of class, philosophical, and political differences when he stated that "the pluralism of ideas, values, and attitudes was a reality because occupational segmentation created differences, in spite of the sense of community."[7] But these cleavages are not the foremost dividing line in the community under study. In many instances the Spanish-surnamed people in Utah who retained ties to the Catholic Church saw clear distinctions between themselves and those who they felt had sold out to Utah's predominant faith. Simultaneously, those individuals who took the plunge and became *Mormones* (Mormons) faced the critical decision of whether or not conversion meant giving up other (or all) aspects of their Mexicano or Mexican American identity. Jessie L. Embry's work "*In His Own*

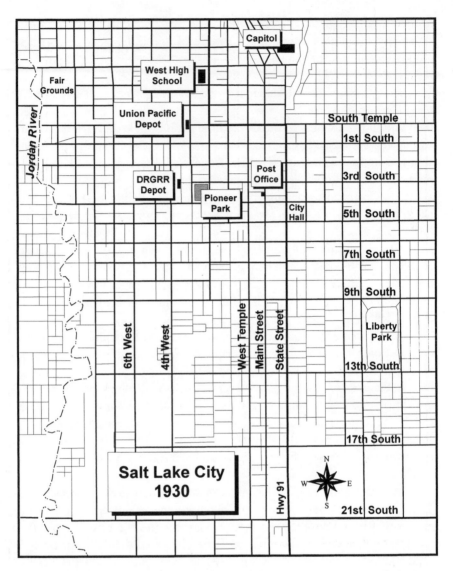

Map 2. Salt Lake City, ca. 1930. The majority of Spanish-speakers lived in an area bounded by South Temple to the north, 9th South to the south, State Street to the east and the Jordan River to the west. *Map by Kevin R. Mulligan*

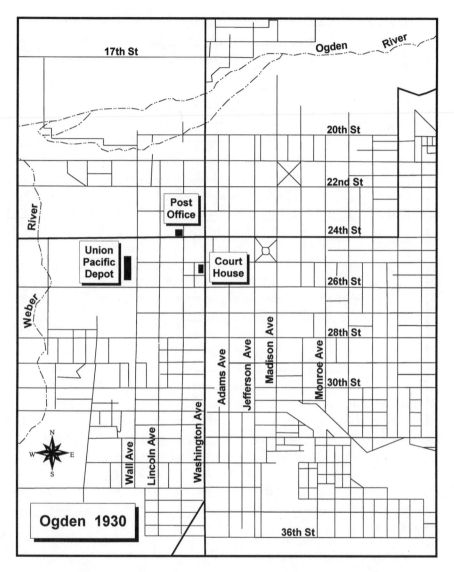

Map 3. Ogden, ca. 1930. The majority of the Spanish-speakers lived in an area bounded by 22nd Street to the north, 28th Street to the south, Washington Avenue to the
east, and Wall Avenue to the west. *Map by Kevin R. Mulligan*

Language": Mormon Spanish Speaking Congregations in the United States examines the varied, and often contradictory, attempts by Mormon leaders to carve out a place for Hispanics in their institution during the early decades of the 1900s.[8]

These considerations, in part, explain why different groups developed in northern Utah and are crucial to an understanding of the primary differentiation that existed within this population: religious affiliation. Sánchez briefly refers to this type of fissuring in the Los Angeles community.[9] In Utah, those who joined the LDS faith plugged into an ethnic network that tied them directly to the majority population. This provided access to social and economic benefits not available to those outside the fellowship. By the late 1920s Catholic Hispanics established their own associations, but they would prove less than effective in meeting some of their needs.

Before 1920 only the Mexican consulate in Salt Lake City dealt directly with the problems of local Mexicanos. The office opened in 1912 (the first consul was José Lozano) and remained accessible even during the most tumultuous years of the Mexican Revolution.[10] During the crisis it was often difficult, if not impossible, for consular offices to function effectively. The situation became so chaotic and grave that for a brief period of time in 1916 E. D. Hashimoto, the labor contractor of Japanese extraction who spoke so disparagingly about Mexicanos to Paul S. Taylor in 1927, acted as Mexican consul.[11] By September, 1920, Salt Lake City's postmaster, in a plea printed in the *Salt Lake Tribune,* urgently called for "some Mexican who can speak and write the Spanish language" to provide "information for use in recommending the appointment of a Mexican consul."[12] The commotion, both in Mexico and in northern Utah, produced a great deal of dissatisfaction among Mexicanos who felt that officials cared little about their daily problems.[13] Faced with a situation in which Mexican representatives were missing, ineffectual, or uncaring, and surrounded by a society that ignored their needs, the growing comunidad of the Beehive State was forced to look to itself and fashion institutions that would respond to their requirements.

The earliest signs of collaboration were informal parties and social gatherings that celebrated cultural traditions and provided some succor to those in distress. Events such as dances, weddings, baptisms, and celebrations of Mexican national holidays allowed these men, women, and children to gather in homes or rented halls to reminisce and enjoy the company of compatriots and family. Lucy Chávez-Hernández, whose family moved to Ogden in 1923, recalls that the Mexicanos and Mexican Americans of the Wall Avenue area held fiestas almost on a weekly basis. Lucy's mother garnered information from the workers she dealt with at a local boardinghouse, and through these types of referrals Ogden-area Spanish-speakers learned about upcoming soirees. For people living far from home in a location where they represented a small percentage of the population, these get-togethers were special and represented a little bit of *la patria* (the motherland) among harsh economic and social conditions.[14]

The celebration of *Cinco de Mayo* (May 5th) in 1920 was important in the evolution of Salt Lake City's Spanish-speaking community. The *Salt Lake Tribune* of May 6 summarized the previous day's festivities. A group calling itself the Mexican Protective Association helped stage the events and reached out to the non-Spanish-surnamed population of Utah's capital city. The celebration featured traditional foods and speeches by local Mexicanos and included the participation of foreign-language professors from the nearby University of Utah.[15] On September 17, 1920, the *Salt Lake Tribune* once again noted the Mexicano and Mexican American presence in the city, estimating the population of the Salt Lake City comunidad to be around 1,000 people.[16] Little other information is available on the activities and goals of the Mexican Protective Association. Its head, a man identified only as A. Monteros, was eventually exposed as a confidence man who preyed upon the goodwill of his fellow countrymen.[17] In addition to staging parties and national holiday fetes, community members formed other groups as events warranted. For example, in April, 1920, an organization was quickly formed to protest what some in the comunidad regarded as the mistreatment of Jesús Chávez, whom Ogden police had accused of robbery. The accusations leveled against Chávez raised the ire of the community, and the people hastily united to raise money for his legal defense.[18]

These informal organizations did much to better the condition and spirit of colonia members. Unfortunately, a lack of connections to the wider Utah society, as well as to each other and to other Hispanic entities elsewhere in the American West and Southwest, limited their impact. Loyalty and volunteerism often lasted only a few days or weeks; upon completion of a celebration, or an individual's release, there was no longer a unifying force around which the group could rally. To render effective assistance, more permanent associations were required—entities that would be able to sustain cluster members in life's most austere moments as well as in daily life and the observation of festive occasions.

Mutuales (mutual aid associations) established in Utah during the 1920s aided in these endeavors. José A. Hernández's 1983 work, *Mutual Aid for Survival,* examines the varied goals and histories of these alliances.[19] Hernández argues that such societies fulfilled three crucial objectives for colonia members: 1) they celebrated the members' culture and holidays without regard to other divisions; 2) they provided (limited) financial assistance against the uncertainties of life; and 3) they offered "expressive" gratification by sponsoring fiestas and other events designed to present a more positive view of the comunidad to the rest of the public. Constituents often felt better about themselves (and their community group) when others viewed their culture and ethnic background more sympathetically.[20]

An example of this type of organization in Salt Lake City was the *Cruz Azul* (the Mexican Blue Cross). Starting in the early 1920s, this group's objective was to help the sick and indigent of the community using internally raised resources. One of the leaders of the organization was Manuel Torres, brother-in-law of Rafael Torres. Manuel arrived in the United States in 1920 and eventually found employment at an ice factory in Helper, Utah. Like Rafael, Manuel eventually found his way to Salt Lake City in hope of improving his economic prospects.[21] The Cruz Azul raised funds by sponsoring dances and other social events. Alfred Córdova's shops often housed these gatherings.[22]

Although the Cruz Azul operated in the Salt Lake City area for a few years (the Cruz eventually disbanded during the years of the Great Depression), the locus of early mutual aid activity for northern Utah's Spanish-surnamed population was among the mineros and their families in Bingham Canyon (southwest of Salt Lake City). Because of the distance between the mines and the west side, the men and women of Bingham were often unable to get to town for festive occasions and events. The physical separation from the rest of the community helped stimulate members of this group to generate their own activities.[23] An early example of an expressive affair staged by a mutual aid society was a fiesta in the Bingham Canyon town of Copperton in 1927. Local Mexicanos felt that the gala was a huge success and provided the rest of the mining community the opportunity to see the positive side of their culture. At the conclusion of the festivities one of the organizers gleefully declared, "not many people knew what a Mexican fiesta was like, the Americans and the other groups, well they thought that we were nothing but a bunch of revolutionaries, they thought that we did not know how to do anything."[24]

Additionally, the society tried to improve its members' educational level by establishing a night school in the basement of the Copper Hotel and offering classes in Spanish literature and language.[25] One of the association's organizers, Jesús Avila, noted a goal of the group known as *Unión y Patria* (Unity and Nation). Avila, who was born in Pasto Ortíz, Michoacán, Mexico, in 1904, worked for U.S. Mines in Bingham during the 1920s. A principal reason for his involvement in the organization was to fight for better treatment of Mexicanos and Mexican Americans by local police. Jesús was disgusted with the manner in which he and his compatriots were stereotyped by local authorities. He claimed, "some of us were dirty but not all of us were and that was the problem I had with the law because they treated us all the same way, I had no problem with them taking care of those who did wrong, but not all of us, and that is why I began to organize."[26]

By the middle of the 1930s Unión y Patria shifted its focus from local to national issues. The group became part of the Comisión Honorífica Mexicana movement (tied to Mexican consulates throughout the United State) that grew to include hundreds of chapters in the West and Southwest. During the Great Depression the Mexican consul in Salt Lake City, Enrique Elizondo (showing a bit more concern and activity than some of his predecessors had in the 1910s), made many trips to Bingham Canyon to carry information and aid to his constituents.[27] Although Unión y Patria surrendered some local autonomy as a result of its attachment to the movement, Avila and his countrymen retained a positive view of the Honorífica's ideals and goals. Elizondo helped by maintaining a meticulous watch over his charges' civil rights and treatment by police. Avila fondly recalled how the consul stood up for his people whenever they were in trouble with the law. Jesús often found that a Mexicano involved in a fight "would be thrown in jail without being given medical attention and the persons who beat him up would be quickly released if they were of another race, I was involved in all of that . . . and if I could not resolve the issue, the consul was always there to help me."[28] Informal associations and mutual aid societies augmented ethnic ties among northern Utah colonia members. However, given the specific texture of American society in this area, the most important groups birthed in the community during the 1920s were religious in nature, and these entities fostered a certain amount of intragroup division and resentment. George J. Sánchez noted this trend among some of his subjects in Los Angeles and stated that conversion to a "new order encouraged the adoption of new values," such as abstention from alcohol and a discarding of traditional chaperoning practices, and often produced intraethnic group divisions.[29]

As early as 1920 LDS missionaries were aggressively pursuing converts among local Spanish speakers. In *Becoming Mexican American* Sánchez states that Protestant denominations in Los Angeles initially failed to show much "inclination to proselytize among Mexican Catholics." But eventually these churches "began to investigate potential areas of social concern" (such as Americanization programs) regarding the Spanish-surnamed population. Initial outreach efforts by Southern California Protestant denominations focused primarily upon what they could do to improve the daily lives of Mexicanos.[30]

Over the past decade several works have examined what some church leaders consider U.S. Protestant churches' "crucial need" for expanding their outreach: ministry and services for the rapidly growing Hispanic population.[31]

For the LDS hierarchy, such temporal concerns were (and are) only part of the equation. Their missionary work sought to return a particular group of people to the proper service and worship of God. Mormons believe that today's Native Americans (and therefore mestizos as well) are the descendants of Jews who migrated to the North American continent in 600 B.C.E. These people eventually separated into the Nephite and Lamanite nations. Through years of turmoil and strife the Nephites (and other groups) were destroyed. Only the Lamanites (who by this time had turned away from God) survived this carnage. Mormons believe that until all of the Lamanites' descendants are converted to the faith, the millennial kingdom of Christ cannot begin. Therefore, it is imperative for Mormons to reach out to the Spanish-speaking people of the Americas. "Although the Book of Mormon's message was directed to all peoples, it was especially relevant to the Lamanites. The first Mormons were so thoroughly convinced of this that shortly after the church was organized in 1830 several elders asked what the Lord had in mind for the 'remnants' of the Lamanites. In accordance with biblical prophecy, all of Israel's descendants would need to be 'gathered' (converted and baptized) before Christ's second coming would initiate a thousand years of peace."[32] At a 1948 conference a church leader described his vision of the future for Hispanics in the Church of Jesus Christ of Latter-day Saints: "I see the Lamanites coming into this Church. Instead of coming in small groups of tens and hundreds, they will be in thousands. I see them organized into wards and stakes with Lamanite people comprising these stakes. I see them filling temples and officiating therein."[33]

The arrival of three Mexicana sisters—Domitila, Agustina, and Dolores Rivera—in Salt Lake City during the late 1910s marks the genesis of the Hispanic LDS presence in the Salt Lake Valley. The women were converts from the town of Chimalhuacán. In a 1975 interview Domitila (or Tila, as she was called) recounted the story of her conversion and early missionary work. Tila's mother converted during the early 1900s and encouraged her daughters to investigate the tenets of her newfound faith. Although their father feared that the girls would be ostracized by neighbors, family, and friends, they joined the Church of Jesus Christ of Latter-day Saints in 1918.[34]

The fear of being branded as outcasts was not the only concern the sisters faced. The commotion caused by the revolutionary war kept the family in constant fear of reprisals, first from national troops and then from the sympathizers of Emiliano Zapata. Amid the chaos Tila's father struggled valiantly to raise enough money in order to send his daughters to safety in Utah; this arduous task was accomplished in 1919. Shortly after their arrival in the heart of the Mormon Zion, the siblings were approached by a bishop,[35] who asked them to minister to *su gente* (your people). During 1919 and 1920 Domitila,

Agustina, and Dolores devoted themselves to spreading their faith among the sugar beet workers on their return to Salt Lake City from southern Idaho and Garland, Utah.[36]

The Riveras' missionary work was paralleled by three men: Juan Ramón Martínez, Francisco Solano, and Margarito Bautista. Martínez was born in Coral de Piedras, New Mexico, in 1874 and converted to Mormonism in November, 1914. By the middle of the 1910s, while living in southern Utah, Juan Ramón believed that God called him to minister to the growing number of Spanish-speaking people of the Salt Lake Valley. He arrived in Salt Lake City with the money he had saved during his lifetime, a total of six hundred dollars. With this capital he established a restaurant on the west side of the city that he used as the first meeting place for local Spanish-surnamed Mormons.[37]

Francisco Solano was born in Morcin, Oviedo, Spain. Solano's father did not want his son to serve in the Spanish army, so he shipped the boy to South America on a freighter when he was two years old. Francisco never saw his parents or native land again. Life as an orphan was quite difficult, and, ironically, he joined the military in order to support himself. While he was stationed in South Africa in 1906 he learned about and joined the Church of Jesus Christ of Latter-day Saints. He arrived in Salt Lake City in 1920.[38]

The final member of this triumvirate was Margarito Bautista, who immigrated to Salt Lake City from Atluatla, Mexico, in 1920. The efforts of these men, as well as those of the Rivera sisters, bore some fruit, and by the end of 1920 about one hundred people were attending weekly services at Martínez's west-side restaurant. The church's hierarchy, impressed with the results of these undertakings, officially recognized the existence of the group (designated the Local Mexican Mission) in April, 1921.[39] In addition to efforts in Salt Lake City, LDS missionaries sought out Spanish-surnamed people in other parts of the West and Southwest. Between the winter of 1915 and March, 1919, emissaries from the church reinitiated the Mexican Mission (which had almost ceased operations in Mexico by 1913) to spread its message to Mexican Americans in Arizona, Texas, Colorado, New Mexico, and California. Church leaders headquartered the reconstituted institution in El Paso, Texas, a central location that would permit the church to be "closer to the Mexican population in the United States and to Mexico."[40]

The Salt Lake City group was led by Bautista and Solano. Margarito was named president and theological instructor; and Solano was chosen first counselor and Bautista's assistant.[41] By August, 1921, the congregation consisted of nineteen permanent members and thirty-three *investigadores* (investigators).[42] In the fall of that year Pioneer Park (located on 300 West and 300 South in downtown Salt Lake City) was the site for LDS services in Spanish. The assembly also sent missionaries to the Mexicano and Mexican American workers and families living near the beet fields of Garland.

Lamentably, Spanish-surnamed leadership of this organization came to an end in 1924. Margarito Bautista was responsible for this change in leadership. Bautista was called to missionary work in his native land at the end of 1922, and Solano was named as his replacement. The mission was reorganized in May of 1923 and renamed the *Rama Mexicana* (the Mexican Branch).[43] A power struggle ensued between the two men; the fealty of many to Bautista caused much trepidation among Solano's supporters. Simultaneously, Bautista began questioning crucial LDS teachings. While in Mexico he claimed to have had a vision in which God called him to be the new prophet to the Lamanites. In addition, Bautista condoned polygamy, a practice that the church disavowed in 1890. Margarito was excommunicated in 1924, and church authorities decided that new leadership was needed at the Rama Mexicana. A Hispanic individual would not be named branch president again until the middle of the 1960s.[44] The divisions caused by this split threatened to tear the Rama apart. Horace H. Cummings, who replaced Solano as president in October, 1924, appealed to his Spanish-speaking charges for harmony and fidelity to church authorities: "I am greatly saddened by what has happened here. We hope that this dispute will be resolved in a satisfactory manner, that all Mexicans join in harmony, that they treat each other with love, without jealousies . . . [that they] sustain [church] authorities, regardless of their race, and that they become a single church and people."[45]

Even though the group was denied a leadership position, bonds forged within this ethnic network tied to Utah's majority population proved beneficial to the spiritual, economic, and psychic lives of the Spanish-surnamed converts. Several events in the life of Rafael Torres demonstrate the advantages of membership in the Rama. Shortly after his arrival in Salt Lake City in 1922 Rafael met Juan, Francisco, and Margarito and became an investigador. Rafael eventually converted because he felt that Mormonism was "the right religion." Interview transcripts leave little doubt as to the sincerity of Torres's conversion. However, they also provide a glimpse into the loneliness single, immigrant men faced in Utah during the early part of the 1920s. The Rama, and the contacts made there, provided spiritual comfort and much more. These gatherings afforded Rafael opportunities to socialize with some of the few *solteras* (single) Mexicanas in northern Utah. During one of these assemblies Rafael met Tila's sister Dolores, and the couple married in 1923. Tila and Agustina also met their future husbands, Cástulo Martínez and Manuel Torres, at Rama Mexicana–sponsored events.

Branch contacts aided the Torres family economically. Margarito helped

Rafael land an assembly-line position with the Nathaniel Baldwin Company in 1923. During the middle of the decade Francisco assisted Rafael in finding construction jobs throughout the city. During the Great Depression, when unemployment surged to 50 percent in parts of the Salt Lake Valley, Anthony R. Ivins, who supervised the Rama during the 1930s, interceded for Torres and helped him procure a bellhop post at the Temple Square Hotel, a job Rafael kept until 1944.[46] Part of his duties at the hotel included working in the coffee shop. He assisted the night clerk and felt, after a few years, that he could competently handle managing the establishment. When the young clerk was promoted to another position within the hotel, he enthusiastically recommended Torres as his replacement. The hotel manager now faced a difficult decision. He liked and respected the hardworking Mexicano, but he ultimately did not promote him because he felt that "not everyone [knew] Rafael" as the staff did and that customers might not like having a dark-skinned person in a supervisory position.[47]

This incident provides important insight into race relations in northern Utah during the first half of the 1900s. Religious contacts helped Rafael get a job, but his association with the LDS network did not overcome all obstacles created by racism. In his 1997 work, *Born Again in Brazil,* R. Andrew Chestnut notes the positive impact of conversion upon the lives of neophyte *creyentes* (believers) in Brazil but acknowledges that limitations based on race continued.[48] Two students of Mormon ethnic history in the United States, Richard L. Jensen and Jessie L. Embry, note similar patterns. In his essay "Mother Tongue: Use of Non-English Languages in the Church of Jesus Christ of Latter-day Saints in the U.S., 1850–1983," Jensen asserts that assimilation has been a dominant theme in church policy for immigrants from northern Europe. However, descendants of Book of Mormon people, such as mestizos, have not been as well accepted by individual church members.[49] Embry's work supports this assertion. Rama Mexicana constituent Arturo Rivera Martínez recalled that prejudice "often came from 'those who held high positions in the Church' . . . some Mormons [were] reluctant to trust Mexicans . . . [and] refused to work with Mexicans, insisting that they were dirty."[50]

Another individual whose religious contacts led to economic advantage was Juan Flores. Juan was born in Mexico but immigrated to the United States in 1918 to top and thin beets in Montana. By 1925 Flores's search for employment brought him to Salt Lake City, where he toiled at a railroad roundhouse. During this time Juan met Rama members and eventually converted to the LDS faith. A bishop then intervened and helped him obtain a better position at Bingham Canyon. Juan worked in the copper industry for the next forty years, retiring in 1967.[51]

Membership in the Rama Mexicana also proved valuable in other aspects of life, such as dealings with the Salt Lake City police department. The case of Eufemio Salazar is instructive in revealing the utility of being a Spanish-surnamed Mormon in the heart of Zion. Eufemio hailed form the town of Ricones (Conejos County), Colorado, and was raised in the LDS faith. Harsh economic conditions in his home region forced him to seek employment in Utah. Upon his arrival he quickly joined the Rama Mexicana. In a 1976 interview Eufemio recalled how this crucial affiliation served him during an unpleasant incident with local authorities. Apparently the constables were on the lookout for a certain suspect, and Salazar happened to fit the general description. Fortunately, once the questioning began, Eufemio played his ace in the hole. In the intereview he stated, "I gave him my genealogy, and all other proper information." Instantly the comportment of the interrogating officer changed drastically. Where before he had seen a potentially dangerous "Mexican" criminal, he now saw a responsible citizen and said, "This man is fine. This man has done nothing wrong. Release him and take him to work."[52] This incident can be contrasted with the treatment of other Mexicanos and Mexican Americans who had dealings with the Salt Lake City police department during the 1920s. "In early 1921 as a result of police raid on 'pool halls and soft drink parlors,' 150 supposed 'vagrants,' mostly Mexican, were checked in connection with a crime for which a Mexican was suspected. Of that number . . . 32 plead guilty to vagrancy, 29 of whom proved that they were men with families who had lost their jobs and were permitted to remain in the city."[53]

Additionally, the Rama served as a place for social activities and networking. Silas Lobato remembered that the meetinghouse was the center of his social life during his teenage years. Silas was born in Las Tablas, New Mexico, in August of 1921. His family moved to Bingham Canyon during the 1920s when his father and uncle procured positions as miners. While in school the young Lobato became interested in scouting, music, and singing. Connections forged at the Rama allowed him the opportunity to participate in all of these activities. As an illustration of Silas's acknowledgment of the importance of this religious/ethnic net, in a 1984 interview he stated: "The LDS religion looks upon the people of Spanish origin or Indian origin, as very—you know, even favorably. And they took me under their wing and I was pretty much set with them."[54] Amy L. Sherman's work *The Soul of Development* examines the value of conversion among creyentes in Central and South America. She reveals some of the important internal/personal changes generated by these relations when she states, "converts enjoy a new range of opportunities for social advancement. . . . Congregants may enjoy access to . . . schools and tuition assistance from their church. Perhaps even more important, membership . . .

may expose congregants to the world outside . . . develop relationships with fellow[s] . . . from other areas of the country . . . [and] then increase their awareness of business, jobs, and educational opportunities."[55] For Silas Lobato and other young Spanish-surnamed converts, membership provided an opportunity to join the Boy Scouts (the LDS Church began sponsoring troops within wards and missions in 1913), as well as the chance to receive training in music and other fields designed to build individual skills and self-esteem.[56] Silas used his musical training to build a career and toured most of the western United States with his own band.[57]

Although a Hispanic did not head the Rama Mexicana again until the 1960s, the branch provided members of both sexes with opportunities to direct in-house groups. From the mission's earliest days (starting in April, 1921) Spanish-surnamed individuals led activities such as Sunday school. Juan R. Martínez was the first superintendent, Margarito Bautista was selected as theological instructor, and Francisco Solano was assistant. Between 1928 and 1931 seven Mexicanos or Mexican Americans served the Rama as first or second counselors. Starting in October, 1923, the mujeres of the congregation organized a *Sociedad de Socorro* (Relief Society). Not surprisingly, the three Rivera sisters occupied leadership positions. Agustina was named president, Dolores served as first counselor, and Tila performed the society's secretarial functions. This relief organization helped sick or injured constituents, raised money for the needy through bake sales and bazaars, and established a quilting circle that distributed blankets to member families.[58] The branch also housed Mutual Improvement Associations (for men and women) starting in April, 1925. Members of the Rivera, Torres, and Martínez clans provided leaders for both branches of *las asociaciónes de mejoramiento mutuo*. Between 1925 and the early 1960s these entities gained a regional reputation within the LDS Church for their Mexican-style dinners (often used to raise money for building construction) and Mexican folklore road shows.[59]

The Rama also sponsored dances and traditional fiestas. Descriptions of these events are helpful for an understanding of Sánchez's notion of a continuum of experience. At these dances many Mexican cultural traditions were celebrated, but other established practices, such as folkloric Mexican Christmas rituals, were undermined. In regard to Yuletide celebrations, the interview with Arturo Rivera Martínez, as cited by Jessie L. Embry, provides much insight. Rivera Martínez claimed that Rama members "were able to retain most of our culture" but then acknowledged that European American elements (such as parties with Santa Claus) eventually crept into the festivities. He explained, "I guess that wasn't part of the Spanish culture, Mexican culture, but we combined them all."[60]

Chaperoning practices declined within the confines of the Rama Mexicana. Clotilda Gómez remembered that her father was strict in chaperoning her during her middle teenage years. Once the family joined the Rama and Clotilda started dating LDS boys, her father eased dating restrictions. Rama Mexicana members preserved some of their ancestral customs, but the safety and security of their new ethnic network made it easier to discard or deemphasize certain practices.[61]

Missionary efforts continued during the 1920s, and by decade's end the Rama had grown to sixty-nine worshipers.[62] As their numbers grew, the rest of the comunidad began to take notice of the converts. The reactions of family, friends, and community to conversion spanned the entire spectrum of emotions from acceptance and ambivalence to confusion and outright hostility. One neophyte, Clotilda Gómez, claimed that to her family, "it was . . . just something that they thought was strange for me to be doing. They didn't resent it . . . we had no problems."[63] As far as Clotilda was concerned, she was still a member in good standing of the broader comunidad and did not wish to lose most of her cultural and ethnic connections.

Clotilda's family and friends may not have resented her decision, but relations between the LDS and non-LDS Hispanics were not always so smooth. Events in the life of Helen Salazar-Benavides illustrate how religious affiliation often worked to divide the Spanish-speaking community. Helen was born in the small town of Manassa, Colorado, in 1918 and was raised in an LDS familia. She recalls that living in a mostly Catholic area made her father fanatical about his beliefs. The family moved to Utah in the late 1920s to work the sugar beet fields of southern Idaho. While in Salt Lake City they lived on the west side and attended services at the Rama Mexicana. During these years the branch had an excellent basketball team which, ironically, consisted mostly of Católico (Catholic) Mexicano and Mexican American boys. This situation was absolutely abhorrent to Helen's father. The boys on this squad were good enough to win games for the Rama in church league play, but not good enough to gain acceptance by many at the branch. Helen described her father as a man who "discriminated against the Mexicans from Mexico. Because they were Catholics. And to him a Catholic was not a Christian." Helen's father did not draw distinctions between himself and other Spanish-speakers because of his occupation, place of residence, birthplace, or ethnicity. Nevertheless, he recognized that religious belief made a dramatic difference in Utah, and he passed this attitude down to his children. Of her childhood in Salt Lake City, Helen remembered: "We never thought anything of . . . being a minority. I couldn't even say we were different from anybody else." Helen claimed that she did not suffer discrimination or racism, but later on in this interview she recalled that during her childhood the Salazar family never traveled east of the city's dividing line, State Street.[64]

The members of the Mexican Branch derived social, economic, and psychic benefits from their religious association. However, they did not totally shed their ethnic identity. In one of the few works on the Spanish-speaking people of Utah produced during the 1970s, Lionel A. Maldonado's and David R. Byrne's *Social Ecology of Chicanos in Utah,* the authors contend that Hispanic Mormon converts were forced to "conform to the denominational culture. . . . and [that the LDS Church tends] to purge ethic dissimilarities."[65] As revealed by the interviews and other materials cited above, this view of the denomination's influence upon colonia constituents appears far too simplistic and one-dimensional. The experiences of Rama Mexicana members were much more complex. They did affiliate with the majority population and its ethnic network, but they refused to jettison all ethnic traits. A member of the El Paso, Texas, branch (in the 1970s) summed up the feelings of many Spanish-surnamed Mormons in Utah when he stated, "We do not feel that (the) added burden of acculturation should be a condition for developing the gospel."[66] Rather, the lives of these individuals and families provide cogent substantiation for Sánchez's notion of a cultural continuum at work.[67]

Before 1920 the Salt Lake Catholic Diocese had little reason to consider the creation of an institution specifically dedicated to the needs of the Spanish-surnamed population of northern Utah.[68] Diocesan records show that only thirteen baptisms for Hispanic children were performed in Utah between 1902 and 1916.[69] The church hierarchy's focus was on the more numerous Italian, Syrian, and Armenian immigrants living on Salt Lake City's west side. By December, 1920, Saint Patrick's Parish, on 400 West and 500 South, was dedicated to serving the needs of Italian Catholics.[70]

Diocesan administrators may not have been aware of the growth of the city's Spanish-speaking population, but a local priest who worked near the city's depots certainly was. In December, 1920, Father Francis M. Alva provided the diocese with a census of ninety-six "Mexican" families living between the Union Pacific Railroad depot on South Temple and 400 West and a similar Denver and Rio Grande Railroad facility on 500 West and 400 South. The document noted that about one hundred Spanish-surnamed children were attending local schools. Each of the families had between three and ten children, all of them baptized by the Catholic Church. Eighty-eight of the couples were married in church services, and eight were wed by civil authorities. Father Alva reached out to this group by offering Spanish-language masses on Sundays and Holy Days after Christmas of 1920. During this time he noted that "assistance to this mass is growing every Sunday."[71]

Alva also suggested a plan of action for reaching out and providing aid to these people. He called for the establishment of a separate school and church to be built in what he called "the mission style" and urged that the name Our Lady of Guadalupe be adopted for the project. This facility would, Alva believed, serve a dual purpose: it would reduce construction costs for the cash-poor diocese; and "its religious beauty and historical remembrance" would remind worshipers of their native land and culture.[72] Concurrently Alva recognized the "danger" posed by the Rivera sisters and their fellow Mormon missionaries. For this reason the priest also suggested that a Spanish-speaking priest be brought in to "protect them against the many preachers of all kind who are after them."[73]

The sense of urgency in Alva's letter did not translate into immediate action by the diocese. The Italian mission did not welcome its first Spanish-speaking priest, Father Perfecto Arellano, until September, 1927. Arellano became the assistant pastor at Saint Patrick's with special duties and responsibilities for the Mexicanos and Mexican Americans of the area. His stay on the west side was brief, lasting only two months. Fathers Antonio and Turibio Galaviz (they were brothers) replaced Arellano. They arrived in December, 1927, and immediately began offering both religious and musical instruction to the children of the area. Antonio and Turibio remained in Salt Lake City until July of 1929, when they were allowed to return to Mexico following the lifting of sanctions against the Catholic Church by the Mexican government. Father Inocencio Martín replaced the brothers but filled the post for only two months.[74]

The rapid turnover of personnel at the mission created a situation that called for a stabilizing presence. Fortunately for the Católicos living in Salt Lake City's west side, the Cristero revolt in Mexico (and the expulsion of church personnel) provided an opportunity for Mexicano priests and nuns to serve their countrymen in various parts of the United States. As Gilberto M. Hinojosa states in *Mexican Americans and the Catholic Church, 1900–1965,* this uprising helped colonia members because "while Mexicanos did not bring their clergy with them, as other immigrants had, Mexican clergy in a sense accompanied them and assisted them, at least temporarily."[75] Nuns from the Order of the Sisters of Perpetual Adoration eventually took on the task of providing continuity and basic services for the Spanish-speaking men, women, and children of the area. In September, 1927, Monsignor Duane G. Hunt contacted the Los Angeles Archdiocese in order to obtain information regarding the use of refugee Mexican clerics and nuns. In a letter to Monsignor Hunt, Father Leroy Callahan described how Mexican sisters taught catechism, directed mothers' and girls' clubs, and performed home visits among the familias living in the barrios of Southern California.[76] Monsignor Hunt determined that a program of this type would be useful and arranged to have six nuns move to Utah. They arrived in Salt Lake City on November 11, 1927.

During their twelve-year stay the sisters, or *las madres* (the mothers), as they were called, became an integral part of the comunidad. They lived and worked out of a west side home located on 528 West 400 South that had been converted into a convent-chapel and given the name Our Lady of Guadalupe (although officially it remained part of Saint Patrick's parish).[77] They inaugurated a kindergarten class, taught Sunday school, and established a summer school program. Las madres participated in so many activities that in 1931 and 1938 their superiors reprimanded them for not keeping a twenty-four-hour vigil of the Holy Eucharist, as is the rule for their order.[78] While the workload brought reprimands from their supervisors, las madres greatly impressed local Catholics with their service and devotion. Mary A. Thompson, who chaired the Mission Circle for the Women's Catholic League, commented that "to have such educated and refined women as these among our foreign born makes for a more cultured group of foreigners. They reach a people with whom we have difficulty getting a contact."[79]

In April, 1930, Father James E. Collins arrived at Guadalupe. Collins, who hailed from Salem, New York, had been an assistant pastor at the Cathedral of the Madeleine in downtown Salt Lake City.[80] From 1930 until his death in August, 1957, Collins provided dedicated and capable administration and service to this overwhelmingly Spanish-speaking congregation. His first task was to learn the native language of his flock. Frances Yánez, whose family arrived in Utah during the 1920s, fondly recalled Father Collins's early attempts to complete a mass in Spanish. As he attempted to navigate through sections of his homily, the majority of the congregation would often call out in unison whenever the good pastor made a mistake.[81] While this led to many comical situations during what should have been a solemn occasion, most of the flock admired Collins because of his efforts to learn *Español* (Spanish) and to serve "his" people.[82]

In addition to providing services to the community, Father Collins also acted as a buffer for Hispanics against the "good Catholic ladies" (such as Mrs. Mary A. Thompson) who tried to help the "unfortunate" Mexicanos and Mexican Americans "but who betrayed snobbish and condescending attitudes toward the poor Spanish-speaking women with their ever present babies and small children."[83] The creation of a Catholic mission on the west side allowed another group of Spanish-speakers to build upon existing ethnic ties. The connections created at Guadalupe mirrored some of those of the Rama Mexicana; the services provided helped colonia members survive in northern Utah while maintaining many aspects of their culture.

The children who participated in the various activities at Guadalupe were affectionately referred to as Father Collins's "kids." One of these was María Dolores González-Mayo. María Dolores was born in 1924 in Santa Fe, New Mexico. Her family owned several small farms but was unable to sustain its self-sufficiency and independence during the Great Depression. In the early 1930s the González clan migrated to Utah in search of jobs. María Dolores's father worked as part of a track gang at Bingham Canyon, while her two brothers toiled in the copper mine. The young girl's mother ran a boardinghouse that served the needs of Spanish-speaking mineros. Amidst all this drudgery and toil the family found both assistance and fellowship at the Catholic mission. María Dolores described family members as devout Catholics "whose life centered around their church." This young girl attended mass on a daily basis and school during the summers, participated in parties (known as *Jamaicas*), and played baseball under the watchful eyes of Collins and las madres. During holiday seasons services at Guadalupe were performed in traditional fashion. A favorite Christmas event of María Dolores was the procession known as the Posadas. Families traveled from house to house in the neighborhood reenacting Mary and Joseph's search for shelter. The occupants of the individual dwellings would refuse entrance to the revelers. This activity would continue until all of the houses in the area had been visited; the procession eventually wound up at the church building where the evening's celebration would culminate in a Christmas mass and feast.[84]

The Guadalupe mission also served as a center for community social events. Bertha Amador-Mayer was one teenager who participated in many church-sponsored dances and cultural programs and productions. Bertha was born in Mexico in 1912. The family moved to the United States in 1926 when her brothers were hired to work the beet fields of Utah and Idaho; the Amador men eventually procured employment at the Garfield Smelter. Bertha was a talented singer who often performed traditional Mexican music at both Guadalupe and the Rama Mexicana. As was the case for the Mormon congregation, young Spanish-speaking teenagers could meet members of the opposite sex at the mission, and there is where Bertha met her future husband, Vicente.[85]

The services provided and social experiences of worshipers at the Rama Mexicana and Guadalupe paralleled in many ways, but there were some crucial differences. Dating customs among the Guadalupe familias, for example, appear to have been more in line with traditional Mexican and Mexican American practices than were those at the Rama. It seems that Catholic parents, with direct ties to their ancestral church and many of its customs, were less willing to forgo the practice of chaperoning. Father Reyes Rodríguez, a *nativo* (native son) of the west side and one of Father Collins's kids, recounted the strict rules followed by his parents while they dated in Salt Lake City during the 1920s: "She [his mother] was always guarded by her aunt. They were all tightly held and watched closely and weren't allowed to go anywhere. You know, it always remains a mystery how they ever got married."[86]

Dating practices were not the only difference. On a more temporal (economic) plane, the LDS network had a distinct advantage in its ability to generate leads for job openings. The oral histories of Rama Mexicana members provide many references of how religious contacts helped in the acquisition of employment. Catholic Hispanics in these collections do not often allude to this type of aid. If in parts of Latin America, where Protestants are a substantial minority, these connections have been shown to help individuals in job searches, it is easy to envision the significant impact of such ties for Utah's Mormones. It is likely that job openings were discussed after masses or during social events at the Catholic mission. However, the principal variance is that the Rama Mexicana afforded better contacts for job recommendations. The Anglo men who led the branch after 1924 had access to Utah's business community that was unavailable to the common laborers who comprised the bulk of the mission's congregation.[87]

As observed with Rama constituents, the members of Guadalupe experienced the full spectrum of relationships with their LDS neighbors. María Dolores González-Mayo's encounters were, on the whole, positive. She recalled that her older brother dated several Rama girls and that Catholics were made to feel welcome at most of their social events. María Dolores also told of having a crush on one young man from the branch: "I don't remember that we ever argued religion. We were just kids, we were [just] having a good time." Although these relationships appear to have been friendly on the surface, there are similarities to Helen Salazar-Benavides's experience; those who were a different faith were often kept at arm's length. The González family socialized with LDS Hispanics, but they insisted that their daughter marry a Católico in order to raise their grandchildren in a "traditional Catholic atmosphere."[88]

Events in the life of Epifanio González demonstrate the more negative side of relations between Catholic colonia members and Mormons. Epifanio was born in California in 1921, and by 1929 he and his family were working the beet fields of Utah. In a 1985 interview Epifanio summarized some of the predicaments of growing up Católico in the heart of the Mormon Zion. A formidable obstacle was the reaction of many LDS members to his skin color. Epifanio was dark skinned and was often told that this "scourge" was a punishment for his sins, or those of his ancestors. A key passage regarding the significance of skin color comes from the Book of Mormon's Alma 3:6: "And the skins of the Lamanites were dark, according to the mark which was set upon their fathers, which was a curse upon them because of their transgression and their rebellion against their brethren, who consisted of Nephi, Jacob, Joseph, and Sam, who were just and holy men." Epifanio's skin color was not the sole barrier to his acceptance into northern Utah society; "the second failure [was] when they found out that you are of the Catholic faith." These psychic traumas caused Epifanio great resentment toward the Church of Jesus Christ of Latter-day Saints and its members—so much resentment that in his later years he would pray for the souls of Mormons because he felt that their beliefs on race (and their actions toward him) had surely condemned them to eternal damnation.[89]

In 1973 Brigham Young University student Martin Alden Johnson completed a doctoral dissertation for the school's Department of Psychology which examined the issue of Mormon attitudes toward racial minorities. His results provide some support of Epifanio's contentions. In his research Johnson's sample population demonstrated that "the Mormons are not significantly different from those of other religious persuasions in their secular racial attitudes toward Negroes, American Indians, and Mexican Americans." This result in some ways contradicts the church's stance that mestizos are part of a people with a particular (crucial?) role to play in bringing about the millennial kingdom. The reason that Epifanio González and other dark-skinned people faced mistreatment, Johnson asserts, is because "possibly the Mormon subjects simply have not attended to these teachings, or have disregarded them. Another possibility . . . is that determinants of prejudice are mediating or overriding the effects of Mormon tenets on secular racial attitudes."[90]

In substantial and important ways the organizations created by northern Utah Hispanics between 1920 and the middle 1930s strengthened the preexisting ties of language and ethnicity. These entities became the institutional manifestations of an existing network. The associations provided some assistance to those in need, fostered a level of cultural pride, and tied individual members of the comunidad to an overarching ethnic identity. These groups also spotlight the most critical differences within this community: Not all individuals maintained the same attachment to traditional cultural customs and practices. The Spanish-speaking men, women, and children who converted to the Church of Jesus Christ of Latter-day Saints connected to another (and within Utah a more effective) network—one tied directly to the majority population. Catholic Hispanics created and participated in their own church and religious association, but with limited resources and (economic) contacts it did not benefit them as much as the Rama benefited the Mormons. In particular, the Mormon net had a greater ability to link creyentes with occupational opportunities. Both religious institutions provided services, cultural havens (to a certain extent), and warm fellowship for constituents during the last years of the 1920s. Unfortunately, the coming of the Great Depression produced a tremendous amount of strain and hardship upon these two assemblages. The Catholic mission was less well equipped to meet the crisis. The 1930s were difficult times for all of Utah's Spanish-speakers, but the LDS network provided Rama Mexicana members with much firmer ground from which to weather the economic storm.

3

"El Diablo Nos Esta Llevando"
Utah's Spanish-Speaking Population and the Great Depression, 1930–40[1]

We're down on Fourth South far from luxury, down where the viaduct spans the D and RG, most unpretentious, but somewhat quaint, with Guadalupe as our patron saint.

—Theme song of the Guadalupe Mission

The spiritual welfare of those on relief must receive especial care and be earnestly and prayerfully fostered. A system which gives relief for work or service will go far in reaching those goals.

—Heber J. Grant, LDS Church president

While many areas of the United States enjoyed levels of economic prosperity during the 1920s, Utah endured a severe post–World War I recession. Decreased demands for metals and a return to full production by European farmers were crushing blows to key state industries. Reductions in these critical areas also touched rail transportation, causing layoffs and cutbacks that further slowed commercial activity.[2] Although there were signs of a gradual recovery by 1925, economic trends during the decade did not keep pace with the rest of the West and nation. By 1929 per capita income for Utah's residents was $537 per year, only 80 percent of the national average.[3]

Although Utah's economy did not boom during the Jazz Age, it still attracted an increasing number of Spanish-speaking men, women, and children to the area.[4] By 1930 more than 4,000 people of Mexican origin lived in Utah, and more than one-half of them lived in Salt Lake and Weber Counties (2,222).[5] These clusters depended upon agriculture (primarily beet-field work in the Cache Valley and southern Idaho), mining, and transportation for their low-paying jobs. The Great Depression devastated industry and the lives of many of its most vulnerable employees. By 1940 the federal census for Utah recorded a 73 percent drop in the number of Mexican-born individuals in the state (from 4,012 to 1,069). As occurred elsewhere, Spanish-speaking employees in Utah were among the first fired during industrial downturns.[6]

This chapter will examine the effects of the Great Depression on work, daily life, organizations, and religious institutions of northern Utah's colonias, comparing local trends with other sections of the country. The downturn's impact upon industry will be explored, as will the participation of Spanish-speakers in government-funded programs. Finally, the efficacy of the Catholic and Latter-day Saint assistance networks will be compared and contrasted.[7]

Utah agriculture benefited greatly from Europe's military turmoil. By the end of World War I the price of sugar beets, the state's most significant crop, had surged from seven dollars to over twelve dollars per ton.[8] The upswing in commodity prices ended in the winter of 1920, and by November, 1921, the price of beets plummeted to less than five dollars per ton. In 1922 farmers in the Cache Valley, the heart of Utah's sugar beet country, decreased acreage planted by more than 60 percent.[9] Lower earnings forced many farmers to slash costs or to leave farming altogether.[10] After enduring a steady decline after the end of World War I, prices for agricultural commodities declined by another 61 percent between 1929 and 1932.[11] A slumping sugar beet industry during the 1920s meant difficult times for the Spanish-surnamed people of the state, but the Great Depression made matters even worse for betabeleros and their familias.[12]

Natural as well as economic disasters ravaged Utah's agricultural industry during the 1930s. A serious drought plagued the state in 1931 and was followed by an even worse one in 1934. The winter of 1933–34 was unusually warm, with disastrous results. By planting season of that year water levels in area lakes were as much as fourteen feet below normal. In 1934 Utah's farmers planted only 30 percent of their normal acreage and managed to harvest but 40 percent of the drastically reduced crop. These circumstances caused a sharp drop in the pay of betabeleros. In Idaho wages decreased from twenty-eight dollars to ten dollars per acre. Conditions were so grim that Salt Lake City's Mexican consulate office issued statements claiming that some of their charges would starve to death if they did not receive immediate assistance.[13] Those who retained employment struggled to increase their earnings; many took their children out of schools to assist in the fields. Many contractors took advantage of this situation and employed only large families (with children older than six years of age). The wages paid to these people remained slightly above the subsistence level in order to keep them coming back to the fields season after season.[14]

The family of Francisca "Pancha" González toiled under these difficult conditions. Pancha was born in Amarillo, Texas, in April of 1918. Her father arrived in Utah during the 1920s to work for the Union Pacific Railroad. Family members supplemented his earnings by working the sugar beet fields. During the winters Pancha's father was often forced to steal coal in order to heat the family's home. By 1930 the clan had mushroomed to seven children. Pancha's parents never planned how they would support their new offspring. She reported: "That's the first thing you do now with the kids. We've got to save money. . . . Heck in those days if you had enough to eat that was good." Tragically, this tenuous strategy for economic and familial survival crumbled at the worst possible time; Pancha's father died in 1930 while his wife was pregnant with their eighth child. This calamity deprived Pancha of even a rudimentary education; the children were now more essential to the family's survival than ever. Pancha became so frustrated with these living conditions that she married at age fourteen in an attempt to escape.[15]

Cruz Campero García's experiences were strikingly similar. Cruz was born in Mexico in 1919. After stops in El Paso and Chicago his family arrived in Salt Lake City during the 1920s. García's father worked for the Denver and Rio Grande Railroad, but his pay did not support the entire family. Cruz quit school at the age of fourteen to supplement the family's income. He worked in the celery fields of Salt Lake County during the winter and did odd jobs throughout the city the rest of the year. Eventually Cruz signed on with a local macaroni manufacturer. His take-home pay for seven days' worth of labor amounted to twelve dollars.[16]

Demand for metals decreased after World War I, and production of gold, silver, lead, and zinc from Utah mines plummeted 54 percent by 1919. In 1920 copper production was 50 percent below 1917 levels.[17] Utah Copper responded to this slowdown by releasing more than six thousand men from their posts at Bingham Canyon.[18] In 1922 conditions began to improve, and by 1929 Bingham experienced a boom. During these years Spanish-surnamed workers held the lowest paying, least skilled, and most dangerous jobs, as they did in mines throughout the West and Southwest.[19] Unfortunately, this level of prosperity did not last long. In 1930 copper began to lose its luster, and by November the metal's price dropped to below the break-even price of twelve cents per pound. Employers attempted to keep as many people on the job as possible, but by 1932 most Bingham employers had shut down or drastically curtailed operations. A disastrous fire on September 8, 1932, compounded the economic crisis. Seventy-five homes were destroyed as the flames swept through and devastated the Highland Boy section of the canyon's living quarters.[20]

The family of Esperanza and Gavino Aguayo managed to scratch out a living in Bingham during the 1930s. Gavino was born in Mexico in 1925, and his sister was born in Bingham in March, 1932. Their parents were farmers who had fled Mexico during its revolutionary turmoil. Esperanza's uncle worked in the mines during the 1920s and eventually convinced his brother to move with his family to the Beehive State. The 1932 fire destroyed the Aguayo home, but the family remained and moved to the neighboring community of Dinkeyville. Esperanza and Gavino were fortunate in that their father never lost his job during these lean years. He kept working, even if only for a day or two per week. The family bartered with neighbors for the goods and services they could not afford and subsisted mostly on tortillas and potatoes prepared by their mother. Conditions were harsh, but the children felt lucky to be as well off as they were. Esperanza and Gavino reported: "You know, we were poor. . . . But really at that time . . . we didn't know it."[21]

No other industry, besides agriculture, attracted a larger amount of Spanish-speaking labor to the Southwest than *el traque* (track work). Most Mexicanos and Mexican Americans toiled in gangs that maintained the lines of the various railroad companies. This job often entailed living next to the tracks. Upon completing their daily labor, these men returned to homes that were nothing more that antiquated boxcars with limited furnishings and outdoor toilet facilities. Railroad labor historian Jeffrey Marcos Garcilazo's work about traqueros provides a vivid description of the conditions that confronted Mexicanos and Mexican American gang laborers and their familias: "Boxcar housing appeared in two basic forms. The first type provided temporary housing for grading and construction gangs (building new roads) and the second type . . . (was) permanent housing for section and extra gangs. . . . Residents in semipermanent housing eventually bought furniture and made basic improvements. . . . Boxcar housing amenities varied from one railroad to another. Some companies equipped boxcars with new wood burning stoves, others had none. . . . Railroads did not always provide proper sanitation services, filling holes and digging new ones, in a timely manner."[22] Conditions for traquero families in Utah conformed to this pattern.[23]

The post–World War I recession damaged Utah's transportation sector, although not as severely as it did agriculture and mining. In 1921 rates, revenues, and employment levels for this industry in Utah decreased, but the slowdown proved to be temporary. Total employment for Utah railroads actually increased slightly (from 7,700 to 8,000, an increase of about 4 percent) during the 1920s. Although healthier than other sections of the state's economy, the railroads were also hard hit by the Great Depression.[24] Spanish-surnamed labor had been a crucial element of the transportation industry in Utah during the preceding decade, especially for the Union Pacific and Denver and Rio

Grande lines. The early 1930s brought dramatic change. The number of His-panic employees of the Union Pacific decreased and would not return to pre-Depression levels until the start of World War II.[25]

María Dolores García grew up near the Denver and Rio Grande Railroad depot in Salt Lake City. María was born in Mexico in April, 1917, and her fam-ily moved to northern Utah in 1923 after her father procured employment with the railroad. Although he never lost his job, it took great effort to make ends meet during the Depression. The Garcías scrimped and saved wherever and whenever they could, buying canned goods in bulk and making all of their clothes at home. Unlike others on the west side, the family managed to have Christmas celebrations every year, although María Dolores's stockings were filled with fruits and nuts rather than the hoped-for toys and games.[26]

José Méndel and his family experienced similar difficulties. He worked on the tracks during the 1930s and, while grateful for the opportunity to work, complained bitterly that the railroad took advantage of its employees. Mén-del's supervisor warned him that he could leave if working conditions were not to his satisfaction; there were more than enough laborers willing to accept his low-paying position. In a 1970 interview José recalled that during the Depres-sion years he earned only thirty-eight cents per hour, or about fourteen dollars for two weeks of work. His family stretched his meager pay by subsisting on potatoes and gravy.[27]

As the economic catastrophe spread and worsened it did not matter whether one was a betabelero, a minero, or a traquero; most colonia members faced daunting challenges to keep body, soul, and family together. Through-out the entire country Spanish-surnamed women played an important role in helping their comunidades and familias persevere. In Utah, and elsewhere, Hispanic women stretched budgets, raised their children, assisted neighbors and strangers, and worked outside their homes.[28]

One of the most insightful examinations of the contributions of Spanish-speaking women to familial survival during this era is Julia Kirk Blackwelder's *Women of the Depression*. This study details the activities, sacrifices, and suffer-ings of Anglo, African American, and Mexican American women in the Alamo City. Blackwelder contends that the three racial groups comprised different castes and that this "system based on race, color, or ethnicity was a dominant force shaping women's lives."[29] Regardless of their class, the Great Depression caused much emotional and physical trauma for Spanish-surnamed women. Middle-class familias in San Antonio had more resources to draw upon, but Blackwelder maintains that even these Mexicana or Mexican American mujeres "could not turn their backs on the misery in their midst."[30] Blackwelder's work presents important insight on the role of race/caste, but ignores the role of religious affiliation as a variable in the lives of Depression-era women. What aid and benefits did the Catholic Church provide for Spanish-speaking women? Did Hispanics affiliated with Protestant denominations experience the Great Depression in the same way as their Catholic vecinos did? These questions are of crucial importance to the stories of women and familias in northern Utah.

John Florez's family managed to survive in Salt Lake City during the depths of the Depression. John, a native of the west side, was born in January, 1932. His father, Reyes Florez, moved to Utah to work for the Denver and Rio Grande line during the late 1910s. Even during the economic crisis he managed to hold his job as a traquero. Family members supplemented his salary by working in the beet fields in the spring and autumn seasons. Florez recalled that the family lived in an old boxcar that had been subdivided into a kitchen and living area. Their "house" was located a mere twenty feet from the tracks. Incarnación, John's mother, fought a never-ending battle to keep the quarters clear of dust and dirt. Her financial responsibilities included figuring a way to elongate her family's meager cash influx; she accomplished this by serving beans and tortillas on a daily basis.

Although the family was poor, Incarnación raised her children with a deep sense of pride in their Mexicano heritage. The Florez children faced a constant battle in school as teachers and peers humiliated them by claiming that their culture and customs were savage and barbaric. Their mother patiently and diligently countered these detrimental influences by teaching her offspring about Aztec history, culture, and art. She also rendered valuable services to the less fortunate of the community. The unemployed frequented the Florez boxcar because they knew that the lady of this "house" provided food to all who requested it.

Concurrently, Incarnación helped colonia members through her work as a *curandera* (healer). E. Ferol Benavides, a student of these practices, describes *curanderismo* as "a combination of folk medicine and faith healing. To some it is all one or the other, but most curanderos/as combine a knowledge of herbal remedies with liberal doses of prayer and religious/superstitious ritual. . . . The curanderos/as . . . never advertise and are often difficult to unearth, particularly for a researcher who is not a member of the subculture."[31] Apparently Incarnación's skills must have been considerable, for she "was well known . . . throughout Utah and neighboring states . . . and practiced her healing arts until her death in 1968."[32] Neighbors often came to John's mother seeking cures for assorted maladies or to have their fortunes told. Sometimes the rituals worked, but more often they merely provided spiritual comfort. Incarnación Florez did much to help her family and community overcome the trials and tribulations of the 1930s. But her magic and beliefs were not powerful enough to ameliorate conditions or to spare her heartache. She lost nine of twelve children to childhood diseases, and the family's poverty was certainly a contributing factor. John summarized the Florez's Great Depression experiences by stating, "people who talk about 'the good old days' do so because they didn't have to live it."[33]

Although the Spanish-surnamed women of northern Utah filled many and varied roles, they, like their sisters in other parts of the United States, felt that their primary task was to raise their children to be *bien educado* (well mannered).[34] Traditional standards were even more crucial now that many of them and their children were living in *lo extranjero* (outside their nation, culture, and traditions). Clotilda (Tilly) Ontiveros-Gómez recalled that her mother emphasized proper manners even during the trying times of the Great Depression. Tilly's family immigrated to the United States to work in the beet fields of Idaho in May, 1919, and stayed for two years. During the early 1920s some of her father's coworkers moved to Utah and procured jobs at the smelter located in the Salt Lake City suburb of Murray; the Ontiveroses soon followed. Tilly's father managed to stay employed during the 1930s as part of a skeleton crew at this facility. The few days that he worked were not enough to support his family, so the children toiled in the beet fields alongside their parents. Still, they often went hungry. Tilly recalls that during these years she was so skinny that her ankles would poke holes in her stockings. Although conditions did not permit the Ontiveros offspring much formal education, their mother continually reminded them "to be clean people, to be good people. And to work hard." Perhaps these customs and beliefs did not do much to mitigate all of the hardships faced, but they did help to reinforce self-esteem. No matter how difficult times became, one could retain a humble pride in being bien educado and remembering lo nuestro.[35]

Additionally, many Hispanic women sought work outside their homes to supplement family income. These wives and mothers were a vital labor source in industries such as domestic work, food processing, and garment manufacturing.[36] María Dolores García helped her traquero husband by working as a maid at the Park Hotel in Salt Lake City. Her pay was minimal, but it provided the young couple with a rent-free apartment. Unfortunately, the marriage did not last because her husband drank too much and would take off to California for weeks at a time. Following the divorce María Dolores took in washing and ironing to support her two small children. She ultimately found permanent employment at a local bakery.[37]

Alex Hurtado's mother chose a different route. Alex's parents each left Mexico during the 1920s, and their families settled in Bingham Canyon. The couple met, married, and had four children while living in the mining town.

Eliza Tostado, Alex's mother, eventually divorced her husband and was faced with the dilemma of supporting her children. Her son described her as "independent as hell" and not interested in accepting her ex-husband's child-support money. Although she could barely read or write English, she put her cooking and domestic skills to use in running a boardinghouse in Bingham. Rooms were let to miners, and Eliza provided about twenty men with three meals a day. This business allowed her to be self-supporting, and she eventually raised a small amount of working capital with which to expand her enterprise. By the early 1940s Tostado had saved enough to operate, along with her new husband, several bars and eating establishments in Bingham, Lark (another mining area), and Ogden.[38]

The combined effects of the post–World War I recession and the Great Depression produced desperate economic circumstances in Utah. The state received so much assistance that a Federal Emergency Relief Administration field representative described Utah as "the prize 'gimme' state of the union."[39] The Hispanic population (which declined drastically during these years) constituted a small percentage of those on relief. Most left the state, and many of those who remained were simply too proud to ask for aid. A number of "survivors" claimed not to have been aware of the availability of programs. In this regard, the Spanish-surnamed populace of Utah mirrored their brethren in other parts of the United States.[40]

Juanita Jiménez's family faced many hardships but did not wish to ask for aid. Juanita was born in Mexico in December, 1908, and moved to the United States to work at her grandmother's boardinghouse in Eureka, Utah, in 1929. The young woman hoped to help her grandmother and also earn some money to "get better dresses" and then go back to Mexico. While there, Juanita met her future husband. The couple eloped, married, and returned to live in the mining town. Her husband continued working as a miner even though it affected his health adversely. Unfortunately, economic conditions in Eureka during the 1930s prevented him from changing jobs, and he died several years later. Juanita was forced to look for work but refused to ask for any governmental assistance. In a 1985 interview she said: "We never got help from the government. We never asked for anything. We don't like that."[41] While many of Utah's Spanish-speakers did not avail themselves of assistance, some claimed not to have known that aid was available. Pancha Gonzalez reported that her family faced difficult times but that "no one ever told us about government programs that could help us."[42]

Some individuals did seek and receive federal and state aid during the 1930s. Roberto Nieves, a native of Puerto Rico, moved to southern Utah when he was nineteen years old to work for the Civilian Conservation Corps. He received training, pay, and room and board. He also took advantage of this opportunity to complete his high school education, receiving his GED in 1941. Roberto served his country in the navy during World War II and returned to his adopted home state after his discharge.[43]

Manuel García, Jr., also sought help from government programs. Manuel was born in Mexico in December, 1909, and was relocated to the United States when he was five years old. His family arrived in Salt Lake City in 1919. His father worked for the Denver and Rio Grande Railroad for about forty years. The boy's parents wanted him to receive a formal education, but he quit school in 1928 and went to work for the Denver line. In a 1985 interview Manuel recalled that his foreman did not care for "Mexicans" and forced him to do "dirty jobs" in an effort to get rid of him. He lasted only a few months before taking off for the beet fields of southern Idaho. During the Depression many of these betabelero jobs disappeared, and Manuel had to stand in bread lines to eat. He eventually procured employment back in Utah with a program that put men to work building and fixing roads in Big Cottonwood Canyon. This job allowed him to subsist until he was rehired by the railroad in 1937.[44]

The Great Depression had a mixed impact upon the Utah colonia's social organizations. The community was reduced in size during these years, and many individuals sought to create closer ties to the Spanish-speakers who remained. Patriotic celebrations, dances, parties, and other cultural events served as rallying points and brief respites from trying circumstances. The austerity of this period also provided the genesis of the most important (secular) Mexicano association in Utah before the Chicano movement years of the late 1960s and early 1970s: the Centro Cívico Mexicano (Mexican Civic Center). Harsh conditions produced the opposite reaction in other colonia members. The time and financial demands of some social groups pushed some away; many were willing to share in festivities but ignored the plight of their suffering brethren.

Bertha Amador-Mayer's social life during the late 1930s revolved around events sponsored by the Centro Cívico Mexicano (CCM). Bertha's family arrived in Salt Lake City in 1926, and she married a Union Pacific traquero, Vicente Mayer, in 1931. Although Vicente remained employed during all of the Depression years, he seldom worked a full week. One of the couple's few joys during these trying times was their involvement with the new organization. Vicente was elected president in 1936. The group rented halls and parks to celebrate Mexican traditions, culture, and holidays. Bertha recalled that the group's most critical function was to teach the children of the west side to take pride in their rich heritage and language.[45]

The CCM was not alone in celebrating lo Mexicano during the years of the Great Depression. In Bingham Canyon the Sociedad Honorífica Mexicana often sponsored events. The association's head was Jesús Avila, who had lived and worked in the area since 1924. The Honorifica organized soirees and, in conjunction with the Salt Lake City Mexican consulate, tried to protect the rights of Mexican citizens. The 1930s proved quite frustrating for a community activist such as Avila. Lacking the cohesion created by the CCM, members often disregarded the Honorífica. Many did not pay their dues; at times the group had only five or six active members. This apathy was difficult for Jesús to comprehend. Jesús complained that instead of uniting to help their compatriots, most *miembros* (members) only appeared for parties.[46]

The occupational trends and harsh realities of daily life in northern Utah led many Spanish-speakers to turn to their religious institutions for spiritual and physical support and aid. For almost 98 percent of the Hispanics in the United States during the years of the Great Depression that meant seeking help from the Catholic Church.[47] The Utah colonias generally fit this pattern, but they also represented a unique situation: the presence of a Hispanic congregation with direct ties to the most influential and powerful network in the state, the Church of Jesus Christ of Latter-day Saints.

The strained resources of the Salt Lake Catholic Diocese restricted the availability of services for the Guadalupe flock. While financially limited, the mission and diocese did provide most colonia members with a psychic and spiritual "home" where they could pray, gather as a community, and celebrate their heritage. Although the number of Spanish-speakers in the area decreased during these years, the congregation at Guadalupe grew from 480 in 1931 to over 700 by 1939. The Sisters of Perpetual Adoration helped the children of the west side by teaching religion classes, Sunday school, and arts and crafts. The mission also sponsored a Boy Scout troop as well as Americanization classes. Father Collins hosted a wide range of sporting events, parties, films, and shows for his kids. As an incentive, the cash-strapped mission inaugurated an auction system for all children's activities in which tokens were awarded for attendance; the community generously donated small articles that served as prizes. Collins contributed part of his meager annual salary to this cause. The mission's major effort was a summer school held between mid June and mid August. Attendance ran as high as 250 children per day, with all faiths and ethnic groups from the west side represented.[48]

María Dolores González-Mayo's family lived in Bingham but traveled to the west side of Salt Lake City to worship at Guadalupe. They could have attended the nearby Holy Rosary Church but preferred the "Mexicano" atmosphere at the mission. María Dolores recalled that her childhood revolved around catechism, daily mass, and choir practice under the watchful eyes of

Father Collins and las madres. Mission activities also celebrated the children's culture and partially sheltered them from the problems faced by their families. María Dolores remembered that Father Collins "certainly made it an enjoyable [time] growing up. We don't remember so much the hardships, I think, as we do the good times."[49]

Reyes Rodríguez and his family did not seek material aid from the programs of the Guadalupe Mission, but they were enriched by the spiritual work of Collins and the nuns. Reyes was the son of a Mexicano immigrant who had moved to the Salt Lake Valley in the early 1920s. Reyes was born on the west side in 1932. During the Depression his father worked as a dishwasher or janitor and avoided taking government assistance. The family lived next door to the mission but chose to forgo direct help. Father Rodríguez recalled that the mission, its staff, and his mother's volunteer work produced a spiritual awakening in him. Collins's humility, spirituality, and caring for the poor produced in Reyes a positive impression of the Catholic clergy. Seeing his mother and Collins assisting others helped Reyes realize "a personal relationship with God" and also a desire to serve the less fortunate. Reyes Rodríguez was ordained a priest in 1968.[50]

The religious ties of local Mormones mitigated many of the effects of racism in Rama Mexicana members' lives during the 1920s, but they did not completely eliminate discrimination. Likewise, the congregation did not completely evade the turmoil of the Great Depression, but constituents had access to crucial links that provided psychic and material assistance that helped them survive. In his important work *Born Again in Brazil* R. Andrew Chestnut notes how the various benefits of conversion often create a positive impact on the daily lives of established members and neophytes of these groups. Through these associations, "converts are able to preserve their physical, psychological, and spiritual well being in the midst of ubiquitous illness . . . spiritual ecstasy, manifested in both the gifts of the Spirit and the baptism of the Holy Spirit, and mutual aid networks fill [the] impoverished . . . with an overwhelming sense of divine power."[51]

Although the LDS Church had a long tradition of assisting members economically, officials came to the realization that this depression "would not soon recede" and that "long lasting solutions" were called for.[52] Salt Lake City was severely impacted by the economic collapse, causing the church to focus its relief efforts there. The Pioneer Stake, on the city's west side, was particularly hard hit (the Rama Mexicana was part of this stake during the 1930s). During the early 1930s more than 50 percent of the workers in this area were unemployed.[53] This created much difficulty for the Rama's members in their attempt to maintain their tithing schedule. Branch records indicate that as late as 1939 more than 50 percent of the congregation was not up to date. Even in June, 1942, more than one-half of the worshipers were exempted from this responsibility.[54]

By 1930 the LDS leadership revived the Deseret Employment Bureau and formed inner-stake groups that attempted to assist individuals in need. An early initiative used church organizations both to search for and create employment opportunities. In October, 1930, Bishop Sylvester Q. Cannon praised this effort for registering eighteen hundred men and placing two-thirds of them in jobs during the previous nine months (most of these men and jobs were located in the Salt Lake Valley). These stakewide organizations also made arrangements with farmers to receive products, store them, and then distribute them to the destitute. Concurrently, individual stakes established community gardens and coal-distribution centers. Finally, church organizations negotiated public aid for needy Mormons from various county governments. Direct (cash) benefits from the church were seen as a last resort for those who could not obtain help elsewhere.[55] These new programs were supplemented by the Relief Society, which provided direct assistance (in the form of goods) to the indigent of the various wards.[56] An examination of Relief Society disbursements reveals the magnitude of the economic calamity in Utah. During the recession of the 1920s the Relief Society spent about $302,000 per year. In fiscal 1930 benefits increased to about $350,000, and other church organizations spent another $185,000 on relief.[57] At the cash-strapped Rama Mexicana the branch's women asked their sisters in other Relief Society chapters for assistance in collecting clothes and blankets for needy members.[58]

From an economic perspective, the LDS assistance network did not eliminate poverty and misery form the lives of Rama Mexicana constituents, but it did make conditions more bearable. This is the most significant distinction between the local Mormones' Great Depression experiences and those of the Católicos. An examination of Rama records reveals the staying power of the five familias that composed the core group of the branch's 1929 congregational roster. In a span that produced a 73 percent decrease in Mexican-born Hispanics in Utah, the families of Manuel and Rafael Torres, Cástulo Martínez, Eufemio Salazar, and José Zúñiga survived the Great Depression with the assistance of the church's welfare network. As the economy improved, these families were in a position to prosper. To a great extent their religious beliefs, and the social connections provided, helped mediate future economic improvement and mobility.[59]

Rafael Torres benefited greatly from the church's relief efforts. After he went from one job to another during the 1920s Rafael's connections helped him acquire a position at the Temple Square Hotel in 1930. Anthony R. Ivins, who worked closely with the Rama Mexicana membership and eventually ascended to the highest levels of the Latter-day Saints' institutional hierarchy, recommended Torres to the hotel's manager. Rafael performed many tasks, such as sweeping halls, cleaning windows, and working as a bellboy. Although his pay was only seventy-five dollars per month, it kept the Torres family housed and fed. Rafael remained at the hotel until 1944, when he joined his brother-in-law's (Manuel Torres) tortilla-making business.

Manuel's family also benefited from the church's employment program. Manuel was hired as a janitor at the downtown Salt Lake City store of Zion's Cooperative Mercantile Institution. While grateful for this position, Torres found it difficult to support his wife and five children on an eighty-dollar monthly salary. By 1937 Manuel had befriended a Mr. Walhause, the manager of the store's delicatessen. Walhause often told Manuel that he was not satisfied with the quality or flavor of the tamales that he purchased for the deli. The two men worked together until they created a workable recipe. Manuel took some of his vacation days to sell his wares throughout the city. He proved to be an able tamale maker and salesman and started his own business in 1938.[60]

In addition to temporal assistance, the Mormones at the Rama Mexicana gained psychic enrichment from their association with the larger community of Mormons and their network. Rafael and Manuel served in leadership positions at the branch during the 1930s and associated with men, such as Anthony Ivins, who held important positions within the LDS Church's hierarchy. R. Andrew Chestnut describes the significance of these benefits by writing: "Possibly even more consequential than the material benefits derived from church membership is the psychological and spiritual support provided by the community of believers. Assembled by the common diseases of poverty, believers experience the healing power . . . of the congregation, and in visits from their spiritual brothers and sisters."[61]

The LDS Church's aid burden was eased by a massive infusion of federal funds into Utah.[62] This helped ameliorate conditions but put the church's hierarchy in a dilemma. Should the Mormons turn in this hour of economic crisis to their church, with its well-developed (and expanding) spiritual-based system of assistance, or to the enlarging governmental welfare apparatus? Between 1933 and 1936 Mormon leaders endeavored to formulate a welfare plan that would provide succor to those in distress yet still retain a work component as well as localized control.[63] The culmination of this effort was a speech called "An Important Message on Relief," which was delivered by President Heber J. Grant on April 6, 1936. Many of the initiatives previously used were incorporated into this grandiose plan. Mormons would receive employment assistance and commodities, not cash benefits as under the government's programs. This system created an extra layer of subsidy unavailable to Hispanics outside of the Rama Mexicana.[64]

As early as the winter of 1931–32 the benefits provided by the LDS Church were creating a delicate problem in northern Utah. Did the church have to extend aid to all Mormons or just practicing ones? What assistance (if any) should be rendered to non-Mormons?[65] This situation perplexed some Spanish-speakers. Circumstances in the comunidad were difficult. Should men and women forgo the religion of their ancestors to obtain desperately needed charity? Reactions to this predicament varied, although relatively few left the Catholic Church and converted to Mormonism.

María Dolores García faced the 1930s as a young divorcee with two young children. The commodities the LDS Church's welfare plan provided would have proved invaluable to García and her children. Yet the pressure to remain Catholic was intense. One of María Dolores's aunts converted and suffered strong condemnation from her family. The woman was admonished simply to "cut [herself] open and let the blood out" for changing something as crucial to her identity as the Catholic faith.[66]

Ruth Torres, daughter of Rafael Torres, believed that while there were some individuals who converted to get help, for most people Rama membership was founded on sincere religious conviction. The aid Mormon Hispanics received produced some tensions, but ethnic ties caused most Spanish-speakers to overlook denominational differences. Neighbors helped neighbors because suffering was widespread. As Ruth recalled in a 1996 interview, "we saw good (and need) in all of our people, both Catholics and Mormons."[67]

The Spanish-surnamed people of northern Utah endured circumstances similar to, if not worse than, those encountered in other parts of the nation. As Utah's economic pillars crumbled, most Hispanics disappeared. For those who remained, daily life was a constant struggle and sacrifice. Most of the survivors of the economic catastrophe refused government help and instead turned to their organizations and places of worship for aid and comfort. For the majority of the comunidad this meant the Catholic Church. The staff at the Guadalupe Mission, given its limited resources, did what it could to mitigate suffering for Father Collins's kids and their familias. Rama Mexicana constituents, while not escaping unscathed, received food, employment, and spiritual and psychic solace from the LDS welfare system. The religious affiliation of colonia members had a bearing on how each weathered the storm of economic catastrophe. The stabilizing impact of church assistance helped some Rama Mexicana families to remain in the city and prosper during the following decades.

The difference in efficacy of the Catholic and Mormon ethnic networks created some animosity within the colonia during the 1930s. But this was not the primary impact of the Great Depression on Spanish speakers. Overall, the Hispanic population, as individuals, families, and organizations, were drawn closer together because of the mass exodus. Often vecinos helped vecinos, regardless of religious affiliation. The worsening economic conditions moved familial and ethnic ties to the forefront of social relations. Class and ethnicity proved strong bonding ties against the centrifugal power of adversity and selfishness.

The difficult circumstances of the Depression years also birthed a group that attempted to rally all Mexicans in this area under a single banner. The Centro Cívico Mexicano sought to maintain the "Mexicanness" of the children of the west side, regardless of their religion. The group sponsored fiestas and classes designed to reinforce cultural traditions in the midst of grinding poverty. As the Spanish-surnamed population of northern Utah struggled to maintain the last vestiges of normalcy, the realization that most of them were in dire straits brought many in the community together. Still, religious divisions mitigated attempts at creating a single, overarching "Mexican" group. In a 1975 interview with Gordon Irving, Arturo Rivera Martínez recalled that "his and the parents of other teenagers refused to let them attend the largely Catholic Centro Cívico Mexicano activities. 'Our social life and most every phase of our life was involved in the Church and in the old Salt Lake Mexican branch.'"[68]

The level of unity the comunidad experienced during the Great Depression, however, would be tested during the war years. As the 1930s receded into memory the war economy began attracting new groups that would create fresh divisions in the Salt Lake City and Ogden clusters. Before the war most Spanish-surnamed men, women, and children in Utah were of Mexicano birth or Mexican American heritage. During the early 1940s, however, the growing number of jobs in Utah's military facilities reinvigorated the movement of "Spanish Americans" (Spanish-speakers from northern New Mexico and southeastern Colorado) to the Beehive State. Many of these individuals did not consider themselves "Mexicanos," and cultural and other differences caused tensions within the comunidad. An increased demand for copper during wartime also furthered diversity by attracting significant numbers of young men from a new source, the island of Puerto Rico.

4

"There Was Much Work To Do"
Utah Hispanics and World War II, 1940–45

Prior to 1930 Utah's predominantly Mormon population (65 percent classified as practicing Mormons in 1930) took justifiable pride in its tradition of self-sufficiency.[1] After a series of long and bitter struggles with various state and federal authorities over economic and social practices, polygamy and statehood in the nineteenth century, many Utahans were wary of governmental encroachment into local affairs. The cataclysmic impact of the Great Depression modified some of these views. During the 1930s local political and business leaders became adroit at pursuing Utah's "fair share" of federal largesse.[2] By 1933 Utah ranked first in the nation in federal relief dollars received per capita.[3] Despite this aid, Utah's economy remained stagnant; in 1939 over forty-eight thousand residents were still on governmental assistance. In the Beehive State, as in other parts of the nation, the advent of World War II finally ended the Great Depression.[4]

Federal military spending, starting in the late 1930s, had a salubrious impact on Utah's economy. By 1942 over sixty thousand civilians were employed at ten bases and facilities established around the state. Between June, 1940, and September, 1945, war supply contracts totaling over $1 billion were received; another $430 million were invested in facilities construction.[5] As a result personal income in Utah, which had languished at around $300 million before 1940, surpassed $700 million by 1943. Per capita income, well below the national norm before the war, soared to almost 103 percent of the national average. The economic bonanza improved (or resuscitated) the manufacturing, construction, and service industries for the economy and led to full employment.[6]

The economic surge produced a strong demand for labor. Spanish-speakers, who had fled Utah in large numbers during the 1930s, eagerly responded. The majority of the new wave of Spanish-surnamed workers to Utah during the war years hailed not from Mexico but from rural farming villages of northern New Mexico and southeastern Colorado.[7] In her important mono-graph on the Spanish-speaking people of this area, *No Separate Refuge*, Sarah Deutsch describes the American conquest of this region, the economic changes it created, and the radical transformation of daily life in these towns. Many villagers were forced to abandon their traditional farming and economic patterns and began wandering throughout the Southwest in search of menial labor.[8]

Although Utah was not the principal destination of these roaming *mani-tos* (a shortened version of the diminutive term *hermanito/ta,* meaning "little brother/sister," this term is used by the Spanish-speakers of this area as a form of self-reference), a few Hispanic families from New Mexico settled in the San Juan County town of Monticello during the early 1900s.[9] The *familias* in Monticello formed part of the Southwest's manito communal web and as-sisted their compatriots in their trek toward northern Utah's industrial centers. The Great Depression greatly reduced this traffic, but the demands of a wartime economy revived it.[10] Governmental facilities and private employers recruited heavily in these areas. Concurrently this labor procurement cam-paign reached out to the Caribbean and brought to Utah a new group of Span-ish-speaking individuals, *islanderos* (islanders) from Puerto Rico.[11]

This chapter will examine the effects of wartime conditions on work, fam-ily, and daily lives in northern Utah's expanding colonias. The economic ex-pansion's impact on workplace conditions for Hispanic men and women will be analyzed, as will social relations within the increasingly diverse Spanish-speaking community and with the larger society. Finally, the military experi-ences of Utah's Spanish-surnamed soldiers will be considered.

Before the war Utah agriculture, particularly the sugar beet industry, had been highly dependent upon Hispanic workers. Even during the years of the Great Depression patterns of migratory labor in areas of the West were not radically transformed; crops had to be harvested, and Spanish-speaking work-ers often accepted jobs that others turned down.[12] Wartime needs altered these circumstances. Under the *bracero* (from the Spanish word *brazo,* meaning "arms," literally hire arms or hands brought to the United States during World War II years) program thousands of Mexican citizens were recruited to work in the fields. Conditions were often difficult, but high demand for labor pro-vided opportunities. Bracero defiance of inhumane treatment increased as these workers realized the value of their labor during the war years.[13] Other Hispanics simply left the fields and sought out better pay and treatment in other industries.

Unlike neighboring states, Utah employed only a handful of braceros. At its peak, in 1944, the agricultural industry employed between six hundred and seven hundred of these Mexicanos.[14] The draw for the Hispanics who flocked to northern Utah between 1940 and 1945 was not agricultural jobs; as in other parts of the nation, they moved into military and industrial employment sectors. Utah's manitos and other Spanish-speakers worked in military supply depots, manufacturing, transportation, and mining in Salt Lake, Weber, Davis, Tooele, and Carbon Counties.

The family and vecinos of Orlando Rivera were among those who filled these jobs. Orlando was born in the town of La Jara, Colorado, in November, 1930. He recalled that the Great Depression produced severe hardships for the Spanish-speaking people of the region. His family had lived in the area for many generations as self-sufficient farmers, but economic changes and the commercial collapse of the 1930s made their way of life untenable.[15] Military and industrial jobs in northern Utah presented a chance to rebuild their lives. Almost entire villages, such as Trampas and Tierra María, were relocated to Ogden, Tooele, and Salt Lake City during the early 1940s.[16]

The establishment and expansion of military facilities produced thousands of jobs and created a new economic pillar for Utah.[17] Other sectors also prospered. Manufacturing output increased by almost 200 percent between 1939 and 1945. Among the key elements of this expansion were the construction of the Remington Small Arms Plant in Salt Lake City and the giant United States Steel Geneva Works in Utah County. These two projects employed almost fifteen thousand when fully operational. The construction of the plants and military bases and facilities also spurred the building trades. Before the war only about five thousand Utahans were involved in construction. By late 1942 their number had ballooned to over thirty-five thousand. The mining and mineral processing sector awoke from a decade-long slumber because of wartime demand. Several processing facilities were added during the early 1940s to facilitate the exploitation of the state's mineral wealth. Coal, copper, gold, gas, iron, dolomite, and limestone were all crucial to the war effort. The copper giants—Utah Copper, Kennecott Copper, and American Smelting and Refining—poured over $15 million into plant expansion. The augmentation of old industries and the creation of new economic sectors helped draw Spanish-speakers to the Beehive State.[18]

Valentín Arambula was attracted to the coalfields of Carbon County because of the comparatively high wages offered during the war. Valentín was born in December of 1911 in the town of Valdez, Colorado. Although his father was a law man in the Trinidad area, the Arambula family still faced financial difficulties. Valentín quit school in 1928 to help his father, taking a job with the Victor American Coal Company and remaining in its employ until 1942. He decided to come to Utah based on the advice of his brother, who worked in the mining town of Sunnyside. The work was arduous, but the pay made it worthwhile. Valentín earned a whole dollar more per day in Utah than he had in his native state. He remained in the industry for over thirty years, eventually being promoted to an inspector position with the Kaiser Corporation.[19]

The transportation sector also benefited from wartime expansion. Railroads were a vital link in the nation's war effort, and both Ogden and Salt Lake City saw increased numbers of passengers and freight.[20] The number of Spanish speakers employed in this sector grew steadily until it matched and then exceeded pre-Depression levels.[21] John Florez's father, Reyes Florez, was one of many Spanish-surnamed laborers who kept the lines in good repair during the war years. Before the conflict the family struggled to survive on Reyes's earnings. In 1940 they left Salt Lake City and returned to Mexico. Reyes hoped to be able to provide a better life for his children in his native land, but things did not work out that way. Schoolmates constantly teased John for being an "Americano" who was pretending to be a "Mexicano." The promise of plentiful work lured the familia back to the Salt Lake Valley at the start of the war. Reyes was rehired by the Denver and Rio Grande Railroad, and the Florez clan once again settled near the railroad tracks on 600 South, between 500 and 600 West.[22]

Ogden was another center for railroad activity. During the 1940s as many as 120 trains per day moved through Union Station in the Wall Avenue area of the city.[23] A large percentage of this traffic involved the movement of troops, and these soldiers provided a ready market for liquor, food, and prostitution. Among the store owners who profited from the trade on "the most dangerous street in the world" was Eliza Tostado, the proprietor of the Whitefront Café on Wall Avenue.[24] An examination of the 1944 Polk City directory for Ogden revealed that most other Spanish-speakers worked for the railroad companies or in the food processing industry.[25]

Spanish-surnamed teenagers also benefited from the large number of troop trains passing through northern Utah. Dan Maldonado, a native of the west side of Salt Lake City, was about twelve when the war started. He and his friends often spent time in the depot watching the trains. As the volume of traffic increased, what started out as a diversion turned into a fairly lucrative moneymaking opportunity. As the transports pulled in, soldiers would ask the young boys to run to the drugstore and buy them candy bars and newspapers. Upon delivering these wares, the youngsters would receive tips for services provided. Dan and his buddies "could make four or five bucks—because none of the guys could get off once they got there. Yeah, we kids were happy to do it."[26]

Utah's wartime job growth also attracted a large number of *Hispanas* (Spanish-speaking women), such as Rose Ortíz. These women took advantage of the increased demand for labor to boost their wages in "traditional" jobs for women such as food processing and domestic work. Important employers of Spanish-speaking women in these fields in northern Utah included Purity Biscuit, Utah Poultry, Sweet Candies, the Hotel Utah, American Laundry, and Star Laundry. For some of these women the war effort even afforded a move into higher paying "men's" work in industry, transportation, and military facilities. These occupations provided Hispanas with a more prosperous life as well as reinvigorating in many a feeling of pride, confidence, and self-worth that had been damaged by the Anglo economy's impact upon the villages of New Mexico and Colorado.[27]

Rose Ortíz filled a traditional food-processing job during the war years. Rose was born in Del Norte, Colorado, in June of 1918 and moved to Salt Lake City with her husband in 1941. She procured employment with the Utah Poultry Company a year later. Her tasks on the factory's "disassembly" line were simple, robotic, and repetitive; she killed and plucked chickens and turkeys. Rose recalled in a 1984 interview that "Mexican" women staffed this section of the plant, with only a few Anglo women present as supervisors. Rose's starting pay was $2.50 per day. She continued at the plant for over twenty years but was never promoted beyond the processing line.[28]

While many northern Utah Hispanic women remained stuck in traditional occupations such as food processing, some broke down barriers by working in fields such as manufacturing and transportation. Clotilda Gómez's wartime résumé included toiling in a Salt Lake City railroad yard. When her husband volunteered for military duty, Clotilda was left to support herself and her four children. To survive she worked as a waitress and clerk. To her dismay, she was fired from her second job because she was not a citizen of the United States. Clotilda eventually procured employment at a railroad yard. Being a pioneer in this field was a heavy burden; female employees did not receive much assistance from their male coworkers. In a 1987 interview Clotilda stated: "The men would stand around and watch you work. . . . See how much you could take of it." Part of her typical workday included various forms of sexual harassment. Clotilda tolerated the slurs and insults in order to provide for her children. Regardless of working conditions, she felt proud of her contribution to the war effort: "I think women changed from that era . . . [they took] this change in their lives in order to make decisions and work. Even among the Mexican families there started being a change with the women because they realized they were equal to men."[29]

The large influx of Spanish-speakers had a profound impact on extant colonia institutions. On January 1, 1944, Father James E. Collins presented Bishop Duane G. Hunt with a letter petitioning the Salt Lake Catholic Diocese to raise Our Lady of Guadalupe Mission to parish status. Before 1941 the mission had served a predominantly Mexican population (with a small number of Basques, Spaniards, Syrians, and Anglos). As a result of the influx during the war Guadalupe now served a community comprised of a wide variety of Spanish-speaking people, primarily Nuevo Mexicanos.[30] The diocese acted quickly and approved the petition. On January 17, 1944, the diocese officially recognized the existence of Our Lady of Guadalupe parish. The newly created entity ministered to eighteen hundred people living within the boundaries of West Temple and 500 West and 100 and 600 South.

The Rama Mexicana also grew during the war years. By 1942 the Mormon congregation counted over 120 members in its flock. As they had done in Garland during the 1920s, Rama members performed missionary work among Spanish-speakers. Once again the story of the Lamanites provided Latter-day Saint messengers with an opportunity to "preach the gospel" and reach out to mineros and braceros.[31] Eduardo Balderas, who arrived in Salt Lake City in 1939 to work as a translator for the LDS Church, recalled that the war years were fruitful ones for Mormon proselytizers: "We had several camps around the valley here, and a good many further north. I was appointed to gather a group of young people and do some entertaining, not necessarily go and immediately begin to preach the gospel. . . . We would go as far as Bingham to teach the gospel. We had to rely a great deal on referrals from our members to their friends and associates, and through this means we accomplished quite a bit of work without having to do too much door-to-door contacting."[32]

While the men, women, and children who converted to the Mormon faith did not wish to sever all connections to the rest of the Spanish-speaking comunidad, their transformation did cause tensions and estrangement from friends and families. Samuel Victor Miera, in an interview, explained: "For example, you take a Mexican family, and they're used to all the things that they've been doing all of their life. To them, when you get together the first thing that you do is take out a beer . . . and you sit down and you smoke and drink beer. But now a person becomes a member of the Church. Now you don't laugh when they tell a shady story, and you hear words said that you don't like said in your house anymore. All of a sudden, you realize you're not getting invitations any more to . . . go out some Saturday evening with them . . . all of a sudden [that] comes to an end, and you're an island."[33]

The inflow of the early 1940s further diversified the local colonia's ethnic composition. Wartime demand for copper led mining companies to seek out laborers as far away as New York City and Puerto Rico. In 1943 Bingham Canyon employers began bringing hundreds of islanderos into northern Utah. The circumstances these men encountered were reminiscent of those experienced by the earlier waves of Mexican, Spanish, and Mexican American mineros of Utah during the 1910s and 1920s. The Puerto Ricans did not bring their families, were transient, and worked the most strenuous and lowest paying jobs in the canyon. Many of the "veteran" Spanish-surnamed laborers in Bingham distanced themselves from these "dangerous" newcomers. Some in the more established group had by the early 1940s acquired small amounts of property, moved into better-paying positions, and even started small businesses. They viewed the young, single Puerto Ricans as threats to their community (particularly as a menace to their daughters). These islanderos might speak the same language as the Mexicanos, but in the view of the veterans of Bingham Canyon, a Puerto Rican was "a 'foreigner' and . . . part Negro."[34] Carlos Grimm, the Mexican consulate, shared this view and claimed that "Spanish blood did not diffuse through Puerto Rico. During the early slave trading days Negro blood mixed with that of the Puerto Ricans."[35] Social, economic, and cultural differences precluded the creation of ties between the "old" and "new" Spanish-speakers of Bingham Canyon.[36]

Bingham Canyon's Mexicanos and manitos found a level of unity in their animosity toward the islanderos. Still, this hostility was not enough to forge the two groups into a unified whole; these two Spanish-speaking groups did not always get along. During the 1920s, when there were fewer manitos in Utah, little friction existed between the old and new Mexicans. Rúben Gómez's experiences provide insight into these interactions. Rúben's family arrived in Salt Lake City in 1918 from Amarillo, Texas. His father worked alongside Spanish-speakers from New Mexico and Colorado at his job with the Denver and Rio Grande Railroad. Rúben believed that relations between the two groups were "pretty good" during the 1920s. But there were differences. Both spoke Spanish, but "you could tell by the way they talked" which individuals belonged to which groups. In Gómez's view these people "were drawn together by a common language, occupations and religion. Still, even among the Latin speaking there were differences."[37] In his 1997 work, *The Myth of Santa Fe,* University of New Mexico historian Chris Wilson supports this contention by stating that "New Mexican natives continued to call themselves '*mexicanos*' in Spanish, but . . . (they) distinguished between *surumatos* (slang for Mexican immigrants) and *manitos*. . . . In English they universally employed *Spanish American* to distinguish themselves from more recent Mexican immigrants."[38]

Tensions between the different colonia constituents became more evident during the war. The experiences of Francisco Solorio shed light upon these complex relations. Francisco was born in Mexico in April, 1910, and his family arrived in Salt Lake City in 1923. The young Mexicano struggled though school until he turned fifteen and then left to work in the beet fields of Rexburg, Idaho. The Solorio family eventually rented a farm, and they remained in Idaho until 1948. High wages brought Francisco back to northern Utah to work for the Union Pacific in 1942. While earning more than in Idaho, Francisco did not enjoy working with the large number of Nuevo Mexicanos. He felt that "those people" were not like him and did not respect the customs and traditions of the "old" country. Manitos were raised differently and did not even have the decency to refer to themselves as "Mexicanos." This, Francisco believed, was a grave insult. The Spanish [and their descendants] had robbed his Indian ancestors of their land, culture, and religion, and now Francisco did not want to deal with their heirs in his everyday life.[39] The recollections of Colorado native Orlando Rivera confirm some of Solorio's assumptions. When family members spoke Spanish to each other in the Rivera household, they often used the term *Mexicano* for self-reference. But if someone from outside the *familia* applied this terminology to the clan, "those were fighting words." The Spanish-speaking people who moved to Utah during the 1940s did not view themselves as being the same as "old" Mexicans. True, they spoke a common language, but cultural traditions were different—a crucial distinction being that manitos did not share in the celebration of Mexican independence days.[40]

In his 1948 study William C. Blair details some of the occupational and other differences among the various Hispanic groups of Bingham Canyon. Although most men in the community worked similar jobs, some had been promoted to higher paying positions such as foreman, brakeman, and car driver. These jobs were primarily based on length of service to the copper companies; therefore, a clear occupational distinction existed between those who had toiled in Bingham since the 1910s and 1920s and the islandero newcomers.[41] Cultural, racial, and religious differences were also evident. It is certain that colonia members created clear lines of demarcation within their own comunidad, but did the Anglo Americans of northern Utah recognize these distinctions or did they simply lump all Spanish speakers together as "Mexicans"? How did Hispanics in this area interact with the racial majority population during the war years?

The pages of the *Salt Lake Tribune* offer clues to Anglo opinion of the Spanish-surnamed population of northern Utah. On May 5th (Cinco de Mayo) and September 16th (Mexican Independence Day) of the war years the *Tribune's* reporters and editorial commentators related the details of "Mexican" festivities throughout Utah. The overall tone of the articles was extremely positive; the *Tribune's* editorial board perceived Mexico as a sister republic doing its share to aid the United States in a global war against fascist foes. Mexican citizens currently living north of the border were represented as hard-working, honest folk who should be honored and praised by all true adherents of democratic principles for their role in the war effort. The articles mixed all Spanish-speakers into one group; there was no mention of manitos or islanderos. One scholar who has examined this subject, Mauricio Mazón in his work *The Zoot-Suit Riots,* found that this trend was common throughout the West and Southwest during the war years. To unify disparate groups in the war effort American propaganda often dissolved class, racial, and other distinctions in an appeal for fraternity and equality. In regard to the Spanish-speaking population during the 1940s, these calls for unity took note of the important contributions made by generations of "Mexicans" in the United States.[42]

While on the surface the majority population of the United States seemed genuinely grateful for the services rendered by the "Mexicans" living and working here during the war, this did not mean that all obstacles and racial discrimination ceased to exist during the conflict.[43] In the workplace there was a ceiling for colonia members, regardless of length of service or quality of work. As Rivera reported, "It was a [buddy] system that if you were in any way different . . . you were stereotyped and less likely to get into the technical, [or] managerial positions."[44]

Many Spanish-speakers prospered during the war years; some positions and industries previously closed to them did open. The northern Utah colonia, in general, earned a measure of respect and gratitude from the majority population. Progress was made, but obstacles and ill feelings remained. A noteworthy manifestation of the negative attitudes was evident in the treatment of *pachucos* (slang for zoot-suiters) in the Salt Lake City area. While most Spanish-surnamed men and women were viewed as contributing to the war effort, pachucos were often the targets of scorn, ridicule, and violence. These young men were seen as too "foreign" to be accepted by the majority population. Concurrently they were considered selfish individuals who spent money on outrageous clothes and a good time rather than supporting the war.[45] Events in Salt Lake City demonstrate how some in the majority population responded to the presence of these "troublemakers."

Dan Maldonado used some of his earnings from his rail-yard "business" to participate in the pachuco scene. As a teenager during the war years he bought a zoot suit and cut his hair in the ducktail style, applying liberal amounts of grease to it. He reveled in the look and enjoyed his tough-guy image in the neighborhoods of the west side. He was also realistic and realized that he might have to pay a price for his attention-grabbing attire and appearance. His circle of friends was exclusively Mexican American and African American, and "if there was a bunch of them, [people thought] there was going to be trouble." Dan and his buddies were often kicked out of dance halls and many times were not even allowed to enter. On one occasion Dan was kicked out of a nightclub because management believed his jitterbugging style was vulgar and indecent. Fights with movie theater ushers were also common. When disturbances took place, the pachucos were accused and asked to leave. When Dan pleaded innocence, ushers often replied that the Spanish-speakers "all looked alike" and that it was therefore impossible for them to tell which specific individual had committed the offense. One incident dramatizes the anger and hatred Dan and his friends often faced. As the pachucos crossed Pioneer Park one evening, several angry (and drunk) white men confronted them by hurling racial epithets. The Hispanics bested the whites in the subsequent melee. "But forty-five minutes later . . . here comes the car down the street." The men fired a pistol at Dan, but no one was injured. The whites returned one more time, on this occasion with several more companions to launch a final assault. Dan decided that discretion was the better part of valor and escaped the situation by jumping on a city bus. The majority populace apparently tolerated the presence of Hispanics as long as they "worked" and "contributed" to the war effort. If they rejected what was considered "acceptable" dress and behavior, then they apparently were fair game for abuse and even racial violence.[46]

Northern Utah's Spanish-speaking clusters contributed much sweat and toil to the home-front effort. They also provided fighting men for the war against fascism. The Rama Mexicana contributed a total of sixteen young men to the war effort.[47] The tasks these soldiers performed ranged from the mundane to the heroic. Rúben Gómez volunteered for military service even though he was the father of four children and could have been deferred. Rúben never saw combat and spent his military career working laundry duty, digging sewers, and operating harbor-dredging equipment.[48]

Epifanio González saw combat and served his nation with distinction. Born in Carlton, California, in 1921, Epifanio was by eight years of age out of school and helping his family work beet fields in Montana. By the late 1930s Epifanio's mother decided to return her children to California. Sadly, the children's stepfather abandoned the family in Salt Lake City without enough money to complete their trip. The González clan struggled through the last years of the Great Depression. When he turned nineteen, Epifanio decided to lighten his mother's economic burden by joining the army. Military life kept him fed, but he endured much discrimination from fellow soldiers. Ironically, he believed that this ill treatment did not have a deleterious impact on his self-esteem. His drive and courage readied him for the rigors and challenges of combat. Epifanio earned a Silver Star for bravery at Monte Casino. His military experiences also steeled him for the circumstances he and other Hispanics would face in Utah after the war.[49]

The Spanish-speaking people who migrated to Utah during the years of World War II worked in all of the state's key industries. Many benefited from the economy's expansion by earning increased wages and moving into positions and sectors that had previously been closed to them. The colonia's members proved themselves able, willing, and productive employees whose hard work earned them a measure of respect and gratitude from the majority population. Although appreciated during the war, Hispanics felt the impact of prejudice and discrimination during and after the conflict. Once the articles of peace were signed, some Anglo Americans believed colonia constituents were no longer needed in northern Utah. Those who remained were now viewed as potential competitors for uncertain postwar jobs.

The 1940s produced important changes in the Spanish-speaking community. The arrival of large numbers of manitos and islanderos changed the group's composition. Continued missionary work by members of the Rama Mexicana increased the number of Mormones within the comunidad, and this divided some families and friends. Disparities in economic standing and social customs also proved to be an obstacle to the creation of colonia-wide ties. Closer relations among the various Spanish-speaking groups would not develop until after the war years. Social tensions were also apparent with whites, in particular for those who did not "fit in."

Hispanic women also felt the social impact of wartime conditions. With many jobs open in manufacturing and transportation, not all women were willing to settle for domestic or food processing jobs. The paychecks they earned provided material benefits for their families and much more. The ability to perform "men's" work created feelings of independence and self-reliance that remained. Antonette Chambers Noble, a historian of Utah women, effectively summarizes the experience of both Anglo American and Spanish-surnamed "Rosies" in Utah: "For some the war generated lasting social and economic changes. . . . Others acknowledged that the war brought unprecedented opportunities for women but characterized these changes as temporary and with few lasting results. The Utah case . . . suggests that elements of both interpretations are valid. The war did spur a changed female labor force . . . [and] personal growth. An invisible revolution, however, may have occurred in the thoughts and expectations of Rosie's children who began to come of age in the 1960s."[50]

Returning war veterans also helped fuel this transformation of thoughts and expectations. Soldiers who had fought for liberty and equality of treatment would not stand idly by and see their fellow Hispanics treated unfairly.

Enduring boot camps, separation from family and friends, and the chaos of battle forged in many of these men a steely desire to seek equality and justice in Utah. The Spanish-speaking population of this area began a period of activity that led to the creation of new social clubs, mutual aid societies, and even a civil rights organization. The wartime generation had helped defeat the nation's external enemies and now turned its attention to attacking the incongruities that existed between America's ideals and social realities. Epifanio Gonzalez summarized these feeling when he asked: "How would you feel if you came [home] decorated, you fought your heart out in the war, and now you say, 'Now I am an American. I'm just as good as anybody.' And then, all of a sudden, you're just a second rate citizen[?]"[51]

Fig. 1. Mexican and Mexicano traqueros at work on Union Pacific tracks in northern Utah, ca. 1920s. *Used by permission, Utah State Historical Society, all rights reserved. Photo no. C-239 #28*

Fig. 2. Mexican or Mexican American couple, Salt Lake City, Utah, ca. 1920s. *Used by permission, Utah State Historical Society, all rights reserved. Photo no. C-239 #12*

Fig. 3. Mexican or Mexican American wedding photo, Salt Lake City, Utah, ca. 1920s. *Used by permission, Utah State Historical Society, all rights reserved. Photo no. C-239 #13*

Fig. 4. Membership of Mexican Branch/Rama Mexicana with Anthony Ivins, Salt Lake City, Utah, ca. 1929. *Used by permission, Utah State Historical Society, all rights reserved. Photo no. C-239 #26*

Fig. 5. Mexican Branch/Rama Mexicana membership, Salt Lake City, Utah, ca. 1930s. *Used by permission, Utah State Historical Society, all rights reserved. Photo no. C-239 #24*

Fig. 6. Performers from a Salt Lake City, Utah–based Mexican troupe, ca. 1925. *Used by permission, Utah State Historical Society, all rights reserved. Photo no. C-239 #1*

Fig. 7. Mexicano and Mexican American dancers participating in a community celebration (Galena Days) in Bingham Canyon, Utah, 1951. *Used by permission, Utah State Historical Society, all rights reserved. Photo no. C-239 #20*

Fig. 8. Relief Society members, Mexican Branch/Rama Mexicana, Salt Lake City, Utah, ca. 1920s. *Used by permission, Utah State Historical Society, all rights reserved. Photo no. C-239 #27*

Fig. 9. Interior of Our Lady of Guadalupe Church, Salt Lake City, Utah, ca. 1948. *Used by permission, Utah State Historical Society, all rights reserved. Photo no. C-239 #23*

Fig. 10. Sociedad Mutualista Miguel Aleman, Fourth of July celebration, Bingham Canyon, Utah, ca. 1940s. *Used by permission, Utah State Historical Society, all rights reserved. Photo no. C-239 #21*

Fig. 11. Jesus Araniz's employee identification photo, Utah Copper Company, 1942. *Used by permission, Utah State Historical Society, all rights reserved. Photo no. C-239 #33*

Fig. 12. Mineros in Bingham Canyon, ca. 1950s. *Used by permission, Utah State Historical Society, all rights reserved. Photo no. C-239 #32*

Fig. 13. Some of los niños of the west side of Salt Lake City, no date. *Used by permission, Utah State Historical Society, all rights reserved. Photo no. C-239 #4*

Fig. 14. Ballet Folklorico de Utah, Salt Lake City, Utah, ca. 1970s. *Used by permission, Utah State Historical Society, all rights reserved. Photo no. C-239 #3*

5

"Second-Rate Citizens"
Utah Hispanics during the Postwar Years, 1946–67

The Allies' victory in World War II produced both elation and trepidation throughout the West and Utah. Many now feared that the economic surge of the war years would soon give way to another commercial collapse. The anticipated downturn never materialized as industry retooled to meet pent-up consumer demand as well as the needs of the cold war.[1] Utah benefited from this economic expansion due in part to its well-developed defense sector. Military spending "contributed a greater percentage of Utah's total income than . . . in any other state."[2] By 1963 more than seventeen thousand Utahans worked in defense-related industries. Local manufacturing and the public sector also expanded after World War II.[3]

Utah's Spanish-speaking population participated in this growth to a certain extent. Between 1941 and 1945 Hispanics were viewed as valuable members of the American team battling the forces of fascism and dictatorship. Peace, however, raised expectations among some in the state's majority population that life and employment patterns would return to "normal." Spanish-surnamed individuals were to be employed in vital economic sectors and were to be proselytized, but they had to stay in their place. For workers such as Rúben Gomez this meant that unless the boss liked you, "promotions were out of the question."[4]

The conflict might not have altered the attitudes of some Anglo Americans, but many colonia members' views changed. After 1945 many Spanish-speaking people expected their nation to expand opportunities as a reward for their wartime efforts and sacrifices. As Carl Allsup makes clear in his 1982 work, *The American G.I. Forum,* returning veterans (and other elements within the Hispanic communities of the United States) refused to settle for less than full citizenship.[5] Many in the Salt Lake City and Ogden clusters hoped to build upon wartime gains and achieve equal treatment in employment, education, and housing. During the 1950s Hispanics in Utah and throughout the

West and Southwest created and joined groups dedicated to those aims, as well as mutual aid and cultural preservation societies. Through these entities some hoped to preserve their Mexicano and Mexican American customs, and others sought to improve conditions in their neighborhoods and call attention to their economic, social, and political needs and concerns.

The associations established by these men and women provided aid to the community, but they did not generate much change in the conceptions of the wider society. Most of these clubs had limited funds and minimal clout among Utah's governmental, business, and religious leaders. A lack of access to power brokers, however, was not the only obstacle. Between 1946 and 1967 existing ethnic, cultural, and religious divisions within the colonia precluded unification of these varied organizations into a single effective, well-structured, and concerted lobby for social change. For most residents of northern Utah the civil rights struggles of the 1950s and early 1960s were events occurring elsewhere which existed only on their television screens.[6] For local Spanish-speakers this was a period of much organizational futility as well as white indifference and neglect. Still, the bigotry and unconcern that constrained Spanish-speakers' occupational and scholastic opportunities and social mobility (and the impotent response of colonia groups before 1968) had beneficial consequences. Difficult conditions helped foster the notion that only collective action and protest would address grievances. By the late 1960s many in the community set aside differences in education, ethnic background, and religious association and created a united front to battle discrimination and second-class citizenship.

Given the paucity of primary source documents available concerning the Spanish-speaking people of northern Utah, the 1947 work by University of Utah sociologist Joseph E. Allen, "A Sociological Study of Mexican Assimilation in Salt Lake City," is of immense value. This study provides one of the few in-depth examinations of the Salt Lake City colonia written before the late 1960s. The work presents data on cluster members' occupations, educational attainment, geographical concentration, and religious affiliations. Allen generated his information through the use of a questionnaire completed by 491 Spanish-surnamed heads of households. The 876 individuals represented in the study accounted for over 40 percent of the estimated "Mexican" population of the city.[7] Allen's work provides an important step forward (compared to the output of the reporters and editorial writers of the *Salt Lake Tribune*) by recognizing that this comunidad was indeed not monolithic in its ethnic, language, and religious composition. People from New Mexico and Colorado, Allen asserts, saw themselves as separate and distinct from native Mexicanos and Mexican Americans.[8] The sample population reflected the large inflow of Spanish-speaking manitos into the city during the World War II period. Of the 491 respondents, only 82 were Mexican natives. More than 83 percent of the remaining individuals hailed from three states: New Mexico (137), Utah (110), and Colorado (96). While Allen notes this internal differentiation and its importance, he still uses the designation "Mexican" as the umbrella term for the entire community.

The persons surveyed worked in thirty different occupations. The designation "common laborer" was the most numerous, but "a goodly portion of the workers (were engaged) in semi-skilled and skilled work."[9] Those born in the United States were most likely to fill the common laborer position (30 percent of their group). Mexicanos tended to concentrate in jobs related to transportation (39 percent of their group). Domestic worker and retail clerk were other significant occupational categories.

The overall trend of Allen's survey revealed that some of these Hispanics had managed to move into better-paying jobs, but the majority continued toiling in lower-level and low-paying positions.[10] Census figures provide both context and verification for Allen's results. The 1950 federal census designated 11.9 percent of males employed in Salt Lake County as either common laborers (6.8 percent) or railroad workers (5.1 percent). These two occupational categories accounted for only about one of every eight working men in the county but comprised almost one-half (44.5 percent) of Allen's subjects.[11]

Academic achievement was another area of great concern. The 404 respondents over the age of eighteen averaged fewer than seven years of formal education. This was a distinct disadvantage in a county where the average adult had more than twelve years of schooling.[12] One-third of the Mexican-born respondents had never attended an educational institution. Fewer than one in six of the sampled Mexicanos, Mexican Americans, and manitos had graduated from high school.[13] Although valuable for its examination of educational achievement, Allen's study does have one major limitation: it does not break down heads of households by sex, which makes it impossible to compare his figures with census information specifically relating to Spanish-surnamed women. The colonia members' limited scholastic training, however, did not adversely affect their English proficiency. More than 90 percent of the native born and 50 percent of the foreign born were classified as speaking "considerable" English.[14]

While most inhabitants of the Salt Lake City community could communicate with the majority population, few had more than a grade-school education. This meant that they would likely remain mired in low-skilled occupations for the rest of their lives. Hope for a better economic future lay in the colonia's children. Allen's project revealed that some teachers in the local public schools had limited expectations of their Spanish-surnamed charges.

The situation in school mirrored that of the workplace; while not segregated, Spanish speakers certainly were not treated (or expected to perform) as equals. Allen asked a retired junior high school principal, D. R. Coombs, to comment on the characteristics of his "Mexican" students. Coombs noted that these pupils "had little interest in mathematics" but often excelled in sports or art. The former administrator complained that the parents of these children avoided PTA meetings as well as other school functions for adults. His overall assessment was that the Spanish-speaking youths in his charge "were not outstanding in scholarship or leadership."[15]

This study also provides detailed information regarding the unique religious composition of the Salt Lake City comunidad. Most respondents identified themselves as being at least nominally Catholic (84 percent). Most of these individuals attended Our Lady of Guadalupe Parish (in 1946 Spanish speakers comprised 84 percent of the congregation).[16] The primary non-Catholic denomination was, not surprisingly, the Church of Jesus Christ of Latter-day Saints. By 1947 the Rama Mexicana had its own chapel, located on 150 West and 500 South, and had about 150 members. Services were conducted in Spanish, but the branch's Anglo leadership also provided English classes for the congregation.[17]

The spatial distribution of the cluster resembled that of barrios in other parts of the American West and Southwest. An overwhelming majority of the Spanish-surnamed men, women, and children of Salt Lake City lived on the west side of town; more than two-thirds of the sample population lived within a one-mile radius between 800 South and 200 North and West Temple (100 West) and 800 West.[18] Unlike the barrios of California and Texas, however, this area was not recognized as a "little Mexico" in the heart of the Mormon Zion. The area inhabited by these Spanish-speakers included "an even greater number of non-Mexicans." Allen believed that the presence of Anglos, Greeks, Italians, and other ethnic groups helped to break down "traditional (Mexican) family customs" such as chaperoning and parental sanction before marriage.[19]

The most significant manifestation of cultural change and acculturation to "American life" was a precipitous decline in the use of the Spanish language among the people Allen surveyed. A recent study of Nuevo Mexicano cultural history and identity noted this same trend in the Land of Enchantment at the turn of the twentieth century. In *Speaking for Themselves* Doris Meyer asserts that young people were among the first to be lured by the English language and American modes of conduct. This inclination made the "leap from the betrayal of language to the abandonment of blood ties seemed increasingly plausible and threatening" to the Spanish-speaking comunidad.[20]

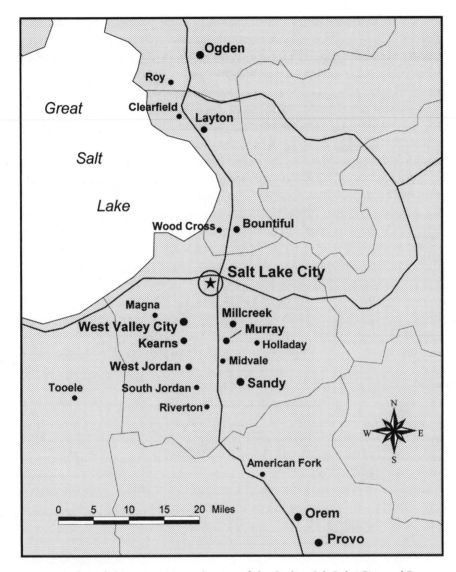

Map 4. A view of the major cities and towns of the Ogden, Salt Lake City, and Provo corridor. *Map by Kevin R. Mulligan*

Living in an area with an overwhelmingly Anglo population, contact with English speakers at job sites, schools, shops, and other aspects of daily life moved Hispanics from what one scholar calls a transitional bilingualism, where usage of both languages overlapped, to a vestigial form that retained only "a few words or expressions in Spanish as ethnic markers."[21] This transformation was well under way by 1947. More than 77 percent of the families surveyed spoke English in their homes at least half the time.[22] For some in this cluster this change was a conscious choice; language proficiency facilitated the ability to fit in and allowed individuals to conform to the society around them. For others, particularly school-age children, there was no option; they believed they had to discard Spanish or face ostracism. One teenager recalled how she felt when her parents "forced" her to speak Spanish in public: "When my parents would speak in Spanish I would answer them in English. In public, many times I would ignore my parents if they spoke to me in Spanish. I was ashamed of being Mexican."[23]

This pattern continued throughout the 1950s and into the 1960s. A 1967 survey of Spanish-surnamed people in Salt Lake City and its suburbs by Helen Mickelsen Crampton offers further evidence of the declining use of Spanish within this population.[24] Crampton focused on English usage by Spanish-surnamed high school students and their parents. Volunteers identified language preferences for public and private conversations; the more often an individual spoke English, the higher his "acculturation score" (to a maximum of fifteen points). The mean grade for the 122 parents interviewed was 10.69; their children tallied 13.18. English usage increased between the generations in all subgroups (Mexican born, Mexican Americans, and manitos) as well. The discarding of Spanish was particularly significant among the Nuevo Mexicanos (adults' average score was 10.41, and their teenagers' was 14.45).[25] The youth involved in this project faced a particularly difficult predicament; many desperately wanted to fit into majority society but achieved only partial acceptance because of their ethnicity or skin color.

This 1967 research provides a starting point from which to analyze northern Utah's clusters during the 1950s and early 1960s. The wartime economic expansion produced some occupational gains, but was this sufficient to assuage higher expectations? There is no doubt that bigotry or indifference at work and school limited options for Spanish-speakers, regardless of how diligent or proficient in English they were. While not as caustic as in other states, discrimination in Utah produced harsh consequences. Allen recognized these problems and called for the passage of legislation that would reduce "the feelings of ill will felt by the minority groups."[26] The activities of the Hispanic population of northern Utah during the 1950s and 1960s indicate that many in the comunidad were unwilling to wait for Joseph E. Allen's views to diffuse throughout the majority population.

The Spanish-surnamed community of northern Utah did not exactly match Richard A. Garcia's model in *Rise of the Mexican American Middle Class*. The first group (the immigrant generation) did not have the same level of economic, class, and political differences found in San Antonio. Rather, their principal dividing line was religious affiliation. But as in Texas, California, and elsewhere, after World War II many local Hispanics accepted and fought for increased equality and opportunity, as did others of the "Mexican American generation." Having sacrificed on the field of battle and done their "fair share" in industry during World War II, many of the Mexicanos, Mexican Americans, and manitos in Utah "unalterably refused to accept second class status and were prepared to wage a protracted struggle for their civil rights."[27]

The Hispanic population of the Beehive State both grew and diversified during the two decades following World War II, but federal census records revealed only part of this increase. The 1950 tract counted 1,396 native-born Mexicans in Utah. These men and women were the parents of 3,925 "native or foreign or mixed parentage" children (for a total "Mexican foreign stock" of 5,321 people).[28] By 1960 this group had expanded slightly to 5,557 individuals. In addition to these "Mexicans," a small number of people from Spain and various Latin American countries lived in the state (1,293 adults and children by 1960). Manitos were not included in these totals; the Spanish-speaking people from New Mexico and Colorado were counted as part of the "white" and "native born" categories.[29] This counting procedure caused the plurality of the state's Spanish-surnamed population to disappear from census figures.

Most of these men, women, and children (75 to 80 percent) resided in Salt Lake, Weber, Tooele, Davis, and Utah Counties.[30] They were not the predominant population in any location of these counties but tended to live in the poorer sections of the state's urban centers. In 1950 the locales with the highest concentrations of native-born Mexicans were Salt Lake City, Ogden, and Bingham Canyon. All of these locations had median family incomes below countywide averages, and more than 25 percent of area families earned under $2,000 per year.[31] Figures from 1960 showed that northern Utah's Hispanics had fallen further behind in this crucial category. The data revealed a median family income of $6,265 in Salt Lake County and $6,313 for Weber County. In both locations the tracts with the highest concentrations of Spanish-speakers had income levels substantially below these totals ($5,174 for Salt Lake County and $5,318 for Weber County).[32]

Between 1940 and 1959 Utah's economic growth helped fuel a 25 percent increase in the state's population. The proliferation of defense and manufacturing jobs drew many laborers to northern Utah.[33] The manufacturing sector expanded between 1946 and 1963 and came to employ almost 20 percent of the labor pool; mining and mineral processing accounted for more than one-third of these jobs.[34] Industry's expansion during these years created some opportunities for limited advancement by Hispanic workers.[35]

Andrés Martínez of Llano, New Mexico, was one manito who worked in Utah's mines. He arrived in Bingham Canyon during the 1930s and toiled in the copper industry for four decades. Andrés, as did most Hispanics, started in the track gang, the lowest-paying and least skilled position. His diligence earned him a "promotion" that provided better pay but much greater risk. The "monkey" slot in the powder gang was as far as most Spanish-speakers climbed in the occupational ladder of the various copper companies during the 1950s. The job entailed scaling down banks to insert blasting powder charges to clear rocks. "The blasting would scatter debris everywhere. It shook every level and sometimes buried an entire next level. It was dangerous work."[36]

When persistence and willingness to risk life and limb did not mean promotions or economic improvement, many of the Spanish-surnamed employees turned to unions. José Fidel Martínez, Andrés's brother, was a loyal supporter of the Mine, Mill and Smelter workers. The group's "radical" ties did not bother José. Some in the union's national leadership were Marxists, but Bingham's miners concerned themselves with bread and butter issues such as pay scales, safety, promotions, and work rules. A 1957 study of Kennecott's labor relations by University of Utah business student John Dale Ensign II concluded that in this case the Mine, Mill and Smelter Workers' reputation did not impair the union's "ability . . . to carry out its primary responsibilities."[37] José appreciated the union's support and willingly fought for better employment terms. During a strike his enthusiastic actions on behalf of the brotherhood gained him a spot on national television. José became involved in a fistfight with a police officer, and the melee nearly turned into a riot. "It took fifteen deputies to control him and get him in the car."[38]

Not all Spanish-speaking workers in the state were as fortunate as those in Bingham. Life for Utah's migrant population was, at best, hard. After 1945 growers in the area faced a tight labor market due to competition from higher-paying industries. Employers sought out a new source of labor for their fields and found it in the Rio Grande Valley of Texas and Mexico.[39] The recruitment of migrants and braceros brought between two thousand and eight thousand field hands to Utah each year between 1949 and 1965. While this number fluctuated, the adverse conditions these men and women faced did not. Local growers were notorious for not providing "adequate migrant housing, medical care, transportation, and full payment and just distribution of wages."[40] Some workers protested this treatment by vandalizing or destroying grower-owned housing. Utah's efforts at enforcing stricter laws regarding conditions in migrant labor camps met with little success. By 1959 twenty-three states had enacted laws regulating labor camps, but Utah was not among them. Conditions during the 1960s improved slightly as federal agencies set minimum wage levels for agricultural labor.[41] This bureaucratic solution produced a new quandary as growers responded to higher wages with increased mechanization that supplanted many betabeleros. Although employers increased their usage of machinery, Spanish-surnamed field hands remained a crucial source of labor for Utah crops.[42]

While Spanish-speaking adults fought to improve pay and working conditions, their offspring struggled to receive an adequate education. A series of local studies conducted during the late 1950s and early 1960s detailed the scholastic life of these students at all grade levels. Stanley H. Henderson's 1958 project examined the learning environment for Hispanic children in Davis County's Central Junior High School. A test of social distance revealed that Anglo pupils often ostracized their minority peers and considered them to be foreigners even though most were United States citizens. These Spanish-surnamed students scored well below schoolwide academic averages in work-study skills, reading, language arts, and mathematics. Central's teachers disproportionately classified their "Mexican" pupils as not being "socially well adjusted."[43]

Orlando A. Rivera's 1959 investigation focused on forty Spanish-surnamed sophomores who enrolled at Salt Lake City's West Senior High School in the autumn of 1955. The majority of these pupils (57 percent) failed to graduate. Only 43 percent received diplomas in 1958 compared to a 72 percent graduation rate for the entire class. Not surprisingly, West High's Hispanic population had a lower grade point average and academic achievement on standardized tests.[44]

Dean O. Stevens's 1962 study measured the social status of Spanish-surnamed children among their classmates and teachers at Layton Elementary. Most of the pupils were Utah natives, but Stevens noted that they were often poorly treated because of their skin color and language. Most were the progeny of migrant workers and tended to have poor language skills and attendance records. These barriers helped produce both peer rejections and lower academic achievement. The instructors' reduced expectations of these Spanish-surnamed charges further compounded social and scholastic obstacles.[45]

Spanish-speaking students met with difficult conditions in northern Utah schools, but as in other facets of life, the discrimination they faced was not as severe as in other parts of the nation. One West High instructor, who taught in Texas before moving to Salt Lake City, praised local schools for what he considered their enlightened approach in dealing with their Hispanic minors. These pupils could "go to school with the rest of the children and so they learn the same things the others do and also pick up things from them so by the time they go to high school the environment is not as different for them" as it was in Texas.[46]

John Florez was one colonia youth who beat the odds and graduated during the 1950s. From his first day in school peers chastised him for being a "barbarian" and because of his "strange" customs (such as eating tortillas with his hands). John said the taunts caused him much grief because "you are taught that certain things are wrong in school and then you go home and see your parents doing it." Although he faced intolerance in school, the Florez family helped him overcome the bigotry of his classmates. These lessons increased his determination to go to college. He reported, "There was discrimination, but you don't know how far you can get unless you try." John's diligence paid off both in the classroom and on the football field. In his senior year he directed South High's team to the state playoffs and won all-state honors as quarterback. He graduated in 1951 and then attended the University of Utah.[47]

By the 1950s Hispanics were the largest minority group in northern Utah schools, but there were few teachers of this ethnic background in the public classrooms. One of the first was Robert "Archie" Archuleta. Archie was born in July, 1930, in Grand Junction, Colorado. His family moved to Idaho during the Great Depression and struggled to survive as tenant farmers. Archie graduated from high school and attended Idaho State University; he was the first member of his family to enroll in college. Archie hoped to improve the plight of his community and to serve as a role model for Spanish-surnamed youths. He accepted a teaching position with the Salt Lake City school district in 1953.[48]

A well-dispersed colonia became even more so as a result of augmented activity in Bingham Canyon after World War II.[49] Since the 1920s Greek, Slavic, and Hispanic families had lived and worked in the canyon to the rhythm of their employers' schedules. One Spanish-surnamed individual recalled that during his childhood years in Bingham the whistle "blew and we got up to go to school. It blew and we went home for lunch. It blew and our dads came home from work, and we knew we better go home to eat." The mine's expansion eventually consumed towns that were the only homes many Hispanic residents had ever known. By 1962 enclaves such as Dinkeyville, Lark, Highland Boy, and Garfield ceased to exist, forcing inhabitants down into Salt Lake City and its southwestern suburbs.[50]

The 1960 census confirmed this trend. Foreign-born Mexicans and Puerto

Ricans in Salt Lake County lived near the railroads and industrial sights of Salt Lake City, South Salt Lake, Murray, Magna, and Midvale. Records for Weber County revealed a similar pattern. In Ogden, Spanish speakers tended to live near the Union Pacific depot, between the Weber River and Adams Avenue and 23rd Street south to the city limit.[51] As their numbers expanded during the 1950s and 1960s, some Hispanics moved into areas with few, if any, people of color. In their attempts to find suitable housing many families confronted both subtle resistance and outright hostility and redlining.

Epifanio González's experiences illustrate the frustrations of Spanish-surnamed would-be homeowners after World War II. Epifanio, a Silver Star recipient due to his heroics at Monte Casino, discovered that his efforts, sacrifice, and valor on the battlefield did not count for much when he attempted to purchase a residence in an east-side Salt Lake City neighborhood. The seller bluntly informed Epifanio that, medal recipient and war hero or not, houses in the Avenues section of the capital city were not for sale to "Mexicans" or African Americans. This rebuke traumatized González, for it contradicted what he believed he had fought for in the war. He ultimately bought a dwelling on the west side of town, "where they think you belong."[52]

Esperanza and Gavino Aguayo encountered similar circumstances in the Salt Lake City suburb of Midvale. The brother and sister grew up in Dinkeyville and thought they would spend the rest of their lives in Bingham Canyon. The mine's expansion pushed the Aguayos and other families down into the Salt Lake Valley. During his search for a new dwelling Gavino discovered that many houses in Murray (another southwestern suburb of the Utah capital) had restrictive convenants. Fortunately for the Aguayos, increased demand for housing by displaced canyon families made it difficult to enforce these "contracts." A real estate agent advised Gavino that, although he and his sister were "Mexicans," there "would be no trouble" with their purchase.[53]

Although economic and social circumstances for Spanish-speakers in Utah were not as difficult as they were for their counterparts in other U.S. locations, many in the comunidad believed that more could be done to address colonia needs. The older associations, the Centro Cívico Mexicano (CCM), the Guadalupe Parish and Mission, and the Rama Mexicana responded by funding an increased number of community and self-improvement programs. These entities provided some benefits, but a small volunteer base, miniscule financial resources, and intracolonia cleavages limited their impact.

Some of these clubs catered exclusively to Mexican natives. The Sociedad Mutua Cuahotémoc (formed in Salt Lake City in 1949) and the Sociedad Fraternal Benito Juárez (established in Ogden in 1952) joined three existing branches of the Comisión Honorífica Mexicana in presenting forums specifically "oriented toward social and cultural activities for the Mexican immigrant in Utah." These societies celebrated independence days and religious holidays and helped maintain traditional customs.[54]

Centro Cívico Mexicano was the largest and most important organization promoting a unified ethnic and community identity before 1967. A group of friends started the CCM in 1936 to "maintain the hispano-american culture through social, educational, and sporting activities."[55] Members generated revenue through countless fund-raising efforts, and in 1950 the association purchased a small lot and house on 155 South between 500 and 600 West. The center soon became a focal point of Mexican activity in Salt Lake City. Through a myriad of program offerings CCM influenced most aspects of daily life in the comunidad.[56]

The CCM drew its board of directors from the neighborhoods of the west side and established standing committees dedicated to improving conditions. The Comité Femenino (Ladies' Auxiliary), Comité Festejos (Festivities Committee), and Comité Mejoras Materiales (Facilities Maintenance and Improvement Committee) jointly sponsored the two most important events in the colonia's social calendar; the celebrations of Mexico's independence days. The highlight of each observance was the crowning of a *Reina de la fiesta* (festival queen) and her court. Young Hispanas vied for this honor by selling tickets to family and friends; each dollar raised was a vote for the ticket seller's candidacy. The funds collected helped to pay for building upkeep and maintenance.[57]

Centro leaders established the Comité de Propaganda (Propaganda Committee), which informed the public of Mexican news and events in the comunidad. The group's principal effort was its sponsorship of *La Voz del Centro Cívico Mexicano* on radio station KWHO (860 AM). In *Spanish Language Radio in the Southwestern United States* Felix F. Gutierrez and Jorge Reina Schement note a major benefit of this type of programming by asserting that "for many Spanish-speakers who have limited ability to understand English, Spanish language radio is their primary source of news, entertainment and advertising." Broadcasting over the KWHO airwaves permitted the CCM's message entry into a substantial percentage of the homes of northern Utah's Hispanic familias.[58]

Board member Tomás Pérez provided the show's *voz* (voice). Pérez moved to the United States from Mexico in 1952 when he was hired as a bracero by a California cotton grower. Tomás did not care for his assignment or working conditions and skipped out on his contract after two months. An uncle advised him to move to Salt Lake City, where Tomás joined the CCM to socialize and assist his countrymen. He volunteered for many tasks but most enjoyed working with

Alfonso Cárdenas on his Spanish-language radio show. When Cárdenas returned to Mexico, Tomás took over the production and broadcasting duties.[59]

The Comité de Beneficiencia (Benefits Committee) functioned as CCM's version of a mutual aid society. It established an emergency fund to serve the needs of injured or infirmed constituents. Worthy individuals received two dollars per day for the first seven days of their illness, and then the stipend declined to one dollar per day until the thirtieth day. If recovery was more prolonged, members took up special collections.[60]

The Centro aided Hispanic youths through its sponsorship of athletic and after-school activities. The Comité de Deportes (Sports Committee) funded basketball and baseball leagues that furnished instruction, guidance, and fellowship. According to one west-side manito youth, the CCM was the only place in town where he could go for recreational activities. In a 1995 interview Judge Andrew Valdez recalled that some Rama Mexicana members did not welcome manitos or Catholics in their basketball league: "The Catholic Youth Organization did not have the money necessary to help. The Centro Cívico Mexicano sponsored a youth league and organized a baseball league."[61] Another service provided by the CCM was through the Comité de Educación (Education Committee), which conducted Spanish-language and Mexican-history classes that helped maintain traditions and ethnic pride among colonia children.[62]

The CCM was Salt Lake City's cultural and social hub for men and women of Mexican descent. But what type of response did non-Mexicanos receive? Officially, the organization abandoned the "prejudices between . . . brothers" and welcomed all Spanish speakers.[63] Andrew Valdez and other teenage manitos, with few options for recreational activities, gravitated toward the CCM's sport, educational, and cultural programs.[64] The group's leadership claimed that place of birth and ethnic affiliation did not create internal divisions, but by 1959 club by-laws restricted full (voting) membership to those of "Mexican nationality or origin." This qualification relegated all other Spanish-speakers to "honorary" (nonvoting) status.[65]

For many in the manito community this partial membership in the CCM was not enough. The Sociedad Protección Mutua de Trabajadores Unidos (Mutual Aid Society of United Workers, or SPMDTU) was in many ways the manito counterpart to the Centro Cívico Mexicano. The SPMDTU began in Antonio, Colorado, in November of 1900. The mutual aid society sought to create a financial and social barrier against the economic hardships and discrimination suffered by Spanish-speakers of this area. Initially all Spanish-surnamed males could join, but a 1929 amendment to the by-laws restricted participation in this association to "Spanish-Americans."[66] By May, 1946, the

large influx of Spanish-surnamed men, women, and children from New Mexico and Colorado spurred the creation of two SPMDTU councils, one each in
Ogden and Salt Lake City. Leo Antencio was the first president of the Ogden
branch, and Rudolfo Espinosa headed the Salt Lake City post. The new entities did not provide the same number of services as did CCM. The groups
functioned primarily as convivial clubs and provided low-cost life and disabil-
ity insurance plans for constituents; the goal of creating a shield against discrimination did not receive much attention.

After World War II, CCM, SPMDTU, and the various fraternal societies
concentrated on community and personal improvement, cultural maintenance, and fellowship but not on working for social change. By the middle
1950s, however, a shift in emphasis occurred. As a result of their performance
on the battlefield during World War II, Spanish-surnamed individuals "destroyed the credibility of Anglo rationalizations regarding the Mexican American." The experiences of many *soldados* (soldiers) in both Europe and the
Pacific (and the incongruities between American ideals and social reality) encouraged certain *veteranos* (veterans) to create an organization (the American
G.I. Forum, or AGIF) dedicated to procuring full civil rights for the Spanish-
speaking people of the United States.[67] The establishment of AGIF branches
in Ogden (1954) and Salt Lake City (1955) were the first tentative steps taken
toward a civil rights campaign for the Spanish-surnamed population of Utah.
Both national and northern Utah AGIF leaders called for equal rights and benefits for veteranos, raised money for scholarships, fought to decrease drop-out
rates, sought better treatment for migrant workers, and struggled to end both
job and housing discrimination.[68]

The Ogden AGIF commenced operations in August, 1954, with thirteen
paid members. Abel Medina was the first chairman, but Molly Gálvan, a secretary at Hill Air Force Base (near Ogden), was the organization's driving force.
During the rest of 1954 and 1955 the group worked to build up its treasury, established a ladies' auxiliary, and held a back-to-school drive.[69] Forum leaders
met with Dr. T. O. Smith, superintendent of Ogden schools, and presented
complaints and suggestions for reducing the drop-out rate and improving attendance of Spanish-surnamed students.[70] Molly supplemented this local initiative with a letter to Congressman H. A. Dixon detailing what she perceived
as the discriminatory climate that existed in Weber County. The representative expressed utter amazement and surprise because he "supposed that race
prejudice in Utah was at a minimum."[71]

In June of 1955 Molly, with the assistance of Father Collins, established an
AGIF branch in Salt Lake City. By September seventeen individuals had
joined, and Larry Jaramillo, an instructor at Westminster College, became the

group's chairman.[72] Like their Ogden colleagues, members of the Salt Lake City chapter held fund-raisers and back-to-school drives. Forum members solicited aid from local charities and collected money and clothes to help dress colonia children for the first day of school.[73] The AGIF's national office had high hopes that the Salt Lake City branch would become large and active, but two severe blows in rapid succession doomed the post. First, Larry Jaramillo accepted a teaching position at Carbon College in Helper, Utah, removing an articulate and effective spokesman for the Hispanic cluster. Second, a controversy developed when supposed "communist elements" attempted to "infiltrate" the fledgling group.[74]

On September 15, 1955, Molly received a letter from Carmen M. López of Bingham Canyon asking for assistance in establishing a "Mexican American organization for our people." Gálvan became suspicious of López when she mentioned her friendship with a woman named Anna Correa-Barry. Recent AGIF bulletins warned members against association with Correa-Barry because of her supposed ties to a series of "communist front groups." Molly investigated and found that López had attempted to "penetrate" the Sociedad Mutualista Mexicana de Miguel Aleman in Bingham Canyon. The society's officials advised Gálvan to avoid contact with Carmen López because she "was an agitator and troublemaker." Following AGIF policy guidelines, the Salt Lake City council contacted the local field office of the Federal Bureau of Investigation.[75] Although the AGIF sought to maintain its "purity" and banish any suspected "reds" from their midst, some individuals in northern Utah considered the AGIF as being comprised of unpatriotic "troublemakers." In 1956 the AGIF attempted to place a new chapter in Tooele, but because of concerns over the groups' potential for "radicalism," the local parish priest refused to recommend the organization to his parishioners until federal officials vouched for the AGIF's patriotism.[76]

The AGIF walked a philosophical and political tightrope in northern Utah and nationally during the late 1950s. The association attempted to fight discrimination while not being overly critical of a bigoted society.[77] The official publication of the Ogden branch, the *Ogden Forum Bulletin,* revealed the contradictions in philosophy and goals that, in many ways, stymied AGIF's fight for civil rights. Constituents wanted a nation in which Spanish-speakers received equal treatment, but they hoped to work within the existing system for change. Molly asserted that Utah's AGIF clubs consisted of people of "unquestionable integrity" who aimed to "thwart the efforts of those who would be wolves in sheep's clothing."[78] An incessant fixation on the communist threat derailed AGIF's ability to articulate its demands for social justice and educational opportunities effectively.

By the late 1940s Spanish-speakers composed the overwhelming majority of Our Lady of Guadalupe's congregation. The development of Salt Lake City's Rose Park subdivision further increased this percentage. As more Spanish-surnamed families moved into the city's northwest section, the parish required the construction of new facilities and the establishment of new programs. On May 16, 1948, a larger church building was dedicated on 715 West 200 North. During the 1950s the Salt Lake Diocese erected a Catholic elementary school (called the Bishop Glass school), funded a community clinic, and trained male volunteers to provide social services for the west side's needy.[79]

After Father James E. Collins died on August 31, 1957, several priests came and went in rapid succession, as had occurred before he arrived.[80] Collins had done much to help the community on Salt Lake City's west side; he directed a wide array of programs which helped maintain the flock's cultural traditions, and he acted as a foil against negative stereotyping of Hispanics by other Catholics. But Collins did not use his position as pastor directly to challenge and protest the poverty and other negative social conditions extant in the comunidad. In this sense Collins fits a pattern of action (inaction?) described by Gilberto Hinojosa in *Mexican Americans and the Catholic Church, 1900–1965*. Although individual priests left "legacies of service with *el pueblo*," Hinojosa asserts, before the 1950s "the Church saw its role primarily as a spiritual one. Its principal goal was to sustain the life of grace of the immigrants by dispensing the sacraments and to safeguard them from encroaching Protestantism."[81]

The clergyman who would greatly expand the parish's role in the colonia arrived in January, 1961. Father Jerald H. Merrill worked out of the old mission house (what had once been the residence of las madres) and took charge of the spiritual welfare of forty-five families. Merrill helped create a branch of the Guadalupana Society that met monthly to discuss neighborhood problems and potential solutions. In 1962 the group rented a room in the Rio Grande Hotel in downtown Salt Lake City and established a community center. The Guadalupana fellowship moved into larger quarters at 346 West 100 South in 1966. The concept of the Guadalupe Center was to establish a gathering place where people from the community could plan projects and organizations answering to their needs. Among the programs created were a Catholic credit union, adult literacy courses, and a cooperative food market.[82] Father Collins in many ways typified the priests who worked with Mexicano and Mexican American congregations from the 1930s through the 1950s. Merrill, however, represented a new era and focus. He was a more "activist" clergyman who during the 1960s and 1970s used cursillos and other programs to stimulate social action and reenergize the spiritual life of his assembly.[83]

The rolls of the LDS Mexican Branch reflected both the growth and increased diversity of northern Utah's Spanish-surnamed population. Between 1946 and 1966 Rama membership swelled by more than 200 percent (increasing to a total of 467 members).[84] By June, 1960, this group's size warranted a change in status from branch to ward.[85] The reorganized Rama Mexicana became known as the Lucero (Bright Star) Ward. The new assembly's composition was markedly different from the Rama's beginnings in the 1920s; manitos and *Latino Americanos* (Latin Americans) now comprised the majority.[86] Continued missionary work, both locally and in South and Central America, produced more Spanish-speaking converts by the late 1960s. During those years Samuel Victor Miera and other missionaries used the local white pages as their principal tool with which to find potential Hispanic converts. These individuals lived throughout the Salt Lake Valley but were most concentrated in the suburbs of Sandy, Midvale, and West Jordan (all of these cities are suburbs of Salt Lake City and are located to the south and west). Eventually two new branches were created to serve the needs of the growing number of Mormones. A branch called Cumorah[87] began operation in April, 1962, and served the Spanish speakers in the southern end of Salt Lake County (bounded by 3900 South). Cumorah, like Lucero, provided a broad range of activities for its membership. Among these were Mexican fiestas and "a choir, a basketball team . . . and a folk dancing group." A second unit, the Haleman Branch, ministered to those who lived west of Redwood Road (1700 West).[88]

As in previous decades, conversion did not break all ethnic ties; Hispanic neophytes still considered themselves part of the larger comunidad. Social affiliations and religious beliefs, however, did produce some cleavages among vecinos. Andrew Valdez recalled that during the early 1960s the people at the Lucero Ward "had more support and services," and he viewed them as being "a closed community . . . separate and distinct" from other Spanish-speakers.[89] Lucero's leaders continued the Depression-era practice of aiding individuals who required assistance for their "financial beginnings."[90] Ward ties provided access to job information and other benefits not available to those outside the fold. In addition to increased services and benefits Mormon religious practice, and the time devoted to it, often limited converts' contact with the rest of the Spanish-speaking community. This reduced interaction with others in the comunidad and sometimes generated feelings of hostility and betrayal.[91]

Robert H. Burton, the Lucero Ward's first president, was clearly sympathetic to the spiritual and (to a lesser degree) monetary needs of ward members. But he was not assiduous in addressing wider colonia concerns. Although Spanish-surnamed Mormons had certain advantages over their Catholic brethren, they too endured bigotry and discrimination. Burton challenged his charges to develop their English skills and pursue an education, yet he refrained from calling for programs to improve social and economic conditions. By the late 1960s this approach was clearly out of step with the demands of the Chicano and civil rights movements going on in other parts of the United States. Burton's successor at Lucero's helm, Dr. Orlando Rivera (1966), chose a different route. The injustice of racism, he felt, affected all Spanish-surnamed people of northern Utah, regardless of denominational affiliation. This realization provided Rivera and Father Jerald Merrill an incentive to cut across both religious lines and cultural divisions and create an organization that would unite all Hispanics. This partnership led to the founding in December, 1967, of a group called SOCIO, an acronym for Spanish-Speaking Organization for Community, Integrity, and Opportunity (*socio* means "good friend"). For the first time the Spanish-surnamed people of Utah established an alliance designed to work at the grass roots to solve social problems and improve living conditions without regard to ethnic or religious distinctions.

After 1945 many of northern Utah's colonia constituents had assumed that their wartime efforts would earn them equal treatment in employment, education, and housing. Between 1946 and 1967 Anglo inattention to the circumstances faced by Utah's Hispanics dashed these fragile hopes. Although the Beehive State underwent a significant postwar expansion, the majority of Spanish-speakers remained confined to low-skilled jobs. Schools failed the comunidad as well, and drop-out rates remained alarmingly high. The search for housing found Spanish-surnamed familias often unwelcome outside of Salt Lake City's west side and other poor neighborhoods.

White intolerance and indifference were not the sole reasons for lack of Hispanic social progress. The Spanish-speaking people's own divisions prevented them from competently and effectively lobbying for redress. During the 1950s local Hispanic men and women joined organizations such as the CCM, SPMDTU, Our Lady of Guadalupe Parish, the Guadalupana Society, Lucero Ward, and the AGIF. Although these groups provided fellowship, financial services, and cultural preservation, each failed to furnish a justification for surmounting intracolonia differences. The disregard of Hispanics' needs (and the development of the civil rights and Chicano movements in other areas of the United States) in part helped overcome internal divisions and brought about the birth of SOCIO. During the late 1960s and early 1970s this organization worked at the grassroots level and helped forge unity and panethnic identification among the various Spanish-speaking people of northern Utah.

6

"The Advocacy Battle for Our People"
Hispanic Activism in Northern Utah, 1968–86

During the two decades following World War II, Utah's economic development reflected conditions present in other parts of the West.[1] The growth of manufacturing, defense, and the public service sector fueled commercial expansion. All three of these areas posted significant increases in employment levels in Utah.[2] The industrial upsurge had a salubrious impact upon the state's Spanish-speaking population. Some laborers parlayed diligence and union membership into higher-skilled, better-paying occupations. This was positive but did not mean an end to workplace discrimination.

In the decades after 1965 economic trends reduced this window of opportunity. The Beehive State's economy followed national patterns and shifted toward the creation of service-sector jobs.[3] Hispanic workers saw improvement diminish with the decline of industrial positions. The new slots created during the 1970s required more than a strong back and a willingness to risk life and limb, and many simply could not, or would not be allowed to, compete for these jobs. By the end of the 1960s it was apparent that northern Utah schools were not educating the children of the comunidad to survive in this more competitive environment. In 1969 Spanish-surnamed students in area schools were dropping out at an alarmingly high (66 percent) rate.[4]

In December, 1967, in a meeting held at the Guadalupe Center in Salt Lake City, Father Jerald H. Merrill and more than 150 concerned individuals launched a group that they hoped would rally colonia constituents behind the struggle for greater economic and social equality. The nondenominational association SOCIO (Spanish-Speaking Organization for Community, Integrity, and Opportunity) officially began operation on March 21, 1968. Its stated purpose was to "act consistently and lawfully to establish and maintain justice in all areas affecting the well being of the Spanish-speaking person and community." The organization's leadership believed that cooperation with local and state authorities would accomplish these goals. SOCIO was envisioned as being able to "work with the system in such a way that changes some rules that amount to . . . artificial barriers."[5] Members pledged to toil at the grassroots level for improved conditions in employment, education, and social welfare.[6] Father Merrill, Orlando Rivera, and others in the community believed that Hispanics would unite and support this panethnic vehicle and "overcome the confusion caused by fragmentation . . . identify problems, establish needs, select action, and move to implement action."[7] The time had come to go beyond fraternal celebrations and fellowship and to "fight the advocacy battle for our people in this state."[8]

During the 1970s SOCIO lobbied for civil rights and served as the most important, though not the only, voice representing the concerns, complaints, and hopes of the Spanish-surnamed people of Utah to political, business, educational, and religious leaders. By 1986 some of SOCIO's original aims were reality: an increased number of Hispanics worked in law enforcement and other governmental jobs; the quantity of minority students at the University of Utah and the rest of the state's colleges and universities had expanded dramatically; and the level and effectiveness of social services provided to the colonia's members had improved. Between 1968 and 1986 SOCIO successfully challenged impediments to social and economic opportunity for Utah's Spanish-speakers, but this success ultimately helped cause the organization's demise.[9]

The 1960 federal census counted only 6,850 Spanish-speakers in the Beehive State.[10] This number included people of Mexican, Spanish, and Latin American birth or descent but did not account for the Spanish-surnamed manitos from New Mexico and Colorado. These people vanished into the "white" and "native born" columns, producing a severe undercount of the state's largest minority group. For the 1970 census the Department of Commerce attempted to correct this situation by creating a new, broad self-identification category, "Persons of Spanish Language."[11] In Utah this modification yielded dramatic results; in the span of ten years the Spanish-speaking population of the state "increased" by more than 635 percent to 43,550.[12] This new classification scheme provided a better estimate of the group's actual size and generated a significant amount of information on residential concentration, employment patterns, income levels, and poverty rates.

Between 1960 and 1970 Hispanics became more dispersed within the state's urban core. More than 87 percent lived along the Wasatch Front counties of Salt Lake, Weber, and Tooele.[13] The Salt Lake City and Ogden areas remained the primary centers of activity and concentration, but more than 400 Spanish-speakers now lived in each of the following townships and cities:

Brigham City, Clearfield, Holladay, Kearns, Layton, Midvale, Orem, Provo, Roy, and Tooele.[14] The overwhelming majority of these people (41,183, or 94.5 percent) were United States natives, and only 2,132 (4.9 percent) of the 43,550 claimed Spanish as their native tongue.[15]

In 1970 the plurality of colonia men (sixteen years and older) continued working in menial jobs, but census tracts confirmed some movement into better-paying, skilled positions.[16] They toiled primarily in Utah's factories (producing durable and nondurable goods) and in non-farm-related common labor (such as freight and material handling). These three categories accounted for almost one-half of urban, Spanish-surnamed employees in the state. Unlike earlier decades, however, a significant number filled higher-level posts. Two notable areas of concentration were craft occupations (such as mechanics, repairmen, and carpenters) and professional and technical employees (mostly as elementary and secondary teachers and health workers). The vocational status of many colonia constituents had improved since World War II.[17] Hispanas had more limited employment opportunities. The working women of the Spanish-speaking comunidad most likely worked in service industries (the majority in food processing) or in low-paying clerical posts (as secretaries and typists).[18] The overall trend revealed some advancement, but most Spanish-surnamed people were still stuck in menial jobs and faced a much higher unemployment rate than did whites (10.1 percent versus 5.8 percent throughout the state in 1969).[19]

The Spanish-surnamed population also trailed in educational achievement, although the gap had narrowed since the 1940s and 1950s. In Joseph E. Allen's 1947 study of Salt Lake City's "Mexican" population, his subjects over eighteen years of age averaged less than seven years of formal education.[20] By 1970 most *adultos* (adults) in the comunidad had almost eleven years of formal schooling; men attained 10.7 years and women 10.5 (compared to a statewide average of 12.4).[21] The percentage of high school graduates more than doubled, increasing from less than 17 percent to 39.5 percent. Still, colonia members faced a severe disadvantage and had much less preparation than those with whom they competed for jobs. Statewide, 67.3 percent of Utahans over age twenty-five had secondary-school diplomas. More than 37 percent of all Spanish speakers attended high school for less than one year compared to only 13.6 percent of whites. A similar discrepancy existed in the number of individuals with college degrees; only 5.8 percent of Spanish-surnamed people had university diplomas compared with 14.0 percent of the majority population.[22]

The variance in education greatly affected occupational patterns. Many positions in industry required at least a high school diploma, and this prerequisite often eliminated otherwise qualified Hispanics from consideration for higher-skilled or managerial positions. In many cases the requirement became an artificial barrier. Differences in job status helped generate a wide gap in family and per capita income. Spanish-surnamed familias throughout Utah earned a median income of $7,833 and mean earnings of $8,215. The corresponding figures for whites were $9,356 and $10,472. In the state's urban areas the differences were even more pronounced (medians of $7,875 versus $9,636 and means of $8,320 versus $10,820).

Individual salaries provide further evidence of this disparity. Median pay for white males in the state (sixteen years and older, employed for fifty-two weeks in 1969) amounted to $8,381; for cluster members this figure amounted to only $7,367.[23] In urban centers the totals were $8,712 and $7,440.[24] Census tracts revealed similar levels of disparity for Hispanas. Throughout Utah, Spanish-surnamed women who labored the entire year (1969) received median wages of $3,842, and they earned only $2,376 if they worked less than fifty-two weeks. White women averaged $4,312 and $2,917, respectively. In the Salt Lake City Standard Metropolitan Statistical Area the figures were $3,733 and $2,556 for Hispanas and $4,426 and $3,191 for whites.[25] On average, Utah's Spanish speakers received about $0.81 for each dollar earned by whites.[26]

Lower pay and educational achievement combined to produce a disproportionately high poverty rate among Hispanics. The 1970 census estimated that 13.8 percent of Utah's "Persons of Spanish Language" received some sort of public assistance (compared with a statewide figure of 4.6 percent of the majority population). Most of these poor familias resided in the state's urban areas. Of a total of 8,955 Spanish-speaking families in the state, 1,573 (17.6 percent) lived on a mean income of $2,339. Single women headed almost one-half (45 percent) of those homes.[27]

The 1970 census provides a starting point from which to analyze the social and economic circumstances of this minority group. The postwar economic growth produced some educational and occupational gains, but Spanish-speakers still lagged behind in these crucial categories. Through a myriad of programs and activities SOCIO and other organizations worked to narrow existing disparities, promoted ethnic awareness, and agitated for greater equality.

Félix M. Padilla's 1985 work, *Latino Ethnic Consciousness,* provides an effective framework for understanding the creation of SOCIO as well as its beliefs and goals. As in Salt Lake City, the Spanish-surnamed people of Chicago endured discrimination in employment, education, and housing. Mexican Americans and Puerto Ricans shared a common language and financial circumstances; both groups lived in the poorer sections of the city; and most individuals labored in low-paying, menial occupations. Still, Padilla asserts, these difficult conditions were insufficient to stimulate a movement designed to overcome intraethnic divisions. Existing cleavages limited the efficacy of individual organizations when they presented grievances to local officials. These atomized entities were simply too weak to contend for redress.[28] In the case of northern Utah, Hispanics were divided along ethnic and religious lines, and these fissures prevented much cooperation among the CCM, AGIF, the Guadalupe Parish, and the Lucero Ward in the fight for civil rights and greater equality.

Padilla acknowledges that institutional inequalities played a significant role in ethnic mobilizations but rightly claims that other forces were more crucial in the development of *el movimiento* (the movement). It was the expansion of the role of government (and private charitable organizations) in American society and the creation of "participation programs" (such as civil rights laws, equal employment opportunities, welfare programs, and affirmative action) that facilitated interaction and mobilization of Spanish-speakers in Chicago. These trends unified Spanish-surnamed peoples of various ethnic backgrounds into "ethnic contenders" who were willing and able to vie for political, corporate, and governmental largesse.[29] In northern Utah Mormones, Católicos, manitos, Mexicanos, Mexican Americans, middle class, and poor united behind SOCIO in order to improve their lives.

In addition to secular and community based entities, the Catholic Church (and other denominations as well) were part of the ethnic-contender movement. The expansion of cursillos and other participatory programs (in particular after Second Vatican Council) brought Hispanic social issues to the forefront of U.S. Catholic policy debates. Whereas during the first decades of the twentieth century the church emphasized its spiritual role (as typified by Father Collins and las madres at Guadalupe), after World War II there was greater emphasis on the quest for social justice (as epitomized by Father Merrill).[30] This drive for greater economic equality reached its peak, according to Ana María Díaz-Stevens and Anthony M. Stevens-Arroyo, during the years 1967–84. These authors describe this internal church debate as intense and of long standing: "They are not mutually exclusive, since both are firmly rooted in the Catholic teaching about faith and . . . good works essential for salvation. But . . . in the historical process of deciding priorities, these notions generate different positions, often similar to the conservative-liberal division within a political party. The first approach emphasizes the administration of sacraments, church attendance, and piety; the other views the church's mission in terms of aid in matters like housing, health services, job opportunity, and social organization." This emphasis by the Catholic hierarchy coincided with el movimiento's demands for social justice and opportunity. Díaz-Stevens and Stevens-Arroyo compare the ties between secular and religious groups during this era to an alignment of celestial bodies. For a short period of time "the radical demands of Latino student militants, the resources of the Catholic and Protestant churches, and the piety of Latino cursillistas had come into syzygy."[31]

In SOCIO's articles of incorporation the board of trustees welcomed the opportunity to "cooperate fully with all . . . within the community whose aims were not inconsistent" with their own. SOCIO's by-laws created a volunteer group with an elected president, four vice presidents charged with specific areas of activity (government affairs, economics, organizations, and social action), a secretary, and a treasurer.[32] The incorporators conceived of SOCIO as an inclusive, proactive entity. But not all Hispanics in the area endured equally harsh treatment, and the comunidad was not monolithic in its agenda for reform. Even with a primary ethnic contender (such as SOCIO) in place, other associations formed and agitated for change.[33] The individuals who created and initially headed SOCIO were middle-class men who had ties to the most powerful and influential entities (social and political) in the state of Utah. This influenced the type of action which this organization would sponsor and support. As Padilla states, "The degree of integration of an ethnic group (or individuals) in the institutional life of the larger society determines, in part, the kinds of strategies . . . that such a group would create to relate to circumstances of social inequality."[34] SOCIO's founders and early leaders were content to bargain with the existing "power structure" in order to remove the "obstructions" which they saw as impeding the progress of the Hispanic population.[35]

Moderate demands and methods helped make SOCIO an effective representative, but there were two other crucial factors that helped account for its success. First, although the Hispanic populace of Utah had grown dramatically since World War II, by 1970 it still comprised only 4 percent of the state's inhabitants.[36] Other studies have shown that in areas where minorities comprise a small percentage of the total population, the majority has often "indulged" in toleration for moderate social change.[37] In his 1999 essay "'Where Have All the Nationalists Gone?'" Mártin Sánchez Jankowski provides further substantiation for this assertion. The author explains why his research project uncovered a greater preponderance of Chicano nationalist "radicals" in Albuquerque and Los Angeles than in San Antonio during the middle 1980s. Sánchez Jankowski contends that those two cities "have the type of political culture, nurtured by their particular local economies and social demographics, which stimulates and tolerates a wide variety of political beliefs, including a variety of nationalist beliefs."[38] The situation for Chicano activists in Salt Lake City during the 1960s was the exact opposite. In northern Utah "the specific texture of American society" was not conducive to radicalized pronouncements and activities. At the same time, aware of the tribulations caused by more militant Chicano groups in California and Texas, many local whites agreed to work with SOCIO rather than face the possibility of a more dangerous and revolutionary community.

Second, the beliefs of the Church of Jesus Christ of Latter-day Saints greatly influenced the hierarchy's perception of this new civil rights group. The involvement of Dr. Orlando Rivera, a University of Utah professor and the first Hispanic bishop of the Lucero Ward, surely inspired confidence in the movement. In addition, the church needed to continue its work among the Lamanites' descendants in order to bring about Christ's millennial kingdom. By the early 1960s some individuals in the hierarchy were expressing concern about how Hispanics in northern Utah viewed the LDS Church. Samuel Victor Miera, who had worked to bring Spanish speakers into the Mormon fold since the late 1950s, believed that the church had a poor reputation among many in the comunidad: "In other parts of the United States the Chicanos and blacks and everybody else blame all their troubles on the white Anglos, you know. Here in Utah they don't do that. They blame it on the Mormons. The image of the Church is terrible."[39] If the church did not stand in the way of the expansion of civil rights and benefits for the Spanish-speaking population in Zion, perhaps some of these individuals would be more receptive to its message. As Bishop Rivera stated before a church leadership group, "when something as American as Mormonism is presented to us, my people do not find in it anything to embrace very readily. This is part of the explanation why Mexican-Americans in the United States do not embrace Mormonism with much enthusiasm."[40]

These problems could be transcended, Rivera advised, if church leaders stressed two arguments to potential Spanish-surnamed converts. First, he felt that emphasis should be placed on the significant role of the Lamanites in the overall scheme of salvation: "We call ourselves Chicanos, and all Chicanos think of themselves as having an Indo-Hispanic background, of having ancestral roots native to America as well as to Europe. Thus, you considering us Lamanites is in no way offensive, but rather acceptable to our people. We are proud of our native American progenitors."[41] Second, he felt that the church should clearly articulate its theological tenets on family life and accentuate similarities between their views and those of most Hispanics: "Cultural characteristics of our people include family solidarity and a family-oriented lifestyle. . . . Why give up these cultural characteristics? I think they are beautiful ones, and they are imminently compatible with Mormon values."[42]

Before SOCIO's founding, northern Utah's Hispanics created several fraternal, religious, and mutual aid societies designed to preserve cultural traditions as well as provide limited financial benefits. A tentative step toward a civil rights campaign occurred with the establishment of the American G.I. Forum (AGIF) chapters in both Ogden and Salt Lake City. These groups were small, had limited resources, and seldom coordinated efforts with other Hispanic organizations to campaign for social change. By the late 1960s many local Spanish-speaking organizations had shifted their attention to less weighty matters, such as staging social gatherings and fund-raising. Ceremonies commemorating the completion of a new Centro Cívico Mexicano building typified this tendency. The dedication of the new edifice and facilities took place on December 1, 1968, and club officials proudly announced that it would be used for entertainment, sporting events, and other recreational activities. The Lucero Ward conformed to this pattern. During the 1960s and 1970s the congregation's principal nonreligious program was its sponsorship of a Mexican dance troupe. While these programs and events were worthwhile and helped maintain a connection to the *cultura* (culture) of the various Spanish-speaking groups, they did not focus on addressing the conditions that caused social problems and poverty within the comunidad.[43]

Not all agreed with this trend.[44] Father Jerald Merrill, Dr. Orlando Rivera, Archie Archuleta, Jorge Arcé-Larreta, Roberto Nieves, and others believed that local clubs did a great deal of good but ignored many serious problems. These individuals created SOCIO in order to establish an organization that would rally all Spanish-speakers in the Beehive State under one banner to take advantage of the political and social changes taking place during the late 1960s. In order to accomplish their goals, SOCIO's leadership had to forge a feeling of unity among a diverse group of Spanish-surnamed people and show them that they could succeed through collective action. The leadership had to make colonia constituents realize that "members are linked to each other . . . because they live in the same areas, have similar values, and face the same economic difficulties."[45]

In addition to generating communal unity and a sense of belonging and identity, SOCIO needed to have access to the "power structure" of the state.[46] In her recent work *Politics at the Margin* political scientist Susan Herbst describes the value of these ties to an organization like SOCIO. The group's early cadre of leaders contained individuals in positions within Utah's most important governmental and private organizations who provided the fledgling association with access to important leaders and policy makers in state and local governments, school districts, the University of Utah, and both the Catholic and LDS Churches.[47] These ties assured that the state's authorities and elites would not ignore SOCIO or its demands.

Father Merrill had lived and worked on Salt Lake City's west side for seven years and, through his own initiative and Salt Lake Catholic Diocese sponsorship, had tried to reduce the suffering of the area's working poor. He sponsored the Guadalupana Society, which sought to develop community-based programs with the goal of improving conditions in west-side neighborhoods. In addition, Merrill helped push individuals within the parish to participate in cursillos designed to heighten a person's sense of social responsibility as well as reenergizing spiritual beliefs.[48] Dr. Orlando Rivera, bishop of the Lucero Ward, worked in the educational psychology department at the University of Utah and had conducted extensive research concerning the circumstances confronting Spanish-surnamed children in northern Utah schools. Rivera took a more activist approach toward community problems than did Robert H. Burton, his predecessor as bishop at the Lucero Ward. Burton advised his charges to learn English and pursue an education. While this argument may have resonated with many of the "Mexican American generation," by the late 1960s conditions, as well as political and social beliefs, had changed drastically. Within the LDS Church this call for greater attention to the unique needs of Spanish-speaking members led to a heated debate regarding the church's policy on "ethnic" or "language based" wards and missions.[49]

Other individuals involved in SOCIO's early leadership cadre included Archie Archuleta, who had taught in the Salt Lake School District since 1953; Jorge Arcé-Larreta, a Peruvian-born University of Utah graduate who toiled for the state's Manpower Council;[50] and Roberto Nieves, a native of Puerto Rico, World War II navy veteran, and Moab-area businessman who had formed several organizations in southern Utah and battled for civil rights.[51] All of these individuals were familiar with the workings of governmental, corporate, educational, and religious bureaucracies, and they initially called for SOCIO to work within the system. In a *Salt Lake Tribune* article one SOCIO leader stated: "The Negroes have gained attention through their riots. But we do not want that, we think there is a better way to prove our point."[52] Initially the overarching goal was not to meet immediate needs, such as food and shelter, but to broaden opportunities so that in the future the Spanish-speakers of the state could "find honest work so that they could provide for themselves." Dr. Orlando Rivera summed up his tenure as president of SOCIO (1970) by stating that he used the preponderance of his time and energy while in office in solving problems, "not in calling the people to a mass meeting to tell them how poor they were."[53]

Employment status and discrimination were areas of key concern. Many in SOCIO questioned why, given the increase in educational achievement, so many colonia constituents continued to toil in low-level occupations. One commentator at a Chicano conference (held at Brigham Young University in

1974) wondered why Spanish-speakers often trained newly hired whites, only to see promotions go to persons with less experience and training.[54] Why were there so few Hispanic men and women employed by government agencies or in managerial positions in area businesses? These laborers were a valuable resource, and both the public and private sectors underutilized them simply because of their ethnicity. The Spanish-speaking community simply wanted to have "equal access to all opportunities" for work.[55] SOCIO's leaders devised a multipronged attack against the issue of underemployment. They appealed to the decency and morality of employers, challenged unfair and artificial barriers to hiring and promotion, and established training programs that taught technical skills. By the early 1970s SOCIO pursued still another avenue to generate jobs: the organization hired a paid staff and in 1974 established another organization, the Institute for Human Resource Development (IHRD), specifically chartered to hire Hispanics and to create and administer social service projects of benefit to people in the comunidad.

The initial actions taken in this area sought to change the majority's perceptions of the Spanish-surnamed worker. In cooperation with community-based Asian American and African American groups, SOCIO helped start the Minority Advisory Board (MAB) within the Utah State Department of Employment Security (USDES). The MAB provided information to state officials regarding hiring practices and worked to educate whites so that they would not automatically regard minority applicants solely as candidates for menial positions. It was not a lack of talent, the MAB argued that held these employees back; it was the dearth of opportunity.[56] This convinced Jennings M. Lee, office manager of the USDES, to examine his own hiring patterns. He discovered that his bureau, charged with urging others to hire people of color, did not have a single African American or Hispanic in its employ. In one year Lee increased this number to twelve. He accomplished this transformation primarily by "modifying" (reducing the qualifications for) several job descriptions.[57]

Many of northern Utah's politicians responded positively to SOCIO's moral persuasion. In an effort to foster better relations between police and the colonia, both Salt Lake City and Salt Lake County worked to create a ten-week officers' training course to attract African Americans and Spanish-surnamed recruits. In conjunction with the Utah State Department of Vocational Rehabilitation and the University of Utah's Division of Continuing Education, twenty individuals received instruction for jobs in law enforcement. The persons chosen had to meet all existing departmental, physical, intellectual, and moral standards for officers and deputies.[58] James L. Baker, Sr., Salt Lake City's public safety commissioner, strongly supported this program and wanted to do even more; in September, 1970, he questioned the need for administering civil service exams to minority applicants.[59] In March, 1971, Baker encouraged the city's police chief, Calvin L. Whitehead, to investigate the need for a regulation requiring that academy candidates measure at least five feet nine inches in height. Alfredo Pando a University of Utah student and SOCIO member, complained to the Civil Service Commission that the "height requirement is very unfair. We strongly feel it is a major obstacle which keeps many Chicanos out of the police force." SOCIO believed this change in policy would greatly benefit the city. Spanish-speaking officers could be more responsive to community needs and would help decrease tensions.[60]

Business leaders also initiated voluntary hiring drives and voted to enact a timetable for increasing the number of Spanish-speakers on their payrolls. In January, 1970, several entrepreneurs committed themselves, thanks to generous tax incentives from the federal government, to hire more than seven hundred "disadvantaged" employees for firms in Salt Lake and Davis Counties.[61]

In June of 1971 Salt Lake County commissioner William M. Timmins proposed a bold course of action. Timmins wanted the county's government to install a multistep plan designed to increase the employment of African Americans and Hispanics. The proposed steps included the hiring of college students as paid interns, establishing hiring quotas by June of 1972, hiring a full-time recruiter, and increasing in-house training for people of color to prepare them for possible promotions and managerial positions.[62] Salt Lake City implemented a similar scheme and increased minority representation to 5.7 percent of its workforce by June, 1973.[63] Weber County officials, in cooperation with SOCIO, the Ogden branch of the NAACP, and Weber State College, devised comparable programs.[64] Still, these changes did not satisfy all critics. The various agencies hired more "needy" people, but most remained in low-level positions. In December, 1973, Marvin B. Davis complained that while Utah's largest municipal government employed twenty-four African Americans and seventy-seven Chicanos, only seven of those individuals occupied managerial or administrative positions.[65]

At the state level Gov. Calvin L. Rampton negotiated directly with SOCIO and prodded bureaucrats and civilians into reducing employment discrimination. Rampton pushed for the creation of a statewide affirmative action plan and charged Joe Gallegos, a member of SOCIO, to help oversee its implementation. In a 1974 conference held at Brigham Young University (in Provo) Rampton acknowledged that since "several studies indicated that there were some serious deficiencies in . . . hiring procedures, we set out to correct those standards." Jorge Arcé-Larreta co-authored one of those inquiries. On May 28, 1971, SOCIO and the Spanish-speaking Committee on Government

Employment presented recommendations on hiring practices to the Utah State Association of Civil Service Commissioners. The suggestions included appointing minorities to oral interview boards, discarding "culturally biased" merit tests or adding five points to a Hispanic's test score, eliminating "unrealistic" requirements for jobs, restructuring positions, and creating a separate register for African Americans and Spanish-speaking job candidates.[66] Governor Rampton appointed Dr. Orlando Rivera to the State Merit Council and provided colonia members with a voice on state government's pay, hiring, and promotional practices board. These combined efforts generated openings for many individuals, and by June, 1974, people of color accounted for 4.77 percent of Utah's public sector workforce.[67]

Negotiations between the chief executive and SOCIO led to the inception of a Chicano ombudsman office in 1973. The individual selected for this post, Gilbert Ramírez, worked for and with the governor and took community complaints and concerns directly to him. The Spanish-speakers of Utah, who had previously been political and social "outsiders" in the Mormon Zion, now had a direct link to the highest elected office in the state.[68] To reduce private-sector favoritism, Rampton warned contractors to "show a significant increase in employment" of these groups or face cancellation of state contracts. The governor required adherence to various objectives to retain Utah's trade: recruitment for minority apprentices; hiring patterns for construction projects that reflected an area's ethnic composition; and the installation of affirmative action plans.[69]

Concurrent with improving opportunities with industry and government, SOCIO explored the possibility of stimulating entrepreneurial and commercial activity within the colonia.[70] Ricardo Barbero, SOCIO's first state president and a chemical engineer at Hercules, Inc., enlisted the aid of Roy Shaw, a professor at the University of Utah's School of Business, to provide instruction in marketing, management, and finance for potential *comerciantes* (business owners).[71]

Even the best trained of these candidates needed assistance in overcoming a still more daunting obstacle: the lack of start-up capital. Father Merrill and the Guadalupana Society helped address this problem in a creative manner. In 1966, three months after establishing the Guadalupe Center in downtown Salt Lake City, the organization's board of directors voted to spend all of its savings—$8,000—on the creation of the La Morena Café. The "Brown Lady" (named in honor of the Virgin of Guadalupe) began operations with ten tables and a few dollars in a checking account.[72] During the first months the staff considered daily revenue of $50 "a busy day." By April, 1970, the once-struggling enterprise had begun to turn a profit; it now employed twenty-nine full- and part-time workers and had a weekly payroll of $1,200. By 1983 the café had become quite popular with downtown office workers; gross yearly sales soared to $675,000.[73] Earnings generated by the restaurant funded several programs. One of these, Hispanamer, Inc., functioned as a development fund that made loans to Spanish-speakers who wished to enter the business world.[74]

To complement this project, Father Merrill helped start a credit union to provide financial services for the rest of the colonia. The Westside Catholic Credit Union, funded with the assistance of the Utah Central Credit Union League, served the savings and credit needs of the community; by 1973 the credit union had 373 members and $135,000 in assets and had originated more than $1 million in loans.[75] By the late 1970s these attempts at internal development (or what could be termed "brown capitalism") produced a beneficial impact on Hispanic economic activity. The 1977 Survey of Minority Owned Businesses revealed that Utah's Hispanics owned 326 firms with approximately $13.7 million in gross sales. More than 14 percent of these businesses (46) had paid laborers (a total of 379) and generated more than $1.5 million in payroll. Over half (55 percent) of these companies operated in Salt Lake County.[76]

In 1977 Gov. Scott M. Matheson provided another level of assistance for these entrepreneurs. Matheson directed the Utah Department of Development Services, Division of Industrial Promotion, to establish a liaison with the Minority Coalition of Utah for aid in the formation of small minority-owned firms and to provide information on state purchasing procedures. To increase opportunities SOCIO allied with the Minority Economic Development Coalition of Utah (MEDCU) in 1975. This company produced feasibility studies, served as technical adviser, assisted in applying for loans, and aided in soliciting government contracts. During the first quarter of fiscal year 1978 (September 1, 1977, through November 30, 1977) MEDCU helped business owners secure nine procurement contracts, including five with local and state governments. By May of 1978 Jorge Arcé-Larreta headed and administered the organization.[77]

Providing equal occupational opportunities was just one step in achieving the ultimate goal of Hispanic self-sufficiency. If the Spanish-surnamed population were to compete, without special aid, they had to improve their technical and job skills. During the 1970s and 1980s SOCIO, in conjunction with state, local, and charitable funding organizations, developed a broad range of offerings designed to increase competency. One program trained men and women for jobs with the Utah Department of Transportation construction crews. Clients received a stipend and reimbursement for relocation, transportation, and other expenses. Outlays for this course increased from $4,250 in its initial year to more than $27,000 by 1979. The Mountainlands Association of Governments provided a grant to fund and staff an office for résumé collection, job development, referral, and placement. Comparable agencies opened in both Layton (Davis County) and Price (Carbon County). The Salt Lake Employment and Training Administration helped support a survival English course and paid students $2.30 per hour while they learned.[78]

Cognizant that single Hispanas headed the neediest families in the area, SOCIO tailored two courses especially for them. A bilingual secretarial class provided instruction in basic math and grammar skills, office procedures, typing, and shorthand. Companies such as First Security Bank and Kennecott Mineral Company hired graduates with starting pay of approximately $3.50 per hour.[79] Another project, the Minority Women Employment Program, worked to move Spanish-surnamed women into nontraditional, skilled occupations such as carpentry and plumbing. These trades provided both higher starting salaries (about $5.50 per hour in 1981) and the possibility of higher pay after training (journeyman hourly pay for these jobs averaged about $11.50 per hour).[80]

Between 1968 and 1972 SOCIO operated as an association of concerned citizens who worked, in their spare time, to better conditions in their neighborhoods. The efforts of more than 1,050 volunteers throughout the state had increased job opportunities and decreased discriminatory hiring and promotional practices in government and private industry.[81] Circumstances improved and prompted Jack Quintana, Utah's equal employment opportunity coordinator, to advise SOCIO's membership in September, 1973, that "the future holds a 'multitude' of opportunities for Chicanos based on a person being hired for his merits, not ethnic backgrounds."[82] John Q. Montoya, chairman of the newly created Governor's Policy Advisory Committee of Spanish-Speaking Affairs, echoed Quintana's sentiments and stated that it was now possible in Utah for a minority person to "build up his educational, employment, and economic position to equal" that of whites.[83]

The efforts of volunteers had generated substantial but uneven progress. Community concerns often went unaddressed because of a lack of follow-up and a "drastic shortage of funds" which "severely limited the range and efficacy of programs."[84] By the early 1970s SOCIO's administrators believed that hiring a professional, paid staff would allow the organization to maximize its ability to produce results for the community as well as create new jobs. In 1972 the Campaign for Human Development provided an outside source of money; with this subsidy SOCIO's era of grassroots activism began to wane, and its period of bureaucratization began.[85] This funding supported Roberto Nieves's salary (as executive director) and three other positions. Their principal mission was to increase SOCIO's ability to apply for grants and to administer programs. The group would "explore and develop projects . . . which would pay for themselves and generate jobs and training opportunities" for community members.[86] By 1978 SOCIO employed thirteen individuals (nine of them on a full-time basis) and had an annual payroll of more than $85,000.[87]

A more ambitious attempt to create professional employment commenced in 1974 with the founding of the Institute for Human Resource Development (IHRD). Its purpose was to seek funding for social projects and hire Spanish-surnamed staff and managers. Local and state officials had cooperated with SOCIO from its inception, but the organizations and programs they originated often established boards and hired personnel without Chicano representation. This arrangement, activists believed, denied Hispanics the ability to provide direct input regarding culturally appropriate assistance and delivery methods. IHRD generated jobs, but most importantly it permitted persons from the neighborhoods a forum with which to recommend, design, implement, and direct services that affected their communities. Linda Quintana, one of IHRD's original trustees, believed that this "separation" from "white supervision" was one of IHRD's most crucial aspects and that "at last we were experiencing a measure of self determination." By 1993 IHRD employed a staff of 212 and managed grants totaling more than $2.7 million.[88]

Advocacy, consciousness raising, and training reduced some barriers, but significant obstacles remained on the path to Hispanic social betterment in Utah. Many corporations and governmental agencies advised SOCIO that they did not hire colonia constituents for managerial or executive posts because few had the proper academic credentials. These entities stated that if they were given qualified individuals, they would hire them. The best long-range solution to overcoming this impasse was to improve the education of Spanish-surnamed children. SOCIO, the Salt Lake Catholic Diocese, and other groups struggled to better conditions in the schools, but it was a daunting task. During the 1969–70 school year 10,170 Spanish-speaking pupils attended Utah public schools; they comprised 3.4 percent of the student population. The districts with the largest number of Hispanic youths were Salt Lake (2,600), Granite (1,664), and Jordan (960); both Jordan and Granite districts serve the southwestern suburbs of Salt Lake City. In all of these vicinities drop-out rates hovered at about 60 percent.[89]

In early 1970 Richard Gómez, SOCIO's education committee chair, presented Dr. Arthur C. Wiscombe, Salt Lake City's school superintendent, with a series of requests to improve conditions. He called for the hiring of more bicultural instructors, bilingual programs, and increased attention to the special needs of minorities. Dr. Wiscombe's reaction mirrored that of other northern

Utah officials: "I'm very encouraged that the Mexican-American group has this strong desire to work with us in upgrading the quality of education for their young people."[90] By June cultural awareness courses and electives on the history of American people of color were scheduled for the following school year. Huberta Randolph, director of curriculum, noted that the district now recognized "that we are a pluralistic society" as she announced a special in-service program designed to sensitize teachers to the needs of minority children.[91] In December, 1971, a similar scenario took place before Dr. T. H. Bell and the entire Granite School District Board. Luis Medina, a member of SOCIO and a professor of social work at the University of Utah, led concerned *padres* (parents) in petitioning the council for increased recruitment of Chicano instructors, hiring a Spanish-surnamed administrator, the creation of specialized career services programs, and increased use of bicultural materials in the classroom.[92] By 1974 Dr. Bell had hired Chris Segura as a staff assistant to administer Granite's Title I funds and to supervise cultural training programs; the Tooele, Weber, and Salt Lake City districts also hired Hispanic administrators.[93]

Community activists believed these recommendations and courses would improve the educational experience for their offspring and make schoolwork more relevant to these youths. SOCIO and other groups argued that Hispanic personnel would make this possible because "those most closely in touch with the social problems are in the unique position to offer fresh insights to help alleviate the strain."[94] Some of the "strains" encountered by these students (during the 1972–73 school year) included substandard performance scores in IQ and standardized tests and low grade point averages (GPAs).[95]

Between the 1970–71 and 1972–73 school years the number of Spanish-surnamed children in Utah schools increased by 16.8 percent (from 10,170 to 11,879). In his 1947 study Joseph E. Allen had quoted a retired school administrator who believed that these students "were not outstanding in scholarship or leadership." Maldonado and Byrne's findings revealed that there had been little, if any, change in academic performance or in teachers' attitudes toward their Hispanic charges by the early 1970s. Spanish-speakers in urban, suburban, and rural school settings throughout the state of Utah all ranked well below national IQ norms; more than 70 percent failed to achieve the average score of one hundred. Standardized tests revealed a similarly disturbing trend. In all areas measured (mathematics, reading, language, and spelling) colonia youths fared poorly. At least 50 percent clustered in the second through the thirtieth percentiles; this meant that between 70 and 98 percent of the participants showed higher academic achievement. More than one-half of all Spanish-surnamed pupils had GPAs under 2.5, and their averages tended to decline the longer they remained in school. In elementary grades most (65 percent) had GPAs above 2.6, but by the time these pupils enrolled in secondary institutions, the percentages had nearly inverted (60 percent earned below a 2.5 GPA). The authors (Maldonado and Byrne) did not claim that these results proved the existence of overt racism, but they argued that the schools clearly showed "a disposition not to accept as 'good' those values and behaviors" not expressed or supported by the area's dominant group. The replies to a questionnaire mailed to a random sample of state educators supported this contention. A significant number of the respondents believed that a deficiency in the cultural and home life of Spanish-speaking familias was the key reason for the low scholastic achievement of this student population.[96]

In 1975 another survey conducted within Salt Lake City schools offered further evidence of the difficulties faced by Utah's minorities (ethnic and religious) in the classroom. Frederick S. Buchanan and Raymond G. Briscoe's essay "Public Schools as a Vehicle for Social Accommodation in Utah" focused on the impact of religion within the educational system. Buchanan and Briscoe asked 397 men, women, and children (242 Mormons and 155 non-Mormons) to assess the prevalence of Latter-day Saint "ideas and control" in the taxpayer-supported institutions of learning. The results revealed a wide discrepancy in the perception of church influence. Members of minority faiths expressed a great deal of trepidation over Mormon influence in the schools. Those aligned with Utah's predominant religion did not agree. They did not believe that LDS philosophical viewpoints might "be adversely affecting the minority's self-image or unwittingly stifling the promotion of social and individual diversity."[97]

The most effective way to surmount the problem of high drop-out rates and majority influence in the classroom, Maldonado and Byrne claimed, was to hire more bicultural educators, but progress in this area was slow. The Annual Statistical Report of School Districts (for 1972–73) and the Utah Public School Directory (for 1974) showed that some colonia constituents had moved into positions in various school bureaucracies. In 1974 Hispanic men and women filled 257 teaching posts in Utah, but they accounted for less than 2 percent of school board members and administrators.[98] By the late 1970s parents continued to protest the lack of people of color in their children's schools. In the 1978–79 school year there were no Spanish-surnamed instructors at West Senior High (and only twenty-six in the entire Salt Lake School District), although this minority population comprised 13 percent of the student body. Two community groups, the Concerned Parents Committee and Task Force, "blamed their children's drop out rate . . . on uncaring, even racist attitudes by teachers" at West High.[99]

But circumstances were not identical for all Spanish-speaking children in the area. A 1971 study by a University of Utah graduate student contradicts some of the conclusions drawn by Maldonado and Byrne. Douglas Bowen Luke's examination of GPAs and standardized test scores of "Mexican" and white pupils at Layton Senior High School verified lower scholastic averages and test results for the minorities, but the differences were not statistically significant. Contrary to Maldonado and Byrne's results, the GPAs of Spanish-speakers tended to increase by their sophomore and junior years. Instead of instituting programs for the special needs of these students, Bowen Luke believed that they "should be treated and thought of in the same way as non-Mexican classmates."[100] Rose Gurule, a Hispanic teacher from Ogden, agreed with this assertion. She felt that singling out Spanish-speakers harmed their academic and psychological development. Gurule believed that her role as an educator was to "challenge people's attitudes to realize that they are as good as anybody else and sometimes they can even be better, if only they strive to do it."[101]

The high rate of academic deficiency of the Spanish-speakers spurred the Salt Lake Catholic Diocese to create programs designed to improve the early education of the west side's youth. In 1970 profits from La Morena Café and contributions from individuals and corporate entities (including the Episcopal, Greek Orthodox, and LDS Churches) helped fund a primary grade school (kindergarten through third grade) at the Guadalupe Center. The facility provided transportation, meals, reading instruction, regular school curricula, and reduced class size, and the self-esteem needs of minorities were emphasized. By the middle 1970s a full elementary school, the Guadalupe Early Learning Center, was operating and supplied instruction to more than eighty pupils. To aid adults the diocese established a course called the Voluntary Improvement Program. Classes met two times per week, and participants received personalized attention and assistance to help them improve their English listening, speaking, and writing skills.[102]

The poor grades, low scholastic achievement, and negative reinforcement experienced by many in high school severely limited the number of Spanish-speakers who chose to pursue college degrees. Between 1960 and 1970 the percentage of Utah Hispanics with secondary-school diplomas more than doubled, but the number enrolled at the University of Utah remained negligible (fewer than twenty in the 1969 academic year). Some community activists insisted that the school's admission policy unfairly discriminated against Spanish-surnamed individuals and that the state's flagship institution of higher learning expended little effort "to seek out and enroll qualified Mexican-American students." Administrators at the Salt Lake City campus vehemently denied the charges, stating that an applicant's ethnic background did not affect their decisions and that "any high school graduate from the state of Utah may attend the university."[103] An internal investigation of the entrance process noted that "current admission policies at the university are adequate." Still, the panel called for increased resources for recruitment, special curriculum programs, and financial assistance for potential minority students.[104] Lewis M. Rogers, chairman of the Outreach Fundraising Committee, believed the school had a moral obligation to "divest itself of its elitist nature and responsibly reach out to help the economically deprived" and to "actively bring impoverished people to the campus." One of the earliest attempts to address the financial needs of these pupils occurred in January, 1968. SOCIO members lobbied for the creation of the Utah Educational Fund to provide scholarships for deserving minorities (the original funding by the state legislature amounted to less than $70,000; by 1985 it totaled $700,000).[105]

In May, 1969, Dr. Clark S. Knowlton, head of the university's Center for the Study of Social Problems, helped draft a proposal to admit 150 minority students. Knowlton and others trained six individuals to serve as outreach coordinators charged with seeking out "youth whom they feel have the support of their community, their families, and the necessary motivation to begin university training." The beneficiaries received academic deficiency evaluations, personal counseling services, access to living facilities, stipends to cover textbook purchases, and tuition wavers.[106] The proposed budget for the aid package totaled more than $350,000.[107]

A second program designed to help get minorities to the University of Utah campus was funded, in part, by a 1970 Ford Foundation grant which provided nearly $41,000 to aid the disadvantaged. School officials, in cooperation with SOCIO and other community organizations, selected and enrolled sixty individuals (forty Hispanics and twenty Native Americans) in intensive classes designed to provide remedial training and instruction in study skills. The objective was to prepare these young men and women to begin regular course work by September, 1970. A study done after these students had completed two quarters of academic work revealed the benefits of this intensive special session. The participants had a higher GPA than the typical 1970 University of Utah freshman (2.37 versus 2.32) and had completed almost as many credit hours as had their white classmates (24.88 versus 28.00).[108]

Andrew Valdez benefited from the Ford Foundation grant. Andrew had spent his teenage years helping his divorced mother survive by shining shoes, selling newspapers, and doing other odd jobs in downtown Salt Lake City. He attended West High and graduated in the summer of 1970. Although Valdez did fairly well in school, his school counselor advised him to "join the military" or "attend a trade school" after graduation. The young manito considered the first option and assumed that he would never be able to pursue a postsecondary education. Fortunately, recruiters from the University of Utah, armed with funds and programs designed to encourage minority attendance, approached Valdez and offered him an opportunity to improve his skills and pursue an academic degree. Once on campus, Andrew proved himself worthy of the opportunity, and he graduated with a law degree in 1977.[109]

The efforts to increase minority representation produced dramatic results. By the end of the 1970s the university provided SOCIO with office space on campus (located at 1056 Annex Building), established a Chicano Studies Program (headed by Carlos Esqueda), hired twenty-one Spanish-surnamed faculty members, admitted more than 320 Hispanic students, and installed in prominent positions within the bureaucratic structure individuals who had close ties to SOCIO. Among those receiving appointments were Dr. Orlando Rivera as associate academic vice president, John Florez as the head of the Office of Equal Opportunity, and students Fred LeBlanc, Solomon Chacón, and Mike Meléndez as peer counselors.[110]

Although headquartered in Salt Lake City, SOCIO reached out to other institutions of higher learning, and those with Spanish surnames spread its message of civil rights and increased opportunity throughout the state. In the coal town of Price (Carbon County), where Spanish-speakers have labored in the mines since the 1920s, SOCIO volunteers assisted Dr. Alfonso R. Trujillo in establishing an ethnic studies program at the College of Eastern Utah. Trujillo believed that the proposed courses and financial aid package would help motivate youths in Carbon, Grand, and San Juan Counties to finish high school and pursue professional careers, as well as "broaden the cultural and educational goals of the college."[111] By 1975 student organizations existed at Brigham Young University (Mexican American Student Coalition), Weber State College (Los Estudiantes Unidos), Utah State University (MEChA), as well as in high schools in Salt Lake City, Ogden, Tooele, Cyprus, Kearns, Clearfield, Layton, Sandy, Midvale, West Jordan, and Price.[112] These clubs espoused and embraced many of the ideas and goals of the Chicano movement, but the influence and guidance of SOCIO's adult administrators helped temper members' pronouncements and activities. Unlike the course of el movimiento in areas with large Spanish-surnamed populations, the movement in Utah was not guided by students but rather was a cooperative effort between adultos (adults) and jóvenes (youths).[113]

For many young people influenced by more progressive elements of Chicanismo, slow and steady betterment was not enough. In 1970 some Spanish-surnamed youths at the University of Utah established the Chicano Student

Association (CSA). The group worked with SOCIO but criticized the pace of progress achieved by its "middle class" leadership.[114] While critical of some aspects of SOCIO's tactics and philosophy, the CSA's more militant rhetoric proved beneficial to the larger organization. SOCIO's negotiators sometimes used the specter of "Brown Power" and "Chicano militancy" as effective bargaining tools.[115]

Richard A. García's work *Rise of the Mexican American Middle Class* is instructive in explaining this situation. García briefly examines the political and philosophical schism between leaders and followers of Chicanismo and their parents (whom García calls the "Mexican American" generation). Throughout the Southwest, he contends, the cries of those who embraced the views of Ché Guevara and Fidel Castro stymied, or simply overwhelmed, the more moderate calls for social reform and increased opportunity of the 1940s and 1950s.[116] Both SOCIO and student groups used some radical imagery and terminology to force recalcitrant whites into line. National leaders of el movimiento such as Corky Gonzalez, Reies López Tijerina, and José Angel Gutiérrez visited the Beehive State during the early 1970s and angrily lashed out at Utah's majority and its "sponsoring" of "racist" and "genocidal" institutions and policies.[117] But given the specific texture of American society in northern Utah, this rhetoric was tempered by more moderate calls for reform. While López Tijerina called for an "explosion of justice" and Corky Gonzalez lambasted the University of Utah for its "racist" policies, speakers such as Dr. Rudolpho Martínez advised students at the campus, "there is going to be no revolution, but rather an evolutionary change." Instead of inspiring students to take over and burn buildings, establish a separate homeland, and break away from all vestiges of "American" society, Dr. Rivera counseled them to improve their grades, graduate, and aspire to professional careers.[118]

During the remainder of the 1970s SOCIO and the CSA worked to increase scholarship funds and financial aid, and they sponsored service projects to aid the less fortunate of the comunidad.[119] Over the next decade Hispanic clubs on campus shifted their focus from protest to the development of future leaders who could fit into mainstream society rather than a separate Chicano/separatist one. As early as 1973 a Chicano counselor hired by the University of Utah urged caution regarding the potential negative consequences of extreme nationalism and separatism: "I think we have done a disservice to some of our Chicano students by perpetuating the bitterness because we have to make people function, not only in the Chicano community, but also in the Anglo community."[120] By 1983 a pronouncement by Patrick Lucero, CSA's activities director, not only did not reflect the more militant days and views of the 1960s and 1970s, but sounded well in tune with the more conservative mood of the nation during the Reagan years: "The prejudice that may have existed in the past is past. We are interested in the future and what is to be. It is up to the individual to earn respect by his contributions and efforts."[121]

To improve the educational experience of Spanish-surnamed youths, Maldonado and Byrne called for a dramatic increase in the hiring of Chicano teachers, counselors, and administrators. These authors proposed a similar solution to better the delivery of social services to colonia members.[122] Between 1974 and 1986 SOCIO and IHRD personnel worked diligently to implement and administer a wide variety of activities designed to improve the daily lives of the handicapped, troubled teenagers, and the needy and destitute throughout Utah.

The IHRD's staff focused on delivering community health and crime-reduction services. The Utah Division of Rehabilitative Services provided the organization with its first grant. The money funded a project called the Client Assistance Program that served the needs of disabled Spanish-speakers. The federal government's Rehabilitative Services Administration field office in Denver provided IHRD with a large stipend and expanded the program to assist injured or physically impaired migrants and seasonal workers.[123] Utah's Division of Youth Corrections supported an undertaking designed to reduce the disproportionately high number of Spanish-speaking teenagers in state correctional facilities. In their proposal for the Esperanza Para Mañana (Hope for Tomorrow) project, IHRD employees noted that Hispanics comprised more than 15 percent of individuals referred by the Second District Juvenile Court (this district encompassed Salt Lake City and surrounding areas), "an over-representation of 300 percent." In total, minority adolescents made up more than one of every five incarcerated youths in Utah. Esperanza Para Mañana created a residential shelter where juveniles (ages twelve to seventeen) received individual, family, and academic deficiency counseling; classes to help improve their study skills; and job training in a caring, culturally sensitive environment.[124] In 1980 new funding established a similar facility, the Casa de Orgullo (the House of Pride), to serve clients referred by the First District Juvenile Court in Ogden.[125] By 1986 IHRD administered programs that offered mental health services in Spanish (Proyecto Salud, or Project Health), legal counsel at reduced or no cost (Proyecto Abogacía, or Project Advocacy), substance abuse and gang resistance information (the Hispanic Youth Leadership Institute), and educational and nutritional aid to children of seasonal workers (Migrant Head Start Program) in Box Elder, Davis, Weber, Sanpete, Iron, and Utah Counties.[126]

Concurrent with its lobbying, educational, and employment support efforts SOCIO shared occupational responsibility with IHRD for the Esperanza Para Mañana program; operated emergency food banks, distribution centers, and the Utah Migrant Council; directed an organization designed to resettle Cuban (Mariel boat lift) refugees in Salt Lake City; and assisted in the rehabilitation of older parolees. The goal of the Mexican American Community Corrections Support Program was to reduce the recidivism rate (estimated at 37 percent in 1975) of Hispanic adults. SOCIO's personnel provided job training; individual, peer, and family counseling; and educational services; in addition they attempted to bolster the convicts' sense of personal and ethnic pride.[127]

In Weber County the SOCIO branch joined forces with other organizations (such as AGIF, SPMDTU, and other mutual aid and college student associations) in order to provide assistance to Spanish-surnamed familias in need of crisis-intervention services. The Weber Council of Spanish Speaking Organizations (WCSSO) established the Crisis Intervention Program (CIP) in September, 1972, in response to a series of tragic occurrences (a deadly automobile accident and a house fire) which left several families homeless and without assistance. The comunidad of the area did what it could to raise funds for the unfortunate survivors but was unable effectively to call upon city and state welfare agencies to provide further succor. For future emergencies the CIP unit mobilized Spanish-speaking staff in order to assist victims and put them in touch with the governmental agencies that could best address their problems and needs.[128]

Using profits generated by La Morena Café and private donations, the Salt Lake Catholic Diocese, the Guadalupe Center, SOCIO, and other groups helped initiate other operations aimed at reducing youth crime and improving housing for underprivileged families. The Pine Canyon Ranch for Boys began operation on 810 acres (donated by Kennecott, Terracor, and IML Freight corporations) near Tooele in June, 1969. It provided rehabilitation for delinquent youths (ages fifteen to eighteen) by offering vocational training (in cooperation with the nearby Tooele Army Depot), high school classes (at Tooele High School), work experience, recreational activities, and a structured home environment with surrogate parents.[129]

Father Merrill and Roberto Nieves, in conjunction with organizations such as the Utah Housing Coalition and the Utah Nonprofit Housing Corporation, struggled to increase the availability of moderately priced dwellings for the poor. By the early 1970s both SOCIO and the diocese participated in a coalition that lobbied a special session of the state legislature for funding. In November, 1973, the efforts of this partnership contributed to the passage of a $3 million appropriation for the building of low income housing.[130] The Federal Housing Authority committed another $427,000 for construction of 119 apartment units for a development called Escalante Park in Salt Lake City's Rose Park neighborhood (1000 North Redwood Road).[131]

To expand and improve the level and quality of assistance offered to the Spanish-surnamed segment of his pastoral flock, Bishop Joseph Lennox Federal established the Diocesan Office of the Spanish-speaking in 1972. Rúben Jiménez (a member of SOCIO) headed the department that provided religious instruction and sponsored a team of priests who traveled throughout the state offering sacraments and masses in Spanish. During Jiménez's nine-year tenure as director he solicited charitable contributions from the Campaign for Human Development and other foundations. These funds (a total of more than $500,000) supported some of SOCIO's operations, the Guadalupe Center, and during the late 1980s the Utah Immigration Project (UIP), which operated five regional offices that assisted immigrants in preparing residency applications.[132]

By 1980 Spanish-surnamed people comprised more than one-half of Utah's 59,844 Catholics. This demographic reality influenced the Vatican in its selection of a new bishop. William K. Weigand (who was fluent in Spanish and had been pastor of Saint John the Baptist Parish in Cali, Colombia, for ten years) received the appointment to head the Salt Lake Catholic Diocese in September, 1980. Bishop Weigand expanded assistance to outlying areas and established the San Felipe/Saint Phillip Mission in Wendover (to serve the religious needs of a growing number of Mexicano workers in the casino town) and a migrant outreach program in Davis County.[133]

The Church of Jesus Christ of Latter-day Saints did not oppose the reforms proposed by SOCIO, but in the opinion of Dr. Orlando Rivera, most Spanish-speakers were disappointed that the state's largest religious denomination did not take "more visible action to effect change." Officially, the LDS hierarchy continued its welfare, cultural, sports, and scouting programs in the individual congregations (such as the Lucero Ward and the Cumorah Branch), but it did little else to shape the development and trajectory of el movimiento. Although the church did not directly affect the development of the Chicano movement in Utah, its continued and aggressive missionary activity in Central and South America eventually impacted upon the Spanish-speaking comunidad of the area by increasing the level of diversity within the community.[134]

Between 1970 and 1980 Utah's Spanish-surnamed population grew by 37.9 percent. Persons of "Spanish origin" (the new Department of Commerce designation to replace "People of Spanish Language") now totaled 60,045 individuals. Most (87 percent) resided in the Salt Lake City–Ogden Standard Metropolitan Statistical Area that encompassed the Wasatch Front counties (except for Utah County, which became part of the Provo-Orem SMSA). Dur-

ing the 1970s the level of national diversity within the Spanish-surnamed cluster increased and the proportion of native-born Hispanics dropped to 88.8
percent.[135] With the assistance of allies in the majority population and with
their own vibrant organizations, these men and women worked feverishly to
improve their social and economic standing. The tracts of the 1980 census reveal the results of their struggle to better educational patterns, income levels,
poverty rates, and educational achievements.

The implementation of affirmative action plans, recruitment drives, and
hiring quotas and a redesigning of job requirements had a positive impact on
employment status, earnings, and occupational mobility. In 1970 almost seven
of every ten Spanish speakers in Utah (both sexes, ages sixteen years and older)
toiled in blue-collar jobs (38 percent in skilled and semi-skilled and 29 percent in unskilled positions).[136] By the following count this number (statewide)
had declined to 61.5 percent, and a greater proportion of Spanish-surnamed
employees (42.4 percent) now filled skilled or semi-skilled posts. SOCIO's
drive to combat underemployment generated some administrative, managerial,
and sales openings in governmental and corporate bureaucracies. This effort
helped increase the number of Spanish speakers in white-collar positions from
33 to 38.5 percent.

The results of educational reform were both encouraging and discourag-
ing. Despite the increased number of bicultural teachers and administrators,
bilingual programs, and specialized services, the secondary-school completion
rate for Spanish speakers (ages fifteen and older) remained below 50 percent
(the statewide average meanwhile increased to 73.9 percent).[137] In institutions
of higher learning special courses, remedial classes, and scholarships had increased the opportunity to pursue academic training, but few Hispanics graduated from Utah's colleges and universities. Between 1970 and 1980 the
percentage of colonia constituents with degrees decreased from 5.8 percent to
5.5 percent.[138]

On November 8 and 9, 1985, under the direction of President Robert
Archuleta and Executive Director Michael E. Romero, SOCIO held its twentieth statewide meeting in Salt Lake City. Participants heard addresses by
dignitaries such as Raul Yzaguirre (chief executive officer of the National
Coalition of La Raza) and Bishop William Weigand praising their eighteen-
year commitment to charitable work, social improvement, and civil rights.
Attendees participated in a variety of workshops that informed them about
activities and needs in areas such as employment discrimination, economic development, public relations, politics, and mental health. The group's leaders
confidently expected to continue to serve as the preeminent voice of Utah's
Hispanics; some even proposed the purchase of a building (SOCIO personnel

had worked in offices located at the Salt Lake County–owned Redwood Multi-Purpose Center in southwest Salt Lake City since 1976) and wanted to turn it into "a community center and place of business."[139] But within one year of these lofty pronouncements SOCIO ceased operations. How could a coalition that generated so much change vanish so quickly? What were the forces (both inside the organization and in the Spanish-speaking comunidad) that led to the implosion of SOCIO?

In his monograph on reform movements and the mechanics of social change, *Grassroots Resistance,* Robert A. Goldberg describes four variables which, he argues, determine the success or failure of reform organizations: elite members' responses, authorities' stance toward the group, organizational image, and organizational structure.[140] From its inception SOCIO's founders overcame obstacles in the first three areas. The presence of white-collar, professional individuals such as Dr. Orlando Rivera, Jorge Arcé-Larreta, Father Jerald Merrill, and Roberto Nieves provided SOCIO with legitimacy (both inside and outside the Spanish-speaking community) and a connection to some of Utah's polity members (Goldberg defines these persons as individuals or groups with access to political officials and with an ability to influence decisions).[141] SOCIO's early leadership and its ties to important institutions assured Utah's version of el movimiento a positive reaction (or at least not a hostile one) from state agencies, city governments, the Catholic Church, and the Church of Jesus Christ of Latter-day Saints. These entities, assured of SOCIO's reformist goals, embraced the organization as a viable entity and, most important, as a responsible partner in the process of social change, permitting (and in many cases encouraging) the implementation of its agenda.

Because SOCIO was successful in its attempt to secure a measure of inclusion into Utah's institutions and halls of power, the future of the Beehive State's largest minority organization seemed secure. However, failure to manipulate membership rewards (material, solidary, and purposive) properly helped bring about SOCIO's disintegration.[142] During its formative, or grassroots mobilization, period purposive and solidary benefits were usually enough to entice many of Utah's Hispanic population to respond to SOCIO's calls for action. A volunteer network and the development of an effective leadership cadre characterized this era (1968–72). Unpaid workers, scattered throughout the state, challenged existing conditions to redress grievances and increase opportunities. The results of these efforts were often erratic and uneven, but the psychic compensation of membership and the feeling that something was being done for el movimiento helped maintain a high level of activity.

Hiring an office staff and accepting foundation funds initiated SOCIO's period of bureaucratization (1972–86); Dr. Orlando A. Rivera said, "to tell you the truth, I think it was the beginning of the end."[143] From this moment until it folded, SOCIO became "increasingly dependent on outside financial support[,] and the direct participation of its membership . . . decreased as the maintenance of the organization" became the ultimate goal.[144] In his important work, *LULAC*, Benjamin Márquez argues that the establishment of a bureaucracy within a formerly all-volunteer group necessitates a change in the existing reward structure, and SOCIO's leadership failed to accomplish that task. Members felt left out because paid personnel now performed the tasks for which they had previously had responsibility. In order to keep members from drifting away, it was necessary to "increase material rewards and lighten the demands upon general membership."[145] But SOCIO wished to continue its role as advocate (which required high levels of voluntary participation) and at the same time use employees to operate a growing number of programs. In a 1985 interview Roberto Nieves, the former executive director, acknowledged the incompatibility of these two intentions: "You can't [bite] the hand that feeds you, you know. Sometimes you've got something against this part of the 'system,' but they're giving you funds."[146] In his introduction to *Chicano Politics and Society in the Late Twentieth Century* David Montejano affirms this contention when he states that the "pragmatic politics" which Nieves describes create a situation in which the "ethnic perspective is moderated, compromised, or contained by participation in institutionalized politics."[147] Nieves suggested that for SOCIO to retain its viability, it had to separate advocacy and administrative functions. This scenario helps explain why IHRD survived while its predecessor did not; from its inception it functioned as a grant-generating and operational bureaucracy with a salaried staff. IHRD did not need to constantly examine its incentive structures to satisfy psychological needs of constituents.

Incompetent management of reward structures helped doom SOCIO, but one other important element helped seal its fate: its own success in removing barriers to mobility. The new opportunities created in education and employment helped sharpen class distinctions within Utah's Hispanic population. Many of the men and women who benefited from these changes shifted their attention away from community work and focused on embracing their new social and economic status. Many of these individuals did not respond to the same type of compensation that had motivated activists in the late 1960s and early 1970s. The longer the reform group continued to operate, the more its incentives lost effectiveness; group members began to "tire of the struggle" and were more likely to become "distracted by other matters."[148] This shift severely reduced participation by SOCIO's volunteer base. Instead of active involvement in SOCIO, these constituents began enjoying the benefits for which they had labored. Rivera said: "A lot of our people are moving into bet-ter socioeconomic positions . . . they're assimilating into the culture . . . they're moving into the professions. And probably 80, 85 percent [of them] . . . are enjoying a good life."[149] In a recent work on the Chicano movement one historian put Rivera's statement into broader perspective by stating, "When Mexican Americans began to enter the American mainstream through the apertures created by the Movement, they abandoned the Chicano Movement organizations that remained separatist in orientation. In the end, many Mexi-can Americans wanted 'in' to the American mainstream."[150]

El movimiento significantly altered the daily lives of Spanish-speakers throughout the United States. Conditions differed from location to location, but it is clear that groups such as SOCIO engendered attitudinal and social changes among colonia residents and whites. While SOCIO can be connected to the broader historical trends of the Chicano movement, the particular tex-ture of American society in which it operated endowed Utah's version of the movement with some unique characteristics.

In his recent work *Chicanismo* Brigham Young University historian Igna-cio M. García argues that el movimiento passed through four separate and dis-tinct phases or stages which "caused a fundamental shift in the way Mexican Americans saw themselves . . . and accommodated to American society." In the initial stage activists "came to believe that the liberal agenda" [the idea of rewards for hard work and eventual upward social movement for a minority group] "was simply corrupt and a failure." In the next two phases community leaders "saw a need to reinterpret the past [and] affirm a rediscovered pride . . . in their sense of peoplehood. They emphasized their indigenous past and glo-rified the ancient civilizations of Mexico and South America." In the fourth and final stage activists sought to end cultural stereotypes and push the comu-nidad "away from integration into the American mainstream."[151]

All four phases are apparent when studying the years 1968–86 in north-ern Utah. First, although less militant than organizations in other locations, SOCIO (in conjunction with the CSA and others) recognized that the hard work which American society demanded from minorities had not generated upward social mobility or improved conditions for most of the Spanish-surnamed population. This led to the notion that the solutions for these prob-lems would have to come from the comunidad itself. SOCIO, its leaders believed, would be the engine that would drive this change in Salt Lake City and other areas of Utah.

García's second phase is also perceptible in the Beehive State. Through the use of curriculum changes, bilingual programs, and the hiring of bicultural in-structors and counselors, SOCIO and its allies hoped to inform Hispanic children about their past and to provide more culturally sensitive scholastic programs in local schools. The development of a Chicano studies program at the University of Utah, the College of Eastern Utah, and other institutions of higher learning brought the reinterpretation of history to the very heart of the state's educational bureaucracy.

The third stage (with its emphasis on glorification and importance of the indigenous past) appears to have been different in northern Utah than in other locations in the United States. SOCIO, through programs such Casa de Orgullo and Esperanza Para Manaña, among others, worked to generate pride among colonia residents, but it was a change in the strategies and plans of the state's majority religion that increased the importance of *mestizaje* (Indo and Spanish racial mixture) (both locally and in South and Central America). In his recent work on the LDS Church, *The Angel and the Beehive,* Armand L. Mauss asserts that during the 1960s and 1970s the Mormon hierarchy "reached more deeply into their bag of cultural peculiarities to find either symbolic or actual traits that will mark boundaries" between Mormons and other groups.[152] Among these traits was the Mormon belief regarding the need to gather the descendants of the Lamanites to help bring about Christ's millennial kingdom. The church increased its outreach and missionary work in an effort to increase the number of converts among mestizos.[153] Through these efforts the Church of Jesus Christ of Latter-day Saints dramatically increased its Spanish-speaking membership (in the United States and in Latin America), but this effort laid the groundwork for profound changes for Utah's Spanish-speaking community. During the decades of the 1980s and 1990s the number of Mormones and Latino Americanos in the heart of the Mormon Zion increased dramatically, once again changing the composition of the northern Utah comunidad.

García's final stage is also evident, although with one major difference. Through its educational programs, its close ties to various governmental and civic agencies, and its programs to reduce discrimination SOCIO worked to eliminate cultural stereotyping of Hispanics by whites. As a result of these efforts Spanish-speakers could supposedly attend and graduate from institutions of higher learning, fill managerial and other skilled positions, and contribute to the economic and social well-being and development of the state. The evidence gleaned from SOCIO's materials places this organization squarely within broader historical currents of the Chicano Movement; however, the data does not reveal that its leadership had the desire to steer the comunidad away from integration into American society. SOCIO fought against discrimination, poverty, and lack of opportunity but did not champion a split or separation from the larger society. Living, working, and fighting for increased social justice in such a remote corner of Aztlan necessitated different strategies than those used in Texas and California. To be effective in bringing about change SOCIO needed to gain the acceptance and assistance of the majority population.

During its eighteen years of existence SOCIO operated throughout the state of Utah and established programs that fostered ethnic pride as well as academic and economic opportunities through active cooperation with state, local, and corporate entities. The group started as a voluntary association but soon became bureaucratized and almost wholly dependent upon outside funding for survival. This change in managerial structure, without a corresponding alteration of reward structures (to maintain interest and loyalty), destroyed SOCIO.

Forces outside the organization also helped bring about its demise. While not directly challenging or criticizing SOCIO or its programs, the LDS Church had great impact on the organization.. The church expanded its missionary and outreach efforts in Latin America and attracted a growing number of *Chileno, Argentino,* and *Peruano* converts (among others) to the Mormon Zion.[154] During the 1980s and 1990s many Spanish-speakers who did not experience the Chicano movement moved to the area and fostered new divisions which have reduced the level of cohesiveness extant during SOCIO's early history.

In the twelve years since its demise (1987–99) the alliance forged by SOCIO broke down along class, religious, and ethnic lines. Many of the problems confronted in the 1970s continued (or became more acute) during the 1990s, but the comunidad could not (or would not) come together to meet the challenge. In addition to divisions based on ethnic background and religious affiliation, disagreements in strategy and goals among Hispanics who had achieved some level of inclusion (the mainstreamed) and their poorer (and often undocumented) brethren (the polarized) destroyed the solidarity that existed ever so briefly during the years of el movimiento.

7

The Mainstreamed and the Polarized
Hispanics in Northern Utah, 1987–99

In assessing the legacy of el movimiento in the United States historian Ignacio M. García stated: "Its primary goal was not simply finding an identity, but rather liberating Mexican Americans from racism, poverty, political powerlessness, historical neglect, and internal defeatism. Identity became important to the process, but so did the development of progressive politics. Movement activists supported the struggle of all peoples of color, savagely attacked racism, and oriented Chicanos toward compassion for the poor. . . . And most of all it promoted cultural nationalism, because Mexican Americans continued to find themselves outside the American mainstream." While the above can be seen as the overall goals of the movement, García correctly recognized that individual organizations "remained preoccupied with [their] own activities and [their] own societal backlash."[1]

The development, activities, and goals of SOCIO in northern Utah attest to the accuracy of García's position. In addition to distinct conditions existing in varied locations, García also noted that not all individuals and groups working under the banner of Chicanismo shared the same agenda. Although the movement created a sense of unity among grassroots and religious groups, it "never subsumed the inherent contradictions of the [various] political parts."[2] Ana María Díaz-Stevens and Anthony M. Stevens-Arroyo concur that this occurred among ecclesiastical organizations as well. In their opinion, as long as el movimiento "was able to focus on goals that all the diverse interests held in common, the differences did not derail its effectiveness. But within Catholicism, the uneven success . . . eventually produced winners and losers. When John Paul II became pope and Ronald Reagan became president . . . the time of syzygy came to an end."[3] The materials presented here support these contentions. This chapter will show that in the dozen years since the demise of SOCIO class, religious, and ethnic divisions among Spanish-speakers in northern Utah have increased and produced cleavages that shattered the perception of unity created during the preceding eighteen years.

On May 7, 1997, participants at a panel discussion during Chicano Awareness Week at the University of Utah asked Dr. Orlando A. Rivera to reminisce about the achievements of SOCIO and the years of el movimiento. Rivera reported, "The three things we were trying to achieve . . . were justice, opportunity, and respect."[4] Between 1968 and 1986 SOCIO, in conjunction with the Guadalupe Center and Parish, the Salt Lake Catholic Diocese, the Chicano Student Association at the University of Utah, the Institute for Human Resource Development, and other groups, worked to reduce economic disparity and remove the artificial barriers that had previously impeded social progress for Utah's Spanish-speaking population. The struggles of el movimiento proved partially successful, and many colonia constituents pursued college degrees and became members of governmental, private, and corporate bureaucracies. This improved status reflected a national trend among Hispanics, but a rising level of affluence and educational achievement among some obscured the difficult realities of those who had not attained the same levels of "inclusion" into the larger American society. For these "polarized" men, women, and children the 1980s generated "no significant change in status . . . in terms of occupational mobility."[5] Ignacio García noted, "The aperture was class specific. Middle-class Mexican Americans, and those on the rise to the middle class, saw new opportunities in federal and state jobs and in a private sector more aware of the potential 'Hispanic' market. For those who had little education, lacked citizenship . . . the openings were limited. Mexican Americans who could moved toward a less hostile Anglo-American mainstream that rewarded accommodation and integration."[6]

Increased financial (and national group) diversity among Spanish-speakers during the 1980s and 1990s helped reduce the cross-class and panethnic unity that had characterized much of the SOCIO era. The interests of white-collar Hispanics no longer meshed with those of the poor and growing number of undocumented workers (estimated to be fifteen thousand people in Utah in 1987).[7] During these years organizations that tried to rally the entire Spanish-speaking community under one banner garnered only lukewarm responses. The breakup of SOCIO and the rise of smaller and newer entities (often based on class interests or ethnic affiliation) revealed the "failure of the 1960s to generate a lasting political consciousness."[8] By the late 1990s Utah's Spanish-speaking people had not reestablished the ties that once bound them. In reality, they were becoming more atomized. After SOCIO's collapse, individuals in the comunidad gravitated toward new associations formed around specific economic, religious, and ethnic interests. These men and women shared a common language and some mutual concerns, but between 1987 and 1999 they seldom acted as a unified and effective community.

The 1990 federal census detailed growing financial and educational cleavages among Utah's Spanish-surnamed population. Between 1980 and 1990 this population grew by more than 40 percent (to 84,597 individuals) and now represented 4.9 percent of the state's inhabitants.[9] Most (90.6 percent) lived in urban areas, and two-thirds resided in Salt Lake and Weber Counties.[10] Some benefited from the commercial and economic expansion of the Reagan years, but many fell further behind in occupational status. The proportion of Spanish-speakers in white-collar positions (both men and women, sixteen years and older) increased slightly to 41.0 percent from 38.5 percent.[11] Advancement into professional, technical, managerial, and other assignments (as well as a higher labor participation rate) helped lift 12.8 percent of all familias in Utah into the fifty-thousand-dollar-and-higher income tax bracket in 1990.[12]

Economic growth also provided some opportunities for blue-collar workers. Between 1985 and 1995 the state's economy underwent significant restructuring, moving "away from government jobs and goods producing industries toward private employment and service producing industries."[13] This tendency continued during the last years of the 1990s and reversed the trend begun in the 1930s (when the state earned the nickname of "prize 'gimme' state of the union"). Although these were significant blows to the state's economy, Thayne Robson, director of the University of Utah's Bureau of Economic and Business Research, concluded that the restructuring of the previous decade limited the impact of the reduction in governmental spending: "'We are the seventh or eighth most diverse economy in the country.' And diversity translates into stability."[14]

This trend reduced the number of manufacturing positions but generated openings in more vigorous sectors (such as food handling, tourism, and Nevada casinos on the border of Utah). These start-up (or expanding) firms helped create both jobs and new clusters of Spanish-speakers in the state. During a fourteen-year span (1980 to 1994) the Cache Valley's Spanish-surnamed populace increased by more than 400 percent. In Sanpete County (in south-central Utah) this population grew by more than 218 percent.[15] The establishment of processing plants (slaughtering cattle and turkeys) pulled Mexicanos and Mexican Americans (many of whom had previously worked as migrant laborers) into these areas. These men and women provided a ready supply of labor that, local employers realized, "will keep coming as long as Mexican employers offer four dollars a day instead of four dollars an hour."[16] Positions at the E. A. Miller facility in the town of Hyrum and the Moroni Processing Plant at Moroni made it possible for some of these Spanish-speakers to pur-

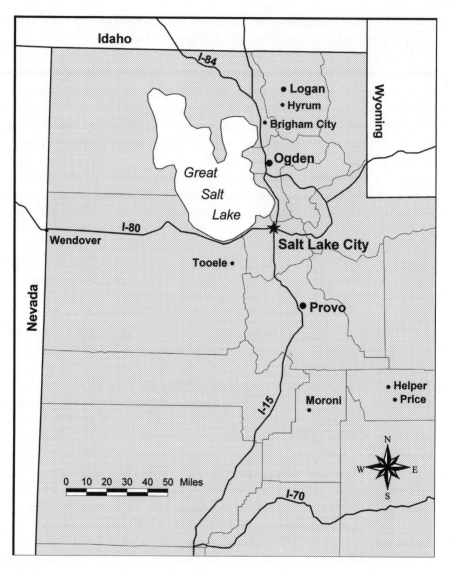

Map. 5. A view of Utah including some of the newer areas of Hispanic concentration such as Moroni. *Map by Kevin R. Mulligan*

chase houses, establish businesses that served the area's "ethnic" clientele, and abandon "nomadic lives to take full time jobs and establish roots in rural towns."[17] While not offering high pay, these jobs were a significant improvement over life in Mexico or as migrant workers for many of these men and women. One immigrant summed up conditions for the most recent wave of Mexicanos to arrive in Utah by stating, "In this country you have a chance to succeed. In Mexico, we would live on beans, tortillas, and coffee. Here we can feed our children. We wanted a better life for them. Now we have grandchildren and they only know America."[18]

A similar pattern has occurred in the resort town of Park City (in Summit County about thirty miles east of Salt Lake City). The development of the ski industry in Utah has dramatically increased the demand for workers in restaurants, clubs, and other tourist attractions. These men and women are vital to the area's economy for they perform tasks that many in the majority population do not wish to do. One former Summit County commissioner recently claimed, "What's happening in Park City are things we will see happening in other parts of the state. If the Hispanics left, [Park City] would be in dire straits."[19]

Another example of the movement by Spanish-speakers into the tourism industry is found in the casino/border town of Wendover (in Tooele County about 120 miles west of Salt Lake City). After World War II local residents worked for potash extraction companies and part-time in nearby casinos (on the Nevada side of the border). In 1980 the ownership group of the area's largest gaming houses, the Stateline and Silversmith casinos, expanded their operations and created an increased demand for change makers, kitchen helpers, maids, janitors, and porters. Two other gambling facilities, the Red Garter and the Peppermill, quickly joined in the town's expansion. This growth produced a new employment sector for locals. The positions available included openings as change makers, kitchen help, maid and janitorial personnel, buspersons, and porters. These jobs provided steady work, although the pay was not much above minimum wage. As the casinos expanded, many locals gladly filled these openings. By the middle of the 1980s news of these opportunities spread to Mexico, and workers, both legal and undocumented, flooded into town.[20] According to Father Reyes Rodríguez, who ministered in Wendover between 1985 and 1987, the arriving Mexicanos and Mexican Americans quickly concentrated in these lower-paying jobs. Many of the Anglos who had previously occupied these slots began moving into higher-paying posts, such as card dealers or managers.[21]

In a 1993 interview Dayle Stewart, the Stateline casino's human resource director, stated that his firm started out most employees at minimum wage.

The pay rate was based on a ten-step scale, based on length of service. Employees could achieve the highest position on this scale if they stayed at their jobs for about nine years. The occupations were not divided by gender; both men and women performed all of the various jobs, from housekeeping to making change. In addition to their pay, many workers lived in company-provided housing. The facilities ranged from dorm rooms for about $6 a day to apartments for families with rents ranging from $200 to $350 dollars per month. The casinos also offered workers employee-paid health insurance plans.[22]

The opinion of personnel from the Salt Lake Catholic Diocese (which established a permanent facility in town, the San Felipe Mission) was split over living conditions in the towns. Father Rodríguez expressed a positive view of circumstances in a 1993 interview. He believed that the casinos treated their employees fairly and that many were provided opportunities to better their occupational skills as well as to learn English.[23] The two nuns who worked full-time at San Felipe (Sisters Burg and Ackerman, who are Racine Dominicans) disagreed. Their primary grievances concerned the employees' pay. It was difficult, they claimed, for these familias to survive when only one person was employed. In most families both the husband and wife worked at the casino; couples often split shifts in order to provide care for their children. Economic difficulties contributed to a low graduation rate among Spanish-surnamed students at Wendover (on the Utah side) High School. In an interview Yolanda Durán, a manager at the Peppermill casino and an officer in a local Hispanic group (called Cinco de Mayo), stated that Wendover High has about four hundred students, roughly 60 percent of whom are Hispanic. Few of these young men and women ever graduate. Durán estimated that the 1993 graduating class only contained about six Spanish-surnamed graduates.[24] In sum, the Wendover experience has produced mixed results for Spanish-speakers. As in Hyrum, Moroni, and Park City, these trabajadores (workers) have taken "jobs that would have gone unfilled."[25] But at what cost? For some, conditions have improved; others appear caught in a cycle of low-wage, low-skilled occupations.

Economic statistics from the 1990 federal census reveal a mixed picture for Utah's Hispanic population. Unemployment levels for colonia constituents remained high (9.3 percent versus 5.0 percent for whites), and the shift away from manufacturing and defense reduced the proportion of Spanish-speakers in skilled and semi-skilled occupations.[26] Those without proper and sufficient training, language skills, or work experience often found it difficult to fit into Utah's more technologically sophisticated and service-oriented economy. The percentage of Spanish-surnamed laborers in unskilled slots actually increased from 19.2 percent in 1980 to 22.4 in 1990.[27] For many of these employees the

1980s, proclaimed by some to be the "Decade of the Hispanic," were ten years of "polarities and contradictions."[28]

Throughout the United States in 1990 a greater number of Spanish-speaking people than ever before enjoyed a middle-class (or higher) lifestyle, but the group did not fully eliminate income disparities with whites. In 1980 Hispanic married couples in Utah (with both spouses working) achieved a median salary equal to 86.1 percent of that earned by whites. By 1990 the figure had dropped to 83.8 percent. Median family incomes for all majority families totaled $33,846; the corresponding amount for Hispanics was $24,941. One important cause of this variance was the low median pay of single Hispanas (who often acted as exclusive caregivers for young children), who earned less than $12,000 per year.[29] Single-parent households accounted for nearly one-half of all Spanish-speakers on public assistance, pushing the group's overall poverty rate to 20.6 percent, nearly three times that of Utah whites (7.6 percent).[30]

Colonia constituents still lagged behind in scholastic achievement. The high school graduation rate for men and women over age twenty-five increased to 61.0 percent, but the figure for all of Utah's adult residents now equaled 86.2 percent.[31] In the 1995–96 academic year 5.3 percent of all public school students (25,120 of 473,666) were Spanish-surnamed, with the highest concentrations in the Granite (4,924), Salt Lake (4,630), and Ogden (2,932) school districts. By the 1996–97 school year these figures increased to 28,447 Hispanic students (out of a total state population of 478,028, or roughly 6 percent). The heaviest concentrations were in the Granite (6,025), Salt Lake (5,102), and Ogden (3,241) districts.[32] Despite the range of services available to these pupils, by 1996 they dropped out at more than three times the rate of whites.[33] Retention and recruitment programs instituted at the state colleges and universities have proved more successful. During the 1980s the percentage of colonia members with postsecondary diplomas increased dramatically, from 5.5 percent to 9.1 percent. The availability of financial assistance (such as the Utah Educational Fund) and recruitment policies lifted the proportion of Spanish-speakers who had attended college to 35.6 percent of those over twenty-five (compared to 58.8 percent of whites).[34] Unfortunately, even with these positive results, the attempt by the University of Utah (and other schools in the state system) to bring even more Hispanics (and other minorities) to campus now faced a new threat. In June, 1997, the University of Utah's president, Arthur K. Smith, commented on the Hopwood case and the impact it might have on recruiting: "While there are those who take satisfaction in these developments, the implications for the American economy, for all of us, are enormous. In Texas and Utah Hispanics constitute the fastest growing ethnic group. They are also the segment of the population whose educational attainment has been relatively low because of historical, socioeconomic and language factors. But just when we must educate more members of this and other under-represented groups, we are being forced to close, rather than open, the door of opportunity."[35]

One of the most auspicious efforts to aid minorities at the University of Utah has been the Chicano Scholarship Endowment (started in 1975). Many award recipients are now members of the state's governmental and educational bureaucracies. Some of these individuals include: Andrew Valdez, Third District Court juvenile judge (Utah's first Spanish-surnamed magistrate); Robert Florez, professor of law, University of Utah College of Law; Renee Jiménez, assistant state attorney general; Felina Ortíz, Immunization Program manager, University of Utah Student Health Services; Lee Martínez, international trade executive for the Americas, Utah State International Business Development Office (and the first Hispanic member of the Salt Lake City commission); and Reyes Aguilar, director of admissions, University of Utah College of Law. A total of 2,847 Spanish-surnamed students registered for classes at public institutions of higher learning for the fall, 1995, quarter (accounting for 2.5 percent of all college students in the state). During the 1995–96 school session this number increased to 3,089 (or 2.7 percent) of the state's college student population. The schools with the largest number of Hispanic enrollees were the University of Utah (680 individuals, or 2.6 percent of the student body) and Salt Lake Community College (1,030 students, or 4.6 percent of the student population).[36]

At the other end of the educational spectrum, many Hispanic dropouts face an uncertain future. With limited employment and advancement possibilities, many of these troubled teenagers have often turned to criminal activity. The young offender population is one section of Utah's society in which the Spanish-surnamed are, unfortunately, overrepresented. Youth of color accounted for 16.3 percent of all admissions to detention in fiscal year 1993. Youth of color account for 8.2 percent of all youth in the state of Utah and 27.5 percent of statewide detention admissions.[37]

In 1995 Hispanic children comprised 48.7 percent of the estimated 2,500 gang members in the Salt Lake Valley.[38] University of Utah sociologist Theresa Martínez claims that the state and local educators are not doing enough to help these individuals, choosing instead to "blame the problem on minority communities, dysfunctional homes . . . and, of course, the welfare mother."[39] Although Martínez does not present information that verifies the existence of such attitudes among state and local officials, incarceration data furnished by the Utah Commission on Criminal and Juvenile Justice is troubling. Confinement figures for minorities (made public in January, 1995) bolster Martínez's assertion that minorities in the juvenile justice system of Utah are treated more harshly than are white criminals. When arrested, minorities usually receive much harsher treatment from the court system and are "three times more likely to be sentenced to community placement . . . five times more likely to be in secure care facilities," even though "the lifetime offending pattern of Caucasian and ethnic minority youths are similar at most stages of the system."[40]

The unequal results in employment and education helped stimulate the formation of a variety of groups. Professional and white-collar colonia members (the "mainstreamed") established organizations designed to assist Spanish-speakers in solidifying their middle- (or upper-) class status, as well as providing avenues for further advancement through networking with corporate, civic, and governmental leaders. One club, Image de Utah, began in May of 1991. Its primary goal was to act as a bridge, "to tie business (private, non-profit, and government) to the . . . community and serve as a referral organization for employment and appointment to councils and boards." On the educational front, Image de Utah worked to recruit colonia teens into job-training, skill-improvement, and mentoring programs. Entities such as the Hispanic Women's Association and SOMOS (an employee group at US West) had similar goals. These organizations wanted to guarantee that the Spanish-speaking community had the opportunity to present its "interests and needs . . . in [the] decision making process."[41]

Concurrent with these efforts, some Hispanics sought to increase the level of entrepreneurial activity among their people. One group, called Impact Business Consultants, Inc., worked with lending institutions, the Small Business Administration (SBA), and SCORE (Service Corp of Retired Executives) in providing potential sole proprietors with technical advice and assistance in securing loans and soliciting sales. The Utah Hispanic Chamber of Commerce promoted the interests of small-business owners and worked to expand the number of state and local government purchasing contracts awarded to comerciantes.[42]

As merchants and *consumidores* (consumers) Utah's Spanish-speakers contributed more than $2 billion to the state's economy in 1996.[43] By 1992 they owned 2,375 firms, employed 2,078 workers, grossed more than $179 million in sales, and paid more than $28 million in payroll.[44] Throughout the northern Utah area white-owned establishments began to stock an increasing variety of *productos latinos* (Latin products) on their shelves to appeal to this expanding market. By the late 1990s colonia residents had the option of shopping in a growing number of *bodegas* (markets), *carnicerias* (butcher shops), *panaderias* (bakeries), *tiendas de ropa* (clothing stores), and *botanicas* (pharmaceutical and religious products) located in Salt Lake City, Murray, Midvale, Ogden, Provo, and even as far north as Logan (Cache Valley).[45]

Hispanic-owned business ventures had become more common in northern Utah by the middle of the 1990s; still, this did not end the level of suspicion that existed among some police officers. A recent raid by city and federal law enforcement agents at the La Diana Bakery (on the west side of Salt Lake City) confirms that some officials believe some of these establishments to be merely fronts for drug manufacturing and distribution operations. A Salt Lake newspaper reported: "They were dressed in black with bullet-proof vests and scarves over their faces. Brandishing rifles and pistols, they ordered everyone— some eighty employees and customers—down on the floor and handcuffed them. Gómez [store owner Rafael Gómez], who was standing near the door when police arrived, says he was struck in the face as they poured in. . . . Police believed more than tortillas were being made in this factory. A confidential informant told them drugs and possibly weapons were being handled there, too." Police officials found nothing. The reassurances of state senator Pete Suazo, who as agent for Impact Business Consultants had helped Gómez get small business loans to establish the enterprise, did not convince officers, who stated that their investigation would continue.[46]

An expanding economy benefited many but did not provide equal bounty for all. The networking and mentoring efforts of Image de Utah and the technical advice of Impact Business Consultants' counselors did little to improve the daily life for the estimated (in 1989) twenty thousand laborers who traversed the state working a variety of agricultural crops. A 1989 Utah Department of Employment Security report detailed the lack of financial progress by these field hands. During the previous ten years their pay had increased by only 6.3 percent.[47] The constant traveling from one part of Utah to another often interrupted migrant children's education, making it difficult for them to complete schooling and break the vicious cycle of poverty.[48] Groups such as IHRD (which funded and operated the Migrant Head Start Program), the Office of Hispanic Affairs of the Salt Lake Catholic Diocese, Catholic Community Services, Utah Legal Services, and the Association for Utah Community Health took up the cause of these "polarized" people. These entities sought to raise the public's awareness of *campesino* (migrant worker) living conditions and to provide some of the basic necessities of life (such as clean water, health services, and educational opportunities). It was a daunting task. A 1986 study of conditions encountered by Salt Lake County field workers revealed that they "consistently presented . . . symptoms of disease which can be an index of poor sanitation, poor hygiene and impure drinking water."[49] High rates of infant mortality, low birth weight, lack of prenatal care, tuberculosis, and measles

among agricultural workers negatively skewed the Hispanic population's overall health indicators.[50] In metropolitan areas of the state "nonethnic" progressive organizations, such as JEDI Women (Justice, Economic Dignity and
Independence for Women) and Food Not Bombs, fed the homeless and called
for greater assistance for the poor, including single Hispanas attempting to
support their children.[51]

The development of new industries, as well as Utah's economic vitality
during the 1990s, pulled thousands of Spanish speakers into the state. Another
crucial factor contributing to this population's dramatic growth was the rapid
expansion of the Church of Jesus Christ of Latter-day Saints. Missionary
efforts and the church's beliefs regarding people of mestizo heritage have made
Mormonism a large, vibrant, and growing denomination in many parts of
South and Central America. A study by LDS officials (released in December,
1996) estimated worldwide membership at 9.6 million people; almost one-
third (32.7 percent) of these faithful lived in Latin America (primarily in Mexico).[52] The arrival of foreigners helped reduce the percentage of native-born
Spanish-speakers living in Utah to 83.8 percent.[53] Most of these individuals
classified themselves as Mexican or Mexican American, but by 1990, 32.8 percent of the state's Hispanic population were born in or traced their ancestry to
Spain or various nations in Latin America.[54] The confidential nature of LDS
membership records does not permit an exact count of Spanish-surnamed
Mormons in Utah, but other evidence attests to their increased numbers. During the early 1970s only three facilities (one ward and two branches) offered
services in Spanish; by 1996 this number had increased to seventeen (fourteen
wards and three branches). The Lucero Ward continued to operate, but the
Cumorah and Haleman branches (in southern and western sections of Salt
Lake County) closed by the middle of the decade.[55]

The growing number of Lamanite descendants has produced some tensions within the church. Jessie L. Embry's study on Mormon Hispanics delves
into the shifting policies of the LDS hierarchy in regard to Spanish-speaking
congregations. The existence of these wards and missions has created much
controversy. On one side of this divide stand Mormons who believe that "the
Church is the same all over the world." Steven Chris Vigil, a Brigham Young
University student and manito from Colorado, told Embry that separate
wards only cause division within the church family: "I believe that by having
these wards . . . it is a way for the Church to suppress the minority people. I
believe that the best way to build relations . . . is for people to intermingle . . .
when you have . . . a white branch, a Lamanite branch or a Hispanic branch,
you begin to segregate people into specific areas. You don't allow them to intermingle and share the culture which is necessary."[56]

On the other side of the equation stand individuals who wish to attend facilities where they feel at home and believe they have a better chance to serve
in leadership positions. Samuel Victor Miera, former president of the Cumorah branch in Salt Lake City, told Jessie Embry that Spanish-speaking congregations want to retain their identity and gain acceptance: "We don't want
to separate ourselves, but we don't want to be mainstreamed either." Ignacio
García expressed similar sentiments when he was called as bishop of his ward
in Tucson, Arizona. Almost immediately he told stake leaders that the Spanish-speaking ward was not a "minor league" members attended until they
spoke enough English to move to the "major league" geographical wards. By
the late 1990s this issue had still not been resolved. In her conclusion Embry
states that she sees "virtue in ethnic and language congregations" but then goes
on to state that the church's goal should be that all members are treated equally
and are recognized as children of God. The solution, it seems to Embry (and
Ignacio García), is for LDS leadership to provide a flexible program that will
permit the making of such decisions at the local level.[57]

Despite a growing number of Mormon (and other) converts, the Catholic
Church and the Guadalupe Parish remained the center of Hispanic community spiritual life. During his tenure as bishop of the Salt Lake Catholic
Diocese, William Weigand expanded the number of services offered to Spanish-speaking worshipers. Weigand hired a full-time administrator to operate
the newly established Office of Hispanic Ministry in 1983, created programs
to address pastoral needs of minorities, assisted the Utah Immigration Project
in its efforts to assist individuals seeking legal residency status, and increased
the number of masses in Spanish from one per week in 1980 to twenty-three
per week by 1984.[58]

In the years after SOCIO's demise the Guadalupe Center continued providing language training to children and adults, but its programs suffered a severe setback because of the closing of its most reliable source of income, La
Morena Café. In the early 1980s real estate developer Adnan Khashoggi un-
veiled plans to build a large retail and office complex in downtown Salt Lake
City. Local officials considered the project to be one of the cornerstones of a
proposed downtown redevelopment scheme.[59] In autumn, 1984, Khashoggi
asked diocesan officials to vacate their property on 100 South and 300 West
to allow for expansion. The Triad Corporation offered La Morena Café space
in one of its towers in exchange for the use of its land. Moving expenses reduced profits and revenues and limited the amount of assistance available
for Guadalupe and other programs. The restaurant folded in 1987 when the
building's ownership group filed for bankruptcy.[60] Emergency infusions of
cash from contributors (including the LDS, Greek Orthodox, and Episcopal

Churches) saved the school in 1985, but administrators now had to find a new and reliable source of funding. By the early 1990s organizations such as the United Way and private charitable trusts (such as the Dolores Dore Eccles Foundation) had become the center's principal benefactors. Private donations surpassed $609,000 in 1993–94, paying for three-fourths of the center's operating budget and providing for the addition of grades four through six to the institution's curriculum.[61]

This example of interfaith cooperation between Utah's two largest denominations did not signify the end of tensions and misunderstanding. Some Católicos persisted in their complaints (as they had done during the 1920s and 1930s) that Hispanic converts to the LDS faith gained significant social and economic advantages over their vecinos: "Here in Utah it is like a Mormon community . . . if you are non-LDS they look at you kind of weird. The LDS members stick together and they don't even try to be friends and neighbors."[62]

Increased diversity of national origin among the state's Hispanics during the 1980s and 1990s helped foster the creation of several clubs dedicated to the observance and preservation of cultural traditions from several countries. The Centro Cívico Mexicano, the oldest and largest of these entities, continued its sponsorship of annual celebrations of Cinco de Mayo and September 16th at their facility on 200 South and 600 West in Salt Lake City. By the 1990s localities such as Midvale, Murray, and Ogden also staged city-sponsored commemorations of Mexican patriotic holidays.[63] But Mexicanos and Mexican Americans were not the only Spanish-speaking ethnic groups staging fiestas along the Wasatch Front during these years; smaller organizations of Argentines, Peruvians, Chileans, Guatemalans, and Cubans gathered in local halls and parks to celebrate their cultures and to commemorate patriotic holidays.[64]

The divergent interests and loyalties of the increasingly varied colonia constituents caused some dissension within the Spanish-speaking cluster, even among Spanish-surnamed students at Utah's colleges and universities. Some individuals continued to embrace the goals of el movimiento and Chicanismo, while others disagreed with those "old-fashioned" aims. A philosophical dispute between two clubs at the University of Utah (after the demise of the Chicano Student Association) typified these tensions and divisions. A branch of MEChA (Movimiento Estudiantil Chicano de Aztlan, or the Chicano Student Movement of Aztlan) began operations on the Salt Lake City campus in the fall of 1993. MEChA's officials, members, and academic adviser (history professor Jeffrey Garcilazo) believed that the organization (along with an allied newspaper called *Venceremos* [We Will Triumph]) should continue the "struggle" of the 1960s and 1970s, agitating for "social and economic equality . . . among all people," and work to build "a democratic multi-cultural society."[65]

Several Latino Americano students did not concur with Garcilazo's ideological perspective and tone and broke away from MEChA, establishing a new organization called the Latino Educational Association (LEA) in May, 1994. Chicanismo, they argued, failed to take their views into account. This 1990s version of el movimiento, they felt, did not recognize that "as Latinos . . . we are not part of *La Raza* movement. We feel that *La Raza* does not represent the spectrum of our culture."[66] In order to make clear the differences between the two clubs, LEA asked MEChA to stop using the term *Latino* in its fliers, publications, and other materials. This difference of opinion was unacceptable to the more "progressively minded" persons in the original organization, who chastised LEA for daring to have a different view. MEChA and Garcilazo contemptuously lampooned LEA as its "conservative counterpart" unwilling to recognize the correctness (infallibility?) of their position and the righteousness of their interpretation of how to continue "the struggle" for greater social justice.[67] Similar cleavages occurred at Weber State University in Ogden. Hispanics (approximately four hundred students during the 1996–97 academic year) split their loyalties between a MEChA branch and Los Estudiantes Unidos (The United Students), who embrace ideas similar to LEA.[68]

The rift on college campuses was duplicated among the larger community. La Alianza Latina, an umbrella group for some of the ethnic organizations created during the 1990s, chose to focus primarily on arranging events designed to sustain, promote, and commemorate the cultural traditions of Latin American nations. Concurrently the more broadly based Utah Coalition of La Raza (UCLR) worked to improve social and economic conditions through "an ongoing dialogue with the social institutions that most directly influence the lives of Utah Hispanics." The UCLR's language and ideology reveal that it hoped to become the 1990s version of SOCIO. The group sponsors an annual meeting (the Hispanic Unity and Youth Leadership Training Conference) to examine such issues as cultural identity, community health, AIDS and HIV, and employment discrimination. The coalition's leadership cadre draws representatives from such entities as the AGIF, CCM, Centro de la Familia (Center for the Family, the new name for the IHRD), Image de Utah, Utah Hispanic Chamber of Commerce, Utah Hispanic Democrats, and Utah Hispanic Republicans.[69] UCLR has succeeded in achieving polity member status,[70] but it has not re-created the community and unity of purpose that existed during the 1960s and 1970s. Unlike SOCIO, this body does not consist of individuals dedicated exclusively to UCLR goals. Member organizations (such as the Hispanic groups for both major political parties) are often at odds with each other regarding tactics, strategies, and solutions to extant community problems. One former SOCIO member has decried these divisions and disunion by harking back to a past time and suggesting that "another strong group . . . is needed today, like the organization . . . we once had."[71]

Since SOCIO disbanded there have been few causes or occasions that have even temporarily united northern Utah's Spanish-speaking people. The mistreatment of Wendover-area casino workers by law enforcement officials was one incident that offered temporary unity. Agents from the Salt Lake City office of the Immigration and Naturalization Service (INS), the Utah Highway Patrol, and the Tooele and Elko (Nevada) sheriffs departments descended upon the gambling town on March 20 and 25, 1986, ostensibly to break up a theft ring that had assaulted "private citizens . . . on the street."[72] To some local inhabitants the tactics used by law enforcement were reminiscent of the Mexican deportation raids of the 1930s. "'Do you have your papers?' one officer demanded. Durán fumbled for his green card and finally showed it to the guests. One man snatched it from him and examined it. Then the men left. No apology, no explanation. 'But don't leave the house for any reason,' one said over his shoulder. 'Why?' Durán asked. 'That's my business,' came the terse reply. Mr. Duran put his children to bed and then listened as the officers pounded on the other apartment doors. 'Open the door you-wetbacks!,' he heard them yell."[73]

In April a coalition calling itself Citizens for Immigration Rights and Justice filed a lawsuit in response to these raids. Condemnation of the officers' tactics came from all quarters of the community. DeLoris Silva Velásquez, director of the Utah Office of Hispanic Affairs (the new designation for the Chicano Ombudsman post), complained that "Hispanics are taught to obey the law, and the illegal entry of people . . . cannot be tolerated, but there is no need to abuse their rights."[74]

Similar incidents occurred throughout the state during the next few years. In 1994 the American Civil Liberties Union accused Provo (Utah County) police of stopping Spanish-speakers and routinely asking them to provide immigration documents.[75] The fear that a person's skin color or appearance might make one a target for harassment had united a diverse group of Spanish-surnamed people in the battle against stereotyping of colonia constituents.[76] Albert Maldonado, a supervisory special agent for the INS in Salt Lake City, expressed the concern of many middle-class Spanish speakers when he stated, "police officers can't come up to me because I look Hispanic and say, 'Let me see your immigration documents.'"[77]

By 1997 the search for illegal immigrants and an attempt to reduce crime around the Pioneer Park area of Salt Lake City took an ominous turn regarding the singling out of northern Utah Hispanics. Under the guise of helping the strapped local INS office, Salt Lake County sheriffs (and eventually Salt

Lake City police as well) received limited powers to assist immigration officials. Federal agents were arresting large numbers of undocumented aliens but did not have the personnel to transport them to larger field offices in Denver and Las Vegas. According to one newspaper, "As a result, many are kept in the Salt Lake County jail, which has contracted with the U.S. Marshal's Office to provide 75 beds. Once those beds are full, the jail had no choice but to start releasing inmates. That is why Salt Lake County Commission has estimated that in 1996 3334 illegal immigrants booked into the county jail were released. Graciela Italiano-Thomas, executive director of the Centro de la Familia de Utah, said that while it is important to crack down on crime, the pilot project has the potential for stereotyping."[78]

While the threat of being singled out as "illegals" did create some cross-class and cross-ethnic unity, examples of disharmony and cleavages were more common during the years after SOCIO's end. The Hispanic-American Festival, held on August 30 and 31, 1996, at Salt Lake City's Franklin Quest Field, represents the most recent unsuccessful attempt to reconstruct the cohesion that SOCIO engendered. Bill García, a local advertising executive, proposed the idea as a way for the majority population of the area to get to know "his heritage and how it contributes and fits in with life in our community today." The celebration featured food, music, and crafts and verified some of the information presented in the 1990 federal census. Representatives of twenty-one Latin American nations attended and hoped to have some fun while educating whites in "the differences between cumbia, salsa, merengue, norteñas, rancheras, and sambas beyond that it is Spanish-style music."[79] Organizers asked the various ethnic organizations to rally around the event in the spirit of latinismo, but separateness prevailed over unity. Some groups protested that the event (sponsored by the State Office of Hispanic Affairs and the Utah Department of Community and Economic Development) was a waste of valuable resources that could have been better spent meeting the pressing needs of the comunidad's poor. Others believed that the planning committee should not have accepted government money.[80] Despite the promoters' best efforts, the festival failed to forge either "a common interest (some kind of need for unity, often political) [or] a common identity, solidified and expressed by some symbol system or 'cultural umbrella' that has the power to appeal across ethnic lines."[81]

The cross-class and panethnic unity that SOCIO helped create shattered after 1986. The growing mosaic of Spanish speakers (estimated to number about 120,000 individuals in 1995) tried, through the efforts of groups such as UCLR and La Alianza Latina, to reestablish a common identity and sense of purpose that characterized much of el movimiento's years.[82] Instead the community has split along economic, ethnic, and religious lines. These men and women share a common language and many of the same concerns (such as their children's high school drop-out rates), but these ties were not sufficient to overcome the atomizing forces pulling manitos, Mexicanos, Mexican Americans, and Latino Americanos apart. Between 1987 and 1999 Hispanics in northern Utah were unable to surmount the barriers that separated those who had achieved a measure of inclusion and success from people (whether legal or undocumented) who still struggle to gain their fair share of the Beehive State's prosperity. Given the growing economic, social and religious differences apparent among the Spanish-speakers in this area, it does not seem that a single organization such as SOCIO will be able to rally the majority of this fractured comunidad under one banner in the near future.

CONCLUSION

"A Place in the American Mosaic"

The 1972 publication of Rodolfo Acuña's *Occupied America: The Chicano's Struggle Toward Liberation* was a critical event in the political and philosophical development of the Chicano movement in the United States. Although this work accurately reflected many of the beliefs of el movimiento, by the end of the decade other scholars had begun questioning some of Acuna's interpretations.

During the 1970s and 1980s authors such as Richard Griswold del Castillo, Ricardo Romo, Mario T. García, and Albert Camarillo produced a series of community studies that examined the discrimination, segregation, and limited economic advancement of Spanish-speakers in California and Texas during the late nineteenth and early twentieth centuries. In some respects these authors agreed with the conclusions of the first edition of *Occupied America;* Mexicanos and Mexican Americans had clearly not been allowed to share equally in the bounty of the American dream. But key differences existed between this new generation of Chicano scholarship and Acuña. Where Acuña saw a monolithic comunidad, works produced in the late 1970s and early 1980s revealed internal divisions (caused by ethnic affiliation, class, and other factors) within barrios. In his 1990 essay, "Recent Chicano Historiography: An Interpretive Essay," Alex M. Saragoza describes the initial edition of Acuna's work as "the quintessential victimization framework . . . [a] book [that] greatly popularized the application of internal colonialism as an interpretive framework for a synthesis of the Chicano experience."[1] The works of Griswold del Castillo, Romo, García, and Camarillo moved the field beyond Acuna's fairly simplistic model of interpretation and began unearthing the complexity of barrio life. Recent works by Arnoldo De León, Richard A. Garcia, George J. Sánchez, David G. Gutiérrez, Vicki L. Ruiz, Sarah Deutsch, Zaragoza Vargas, Erasmo Gamboa, Félix M. Padilla, and Timothy M. Matovina (to name but a few) have further delineated the levels of intricacy visible in the lives of Spanish-surnamed people in the United States. Concurrent with the recognition of these cleavages, some of these authors have broadened the geographical focus of historical research by examining populations living outside traditional areas of concentration. These two trends have provided the framework for this study on the creation, growth, development, and internal differences of the Spanish-speaking population of northern Utah.

Like their brothers and sisters in other parts of the United States, most Hispanics who journeyed to the Beehive State went in search of economic opportunities. They found work but endured discrimination in employment, housing, and education. They created associations designed to improve their daily lives and to help maintain their traditions, customs, and identity. Between 1912 and 1925 the group included some familias, but the bulk of northern Utah's Spanish-speakers consisted of single men from Mexico (as well as a few manitos from New Mexico and Colorado and Spaniards). These trabajadores toiled for beet growers in the Cache Valley and in southern Idaho, for mining concerns (primarily in Bingham Canyon but also in Price, Eureka, and other locations), and for railroad companies.

By the late 1920s the small colonia took on more characteristics of a complete barrio with the arrival of women and children and the development of self-help and religious organizations. The increased number of families and the establishment of a few associations that reflected and nurtured lo nuestro did much to ease adjustment to life in Salt Lake City and Ogden and to maintain cultural identity. By 1930 Spanish-speakers comprised the largest minority in the state, totaling more than four thousand people. The devastating impact of the Great Depression reduced this number by more than 73 percent by 1940.

A second wave of Spanish-surnamed individuals arrived during World War II, responding to openings at military installations, defense-related manufacturing plants, and extractive industries. Manitos responded in large numbers (a smaller number of islanderos from Puerto Rico also responded) to these possibilities. Utah also imported a few hundred braceros to work in agriculture. After 1945 many of these employees expected expanded opportunities as a reward for their efforts and hoped to build upon wartime gains and achieve equal treatment in all areas of life. During the 1950s Hispanics established groups, such as the American G.I. Forum, dedicated to achieving these aims. But these clubs, with few members, little money, and minimal clout among Utah polity members, did not present a viable and effective challenge to discriminatory practices. Ethnic, cultural, and other divisions between Mexicanos, Mexican Americans, and manitos stifled the effectiveness of these organizations.

In the decades after 1965 Utah's economy shifted toward the creation of service-sector jobs. These occupations required more than mere physical strength, and most colonia constituents did not have the educational background required to compete for these positions. The Chicano movement of the 1960s and 1970s provided the context in which to challenge the discrimination and conditions that confronted the community. The establishment of SOCIO in 1968 helped unite many in the Spanish-speaking population in their struggle for greater equality. During its existence SOCIO operated statewide, fostered ethnic pride, lobbied for civil rights, created education and employment programs, and presented the concerns, complaints, and hopes of its membership to the business, governmental, and religious leadership of the state of Utah. Between 1968 and 1986 the association challenged impediments to social and economic opportunity, permitting an increased number of Hispanics to enter institutions of higher learning and to become part of government and business bureaucracies.

The elimination of what many in SOCIO had considered artificial barriers exacerbated economic divisions within the community. Many who benefited from SOCIO's activities moved on, becoming part of what some historians have called the mainstreamed. Their interests no longer meshed with those of the poor and an increasing number of undocumented aliens (the polarized). Since 1987 the cross-class and panethnic ties that SOCIO forged (if only temporarily) have frayed and shattered, and northern Utah's Hispanics have seldom acted as a unified community.

While the Spanish-speaking people of this area share some historical characteristics with other clusters in the American West, they are unique in two ways. The opportunity to find employment in beet fields, mining towns, and railroad gangs has not been the only factor attracting Spanish-speakers to Utah. Since the late 1910s the Church of Jesus Christ of Latter-day Saints has aggressively pursued converts among these people (the descendants of the Lamanites). The church's hierarchy established a mission (the Rama Mexicana) in Salt Lake City in 1923, and membership provided Spanish-surnamed men and women with a direct link to the state's most important and powerful institution. These individuals encountered discrimination in their daily lives, but connection to the Mormon network afforded assistance and contacts unavailable to those of other denominations. The importance of these ties became apparent during the years of the Great Depression. Between 1930 and 1940 Rama Mexicana constituents, while not escaping the economic catastrophe unscathed, received food and employment from the LDS welfare system, helping them survive while more than two-thirds of all Spanish-speakers left the state. A clan's religious affiliation did not break all ties to the rest of the community, but it did have a significant bearing on which families weathered this storm.

Continued missionary work in recent decades has significantly altered the composition of northern Utah's Hispanic populace. The number of people from Argentina, Chile, Peru, Colombia, Ecuador, Guatemala, El Salvador, and other nations residing in the state has increased significantly, while the proportion of native-born Spanish-surnamed people has declined from more than 94 percent to less than 84 percent. Many of these newly arrived Latin Americans are LDS converts. These various national groups have created their own organizations in order to preserve their cultural traditions and customs.

Concurrent with its unique religious composition, the cooperative relationship between SOCIO activists and local business, church, and governmental officials distinguishes the history of this Spanish-speaking community. Demographic realities helped shape and temper SOCIO's objectives, demands, and methods. Although the number of Hispanics in Utah has grown dramatically since World War II, they still account for little more than 6 percent of the state's inhabitants. There are neighborhoods and areas where they comprise as much as 30 percent of residents, but there are no locations in which they form the overwhelming majority of the population.[2] This lack of voting strength has eased majority concerns over certain community demands and permitted a level of cooperation between Hispanics and the state's power structure. These patterns forced the community's leadership to adopt a collaborative (instead of a confrontational and militant) negotiating posture. The partnership between SOCIO and polity members generated social change in Utah without violent incidents. SOCIO's cadre negotiated the creation of affirmative action and recruitment programs, educational reforms, and college scholarship and financial assistance packages. National movimiento figures who visited Utah during the 1970s, such as Corky Gonzalez and Reies López Tijerina, denounced the white majority for its racist and genocidal policies and institutions, but this strident militancy was not the principal thrust of activism in this area. Negotiation and cooperation did more to improve circumstances and remove obstacles than did threats and intimidation.

During the last years of the 1990s local newspapers and magazines have effectively captured the varied aspects of life for Hispanics in northern Utah. These items reveal the mixed results of the era of el movimiento. On one hand, Spanish-speakers are now involved in state and local government, work in law enforcement and the legal profession, own more than two thousand businesses in Utah, and are targeted as a significant (and welcomed) clientele by the largest retailers and financial institutions of the Beehive State.[3] On the other hand, many Hispanics still live in substandard housing, in crime- and drug-infested neighborhoods, and with limited access to the educational programs that they need in order to improve their lives.[4]

   This study provides a preliminary examination of a population previously ignored by students of Mexican American history. True, the Spanish-speaking population of northern Utah is small by comparison with its counterparts in Los Angeles, San Antonio, and Chicago; but the social, economic, religious, and other differences extant in those larger clusters are just as evident and complex in Salt Lake City, Ogden, and their surrounding areas. Intracolonia religious cleavages are more significant in northern Utah than in other locations in the United States. Where else can an individual newly arrived from Central or South America instantly connect with the most powerful institution and network in the state simply by embracing a set of spiritual beliefs? Future research efforts by this writer (and hopefully others) will continue to shed light on this phenomenon. But for now the goal of this manuscript was more limited. This examination of a nontraditional location adds more and different experiences to the expanding narrative of Chicano/Hispanic history and provides Utah's Spanish-speakers with an opportunity to enter "into the larger American mosaic."[5] Hopefully future presentations and materials on differences and ties between Católicos and Mormones in northern Utah will no longer receive expressions of amazement and bewilderment.

NOTES

PREFACE

1. According to the 1990 federal census, Utah's population was 93.8 percent white (by comparison, throughout the rest of the nation whites comprised only 80.3 percent of the population). Hispanics comprised 4.9 percent of the state's inhabitants (by comparison, throughout the rest of the United States, Hispanics comprised 9 percent of the total population). See the following: Office of Planning and Budget, *1990 Census Briefs: Minorities in Utah, Second in a Series of 1990 Census Analysis*, Apr., 1991, pp. iii, 1, 2.

2. A word about the terminology used in this work is appropriate. Representatives of various Spanish-speaking groups have lived in the Salt Lake City and Ogden areas over the past eight decades. I will use the following terms for reference: *Mexicanos* are individuals born in Mexico; during the early years of the period under study (1912–40) this group comprised the majority of the northern Utah community. *Mexican Americans* are persons born in the United States who are of Mexican descent; the majority of these individuals in northern Utah hail, or are descended from, Spanish-surnamed people from northern New Mexico and southern Colorado. The terms *Spanish-speaking, Spanish-speakers, Spanish-surnamed,* and *Hispanics* will be used to refer to the entire community. Finally, the terms *Chicano* and *Latino* will be used when referring to scholarly works that use those terms. For information regarding the debate over the appropriate umbrella term for Spanish-speaking people in the United States see the following: David E. Hayes-Bautista and Jorge Chapa, "Latino Terminology: Conceptual Basis for Standardized Terminology," *American Journal of Public Health* 77 (Jan., 1987): 61–68; Edward Murguía, "On Latino/Hispanic Ethnic Identity," *Latino Studies Journal* 2 (Sept., 1991): 8–18; Alfred Yankauer, "Hispanic/Latino—What's in a Name?," *American Journal of Public Health* 77 (Jan., 1987): 15–17; Fernando M. Treviño, "Standardized Terminology for Hispanic Populations," *American Journal of Public Health* 77 (Jan., 1987): 69–72; Maria Eva Valle, "The Quest for Ethnic Solidarity and a New Public Image among Chicanos and Latinos," *Latino Studies Journal* 2 (Sept., 1991): 72–83; Joseph A. Rodríguez, "Becoming Latinos: Mexican Americans, Chicanos, and the Spanish Myth in the Urban Southwest," *Western Historical Quarterly* 29 (Summer 1998): 166–85; Aida Hurtado and Carlos H. Arce, "Mexicans, Chicanos, Mexican Americans, or Pochos . . . Que Somos? The Impact of Language on Ethnic Labeling," *Aztlan* 17 (Spring 1986): 103–30; and Laurie Kay Sommers, "Inventing Latinismo: The Creation of 'Hispanic' Panethnicity in the United States," *Journal of American Folklore* 104 (Nov., 1991): 32–53.

3. "Latinos' Buying Power on the Rise; Grow in Wealth and Number," *Salt Lake Tribune*, June 20, 1997, p. A1. For recent employment, unemployment, population and home ownership

figures for Spanish-speakers in Utah see: State Office of Hispanic Affairs, *Fiscal Year 1996 Annual Report,* p. 11.

4. Ibid.

5. "Priest Warns against Bigotry in Park City," *Salt Lake Tribune,* Oct. 8, 1997, p. D1. See also: State Office of Hispanic Affairs publication, "Park City Assessment," *Fiscal Year 1997 Annual Report,* pp. 1–7.

6. "WADEN's Police Power Trip: A Lethal Mix of Politics and Profiling in Wasatch County," *The Event Newspaper,* Feb. 15, 1996, pp. 8–11.

7. Ibid., p. 9.

8. Ibid.

9. The term *colonia* refers to a Spanish-speaking community located in the United States.

10. George J. Sánchez, *Becoming Mexican American: Ethnicity, Culture, and Identity in Chicano Los Angeles, 1900–1945,* p. 152.

11. Albert Camarillo, *Chicanos in a Changing Society: From Mexican Pueblos to American Barrios in Santa Barbara and Southern California, 1848–1930;* Richard Griswold del Castillo, *The Los Angeles Barrio, 1850–1890: A Social History;* Ricardo Romo, *History of a Barrio: East Los Angeles;* and Mario T. García, *Desert Immigrants: The Mexicans of El Paso, 1880–1920.*

12. Alex M. Saragoza, "Recent Chicano Historiography: An Interpretive Essay," *Aztlan* 19 (Spring, 1988–90): 1–77, 8.

13. Ibid., p. 11. See also Rodolfo Acuña, *Occupied America: The Chicano's Struggle Toward Liberation.*

14. Griswold del Castillo, *The Los Angeles Barrio,* p. 103; Camarillo, *Chicanos in a Changing Society,* p. 65.

15. In addition to the titles already noted, for an in-depth study of mutual aid societies among Spanish-speaking populations see José A. Hernández, *Mutual Aid for Survival: The Case of the Mexican American.*

16. For a discussion on barrios and their characteristics see the following: Camarillo, *Chicanos in a Changing Society,* pp. 53–78; Romo, *East Los Angeles,* pp. 61–88; and Mario T. García, *Desert Immigrants,* pp. 121–54.

17. Saragoza, "Recent Chicano Historiography," pp. 7, 11–20.

18. Ibid., p. 33. For a detailed examination of differences in ideology among Hispanics throughout the United States, see the following: Félix M. Padilla, *Latino Ethnic Consciousness: The Case of Mexican Americans and Puerto Ricans in Chicago;* David G. Gutiérrez, *Walls and Mirrors: Mexican Americans, Mexican Immigrants and the Politics of Ethnicity,* Joseph A. Rodríguez, "Becoming Latinos: Mexican Americans, Chicanos, and the Spanish Myth in the Urban Southwest," 165–85; and Rodolfo O. de la Garza, Louis DeSipio, F. Chris García, John A. García, and Angelo Falcón, *Latino Voices: Mexican, Puerto Rican, and Cuban Perspectives on American Politics.*

19. Saragoza, "Recent Chicano Historiography," pp. 44–45.

20. For information on the influence of the mass media and consumerism on Mexican Americans see the following: Sánchez, *Becoming Mexican American,* pp. 191–223; Vicki L. Ruiz, "Star Struck: Acculturation, Adolescence, and the Mexican American Woman, 1920–1950," in David G. Gutiérrez, ed., *Between Two Worlds: Mexican Immigrants in the United States,* pp. 125–48; Manuel H. Peña, *The Texas Mexican Conjunto: History of a Working Class Music;* and David Reyes and Tom Waldman, *Land of a Thousand Dances: Chicano Rock 'n' Roll in Southern California.* For an examination of similar issues regarding other ethnic groups see Lizbeth Cohen, *Making a New Deal: Industrial Workers in Chicago, 1919–1939;* and Gustavo Pérez-Firmat,

Life on the Hyphen, The Cuban American Way (especially chap. 4 on the genesis of the "Miami sound").

21. Saragoza, "Recent Chicano Historiography," p. 45.

22. Zaragosa Vargas, *Proletarians of the North: A History of Mexican Industrial Workers in Detroit and the Midwest, 1917–1933;* Erasmo Gamboa, *Mexican Labor and World War II: Braceros in the Pacific Northwest, 1942–1947;* M. L. Miranda, *A History of Hispanics in Southern Nevada;* Juan R. García, *Mexicans in the Midwest, 1900–1932;* Jorge Iber, "'El Diablo Nos Esta Llevando': Utah Hispanics and the Great Depression," *Utah Historical Quarterly* 66 (Spring, 1998): 159–77; and Félix M. Padilla, *Latino Ethnic Conciousness: The Case of Mexican Americans and Puerto Ricans in Chicago.*

23. Arnoldo De León, *Ethnicity in the Sunbelt: A History of Mexican Americans in Houston,* p. xii.

24. Among the growing list of materials on *creyentes* in Central and South America see the following: Virginia Garrard-Burnett and David Stoll, eds., *Rethinking Protestantism in Latin America;* F. Lamond Tullis, *Mormons in Mexico: The Dynamics of Faith and Culture;* Amy L. Sherman, *The Soul of Development: Biblical Christianity and Economic Transformation in Guatemala;* Sheldon Annis, *God and Production in a Guatemalan Town;* David Stoll, "'Jesus Is Lord of Guatemala': Evangelical Reform in a Death-Squad State," in Marty E. Martin and R. Scott Appleby, eds., *Accounting for Fundamentalisms: The Dynamic Character of Movements, Volume 4,* pp. 99–123; Jean-Pierre Bastian, "The Metamorphosis of Latin American Protestant Groups: A Sociohistorical Perspective," *Latin American Research Review* 28 (1993): 33–61; Bryan R. Roberts, "Protestant Groups and Coping with Urban Life in Guatemala City," *American Journal of Sociology* 73 (May 1968): 753–67; and Blanca Muratorio, "Protestantism, Ethnicity, and Class in Chimborazo," in Norman E. Whitten, ed., *Cultural Transformations and Ethnicity in Modern Ecuador,* pp. 506–34. For the few works that examine the impact of conversion upon the lives of Hispanics in the United States, see the following: Clifton L. Holland, *The Religious Dimension in Hispanic Los Angeles: A Protestant Case Study;* Jessie L. Embry, *"In His Own Language": Mormon Spanish-Speaking Congregations in the United States;* and R. Douglas Breckenridge and Francisco O.García-Tetro, *Iglesia Presbitiriana: A History of Presbyterians and Mexican Americans in the Southwest.*

25. The term *Tejano* refers to Texas-born persons of Mexican descent. Timothy M. Matovina, *Tejano Religion and Ethnicity: San Antonio, 1821–1860;* David Montejano, *Anglos and Mexicans in the Making of Texas, 1836–1986,* pp. 34–41; and Armando C. Alonso, *Tejano Legacy: Rancheros and Settlers in South Texas, 1734–1900.*

26. Matovina, *Tejano Religion and Ethnicity,* pp. 15, 65, 93.

27. Ana María Díaz-Stevens and Anthony M. Stevens-Arroyo, *Recognizing the Latino Resurgence in U.S. Religion: The Emmaus Paradigm,* p. 57.

28. Jay P. Dolan and Gilberto Hinojosa, eds., *Mexican Americans and the Catholic Church, 1900–1965;* Jay P. Dolan and Jaime R. Vidal, eds., *Puerto Rican and Cuban Catholics in the U.S., 1900–1965;* and Jay P. Dolan and Allan Figueroa Deck, S.J., eds., *Hispanic Catholic Culture in the U.S.: Issues and Concerns.*

29. Dolan and Hinojosa, eds., *Mexican Americans and the Catholic Church,* p. 3.

30. Ibid., 4, 7, 44, 79, 85, 304. Díaz-Stevens and Stevens-Arroyo examine this trend during the years 1967 through 1984 in a chapter entitled "Syzygy" in *Recognizing the Latino Resurgence.*

31. Richard A. Garcia, *Rise of the Mexican American Middle Class: San Antonio, 1929–1941.*

32. In her recent work *"In His Own Language"* (p. 9) Embry notes that it is not possible to

determine the number of Spanish-speaking Mormons in this country because church records do not list members' nationalities.

33. Vicente Mayer, *Utah: A Hispanic History;* Vicente Mayer, ed., *Working Papers toward a History of the Spanish-Speaking Peoples of Utah;* and Richard O. Ulibarri, "Utah's Ethnic Minorities: A Survey," *Utah Historical Quarterly* 40 (Summer, 1972): 210–32.

34. Spanish-Speaking Peoples of Utah, Ms 96, University of Utah, Marriott Library, Manuscript Division. A second collection, Hispanic Oral Histories, Accession 1369, will also be used in this study. Leslie Kelen conducted these interviews in the early 1980s. Many authors of ethnic histories have recognized the limitations and benefits of oral histories in capturing the historical records of "mute" groups. These works are of crucial importance to the study of Hispanics in Utah because they provide information on a group of people that has been neglected in general histories of the state. For information on the value and limitations of oral histories see: Raquel Rubio-Goldsmith, "Oral History: Considerations and Problems for Its Use in the History of Mexicanas in the United States," in Vicki L. Ruiz and Susan Tiano, eds., *Women on the U.S.-Mexico Border: Responses to Change,* 161–73; Gary Y. Okihiro, "Oral History and the Writing of Ethnic History: A Reconnaissance into Method and Theory," *Oral History Review* 9 (1981): 27–46; and Miranda, *Hispanics in Southern Nevada,* pp. xi–xii.

CHAPTER 1. The Birth of a Colonia, 1900–30

1. Herbert S. Auerbach, ed., "Father Escalante's Journal with Related Documents and Maps," *Utah Historical Quarterly* 11 (Jan.–Oct., 1943): 60.

2. Jerome Stoffel, "The Hesitant Beginnings of the Catholic Church in Utah," *Utah Historical Quarterly* 36 (Winter, 1968): 41–62, 44.

3. For a detailed examination of the roles of these two priests during this mission see Eleanor B. Adams, "Fray Francisco Atanasio Dominguez and Fray Silvestre Velez de Escalante," *Utah Historical Quarterly* 44 (Winter, 1976): 40–58.

4. For information on Spanish slave trading activity in Utah during the early 1850s see Frank McNitt, *The Indian Traders,* pp. 19–20.

5. Paul Morgan and Vicente Mayer, "The Spanish-Speaking Population of Utah: From 1900 to 1935," in Vicente Mayer, ed., *Working Papers toward a History of the Spanish-Speaking Peoples of Utah,* p. 15.

6. Dean May, *Utah: A People's History,* pp. 65–72.

7. Ibid., p. 74. The early Mormon pioneers used the term *gentiles* to refer to those who were not affiliated with their church.

8. Ibid., pp. 80–81. For more information on Mormon cooperative economic activities see Leonard J. Arrington, *Great Basin Kingdom: An Economic History of the Latter-day Saints, 1830–1900.* For a sampling of documents dealing with these activities see Leonard J. Arrington and Ralph W. Hansen, "Mormon Economic Organization: A Sheaf of Illustrative Documents," *Utah Historical Quarterly* 28 (Jan., 1960): 40–55.

9. William H. González and Genaro M. Padilla, "Monticello, the Hispanic Cultural Gateway to Utah," *Utah Historical Quarterly* 52 (Winter, 1984): 9–27; and Don D. Walker, "The Carlisles: Cattle Barons of the Upper Basin," *Utah Historical Quarterly* 32 (Summer, 1964): 268–84, especially 278–80. For information on the sheep industry in southern Utah during the last decades of the nineteenth century see William R. Palmer, "The Early Sheep Industry in Southern Utah," *Utah Historical Quarterly* 42 (Spring, 1974): 178–88.

10. William H. González and Padilla, "Monticello," p. 11.

11. Ibid., 26. See also Vicente Mayer, *Utah,* pp. 37–39.

12. Richard W. Sadler, "The Impact of Mining on Salt Lake City," *Utah Historical Quarterly* 47 (Summer, 1979): 236–53, especially 236–38.

13. Ibid., pp. 239–49. See also Helen Z. Papanikolas, "Life and Labor among the Immigrants of Bingham Canyon," *Utah Historical Quarterly* 33 (Fall, 1965): 289–315; and W. E. Turrentine Jackson, "British Impact on the Utah Mining Industry," *Utah Historical Quarterly* 31 (Fall, 1963): 347–75.

14. Thomas G. Alexander and James B. Allen, *Mormons and Gentiles: A History of Salt Lake City,* pp. 90–91.

15. Leonard J. Arrington, "The Commercialization of Utah's Economy: Trends and Developments from Statehood to 1910," in Dean L. May, ed., *A Dependent Commonwealth: Utah's Economy from Statehood to the Great Depression,* pp. 3–34.

16. Ibid., p. 4.

17. Ibid., pp. 31–33. In addition to mining and commercial agriculture, railroads used their facilities in the Beehive State to build up Salt Lake City as a tourist attraction. See Thomas K. Hafen, "City of Saints, City of Sinners: The Development of Salt Lake City as a Tourist Attraction, 1869–1900," *Western Historical Quarterly* 28 (Autumn, 1997): 343–78.

18. Morgan and Mayer, "The Spanish-Speaking Population of Utah," p. 28.

19. For the results of this oral history project see Leslie G. Kelen, *The Other Utahns: A Photographic Portfolio.*

20. Rafael Torres, interview, Salt Lake City, Utah, 1984, Hispanic Oral Histories, Box 4, Folder 7, Accession 1369, University of Utah, Marriott Library, Manuscript Division. From here on this collection is designated as HOH. See also Ruth Schermocker, "A Study of Various Events in the Life of Juan Valente Trinidad de San Rafael Torres Alvarez," Salt Lake City, Utah, unpublished manuscript.

21. Leonard J. Arrington, "Utah's Pioneer Beet Sugar Plant: The Lehi Factory of the Utah Sugar Company," *Utah Historical Quarterly* 34 (Spring, 1966): 95–120.

22. Ibid., p. 98.

23. Ibid., p. 105.

24. Thomas G. Alexander, "The Burgeoning of Utah's Economy, 1910–1918," in Dean L. May, ed., *A Dependent Commonwealth: Utah's Economy from Statehood to the Great Depression,* pp. 35–56.

25. Arrington, "Utah's Pioneer Beet Sugar Plant," p. 109. See also Leonard J. Arrington, *Beet Sugar in the West: A History of the Utah-Idaho Sugar Company, 1891–1966,* pp. 23–25.

26. Arrington, *Beet Sugar in the West,* p. 90.

27. "Mexican Workers Find Utah Paradise," *Salt Lake Tribune,* June 13, 1920, p. 15. See also Morgan and Mayer, "The Spanish-Speaking Population of Utah," pp. 37–39.

28. "Mexican Workers," *Salt Lake Tribune,* June 13, 1920, p. 15.

29. Rafael Torres, interview, HOH.

30. Frances Yánez, interview, Salt Lake City, Utah, May 21, 1971, Spanish-Speaking Peoples of Utah, Box 1, Folder 3, Ms. 96, University of Utah, Marriott Library, Manuscript Division. From here on this collection is designated as SSPU.

31. Morgan and Mayer, "The Spanish-Speaking Population of Utah," p. 30.

32. Ellen Córdova, interview, Salt Lake City, Utah, June 15, 1973, SSPU, Box 1, Folder 5. Information on Pino and González's agencies is found in: Series 3, Professional Research Projects and Consultant Work, Carton 11, Folders 24–28, Paul Schuster Taylor Papers, BANC MSS

84/38 c, The Bancroft Library, University of California, Berkeley. From here on this collection is designated PSTP.

33. Consolidation of the industry began during the late 1890s with the establishment of Utah Consolidated Mining Company and Boston Consolidated Mining Company. Utah Copper purchased the Boston Consolidated holdings in 1910. See Sadler, "The Impact of Mining on Salt Lake City," pp. 249–53; and Leonard J. Arrington, *The Richest Hole on Earth: A History of the Bingham Copper Mine.*

34. Quoted in Arrington, "The Commercialization of Utah's Economy," p. 24.

35. Papanikolas, "Life and Labor among the Immigrants," pp. 290–92.

36. For information on life in Bingham Canyon during the years of World War I see Helen Z. Papanikolas, "Immigrants, Minorities, and the Great War," *Utah Historical Quarterly* 58 (Fall, 1990): 351–70.

37. Gunther Peck, "Padrones and Protest: 'Old' Radicals and 'New' Immigrants in Bingham, Utah, 1905–1912," *Western Historical Quarterly* 24 (May, 1993): 157–78, especially 162–63.

38. Utah Copper Company, Employee Identification Cards, 1909–19, Accession 1440, University of Utah, Marriott Library, Manuscript Division. From here on this collection is designated as UCC.

39. Utah State Bureau of Immigration, Labor and Statistics, *First Report, 1911–1912,* Salt Lake City, Utah, 1913, pp. 30–31.

40. "Force of Mexicans Arrives at Bingham," *Deseret Evening News,* November 2, 1912, p. 2. See also *Salt Lake Tribune,* November 2, 1912, p. 2.

41. Morgan and Mayer, "The Spanish-Speaking Population of Utah," pp. 22–28. According to 1920 federal census statistics, "Mexican" males outnumbered "Mexican" females in Utah by a ratio of 7 to 3.

42. Santos Cabrerra, interview, Salt Lake City, Utah, Jan. 4, 1971, SSPU, Box 1, Folder 4.

43. Morgan and Mayer, "The Spanish-Speaking Population of Utah," p. 24.

44. Filomeno Ochoa, interview, Salt Lake City, Utah, July, 1972, SSPU, Box 2, Folder 13.

45. Jeffrey Marcos Garcilazo, "Traqueros: Mexican Railroad Workers in the United States, 1870–1930," Ph.D. diss., University of California, Santa Barbara, 1995, pp. 33–34.

46. Vicente Mayer, *Utah,* pp. 39–40.

47. Vicente Mayer, Sr., interview, Bountiful, Utah, Nov. 8, 1970, SSPU, Box 3, Folder 1. For more information on the labor segmentation experienced by Spanish-surnamed track workers see Garcilazo, "Traqueros," pp. 115–49.

48. José Méndel, interview, Woods Cross City, Utah, Oct. 9, 1970, SSPU, Box 1, Folder 1.

49. Lucy Chávez-Hernández, interview, Ogden, Utah, Dec. 9, 1987, HOH, Box 2, Folder 11.

50. PSTP, Carton 11, Folders 24–28. For more information regarding the movement of Spanish-surnamed laborers from Colorado and New Mexico into industrial and railroad work throughout the Southwest, see Sarah Deutsch, *No Separate Refuge: Culture, Class, and Gender on an Anglo Hispanic Frontier, 1880–1940.*

51. For a discussion on barrios and their characteristics, see the following: Camarillo, *Chicanos in a Changing Society,* pp. 53–78; Romo, *East Los Angeles,* pp. 61–88; and Mario T. García, *Desert Immigrants,* pp. 127–54.

52. Morgan and Mayer, "The Spanish-Speaking Population of Utah," p. 25.

53. For a history of the Catholic Diocese of Salt Lake, see Bernice M. Mooney, *Salt of the Earth: The History of the Catholic Church in Utah, 1776–1987.*

54. Joseph E. Allen, "A Sociological Study of Mexican Assimilation in Salt Lake City," Master's thesis, University of Utah, 1947, pp. 35–36, 38, 46–49, 61–66.

55. Dean L. May, *Utah: A People's History*, pp. 173–74.

56. Morgan and Mayer, "The Spanish-Speaking Population of Utah," pp. 34–35.

57. PSTP, Carton 11, Folders 24–28.

58. Robert J. Dwyer, "Catholic Education in Utah: 1875–1975," *Utah Historical Quarterly* 43 (Fall, 1975): 362–78.

59. María Dolores García, interview, Salt Lake City, Utah, Oct. 30, 1984, HOH, Box 2, Folder 2.

60. Ramón García, interview, Salt Lake City, Utah, July 28, 1972, SSPU, Box 2, Folder 20. For an examination of recent dropout figures for Hispanic children in Utah, see Armando Solórzano, "The Quest for Educational Equality: Mexican Americans and Hispanics in Utah," unpublished manuscript, 1997.

61. Edith Meléndez, interview, Midvale, Utah, May 2, 1973, SSPU, Box 3, Folder 14. For further information on this "informal economy" and the role of Mexicanas in these types of commercial activities, see Garcilazo, "Traqueros," 294–302.

CHAPTER 2. "Lo Nuestro":
The Creation of Hispanic Organizations in Northern Utah, 1920–35

1. Morgan and Mayer, "The Spanish-Speaking Population of Utah," pp. 32–38.

2. Sánchez, *Becoming Mexican American*, p. 11.

3. Matovina, *Tejano Religion and Ethnicity*, p. ix; Díaz-Stevens and Stevens-Arroyo, *Recognizing the Latino Resurgence in U.S. Religion*, pp. 57, 84, 96.

4. In his work *Tejano Religion and Ethnicity*, Matovina notes the importance of Catholic religious practices in this scenario; see p. ix.

5. Sánchez, *Becoming Mexican American*, pp. 11–12.

6. Several authors, in addition to Sánchez, have pointed to the economic, social, and other differences that existed, and still exist, within the Spanish-speaking communities in the United States. See: Susan E. Keefe and Amado M. Padilla, *Chicano Ethnicity*; De León, *Ethnicity in the Sunbelt*; David G. Gutiérrez, *Walls and Mirrors*; and Joseph A. Rodríguez, "Becoming Latinos, Mexican Americans, Chicanos, and the Spanish Myth of the Urban Southwest," *Western Historical Quarterly* 29 (Summer, 1998): 165–85.

7. Richard A. Garcia, *Rise of the Mexican American Middle Class*, pp. 79–80.

8. In particular, see p. 24 where Embry quotes a church leader who, in 1952, asserted that the church is not out to force individuals to give up their culture in order to fit into Mormon society.

9. Sánchez, *Becoming Mexican American*, pp. 155–56. Although it does not deal exclusively with the Spanish-speaking population of Los Angeles, a recent article in the *Western Historical Quarterly* provides ample detail regarding the religious diversity in Southern California during the early decades of the twentieth century. See Michael E. Engh, S.J., "'A Multiplicity of Faiths': Religion's Impact on Los Angeles and the Urban West, 1890–1940," *Western Historical Quarterly* 27 (Winter, 1997): 463–92.

10. Morgan and Mayer, "The Spanish-Speaking Population of Utah," p. 45.

11. Ibid., 45–46.

12. *Salt Lake Tribune,* September 17, 1920, p. 18.

13. Morgan and Mayer, "The Spanish-Speaking Population of Utah," p. 46. Historians have documented similar complaints from Mexican nationals in other parts of the United States. See Juan R. García, *Mexicans in the Midwest.*

14. Lucy Chávez-Hernández, interview, Ogden, Utah, Dec. 9, 1987, HOH, Box 2, Folder 11.

15. *Salt Lake Tribune,* May 6, 1920, p. 22.

16. *Salt Lake Tribune,* Sept. 17, 1920, p. 22.

17. *Salt Lake Tribune,* July 16, 1920, p. 1.

18. *Salt Lake Tribune,* Apr. 13, 1920, p. 8.

19. Hernández, *Mutual Aid for Survival.*

20. Ibid., 45.

21. Schermocker, "A Study of Various Events in the Life of Juan Valente Trinidad de San Rafael Torres Alvarez."

22. Ellen Córdova, interview, Salt Lake City, Utah, June 15, 1973, SSPU, Box 1, Folder 5.

23. Morgan and Mayer, "The Spanish-Speaking Population of Utah," p. 53.

24. Jesús Avila, interview, Lark, Utah, May 6, 1973, SSPU, Box 4, Folder 14.

25. Morgan and Mayer, "The Spanish-Speaking Population of Utah," p. 55.

26. Ibid.

27. For more information on the Comisión Honorífica movement, see Francisco E. Balderrama, *In Defense of La Raza: The Los Angeles Mexican Consulate and the Mexican Community, 1929–1936.*

28. Jesús Avila, interview, SSPU.

29. Sánchez, *Becoming Mexican American,* pp. 153–54. See also Dolan and Hinojosa, eds., *Mexican Americans and the Catholic Church,* pp. 95–96.

30. Sánchez, *Becoming Mexican American,* p. 155.

31. See the following: Robert D. Knight, "A Study of the Role of the Episcopal Diocese of Los Angeles in Meeting the Psychosocial Needs of Hispanics," Master's thesis, University of California, Long Beach, 1989; and Enrique Zone-Andrews, "Suggested Competencies for the Hispanic Protestant Church Leader of the Future," Ph.D. diss., Pepperdine University, 1996.

32. See *Book of Mormon,* Book of Ether, 4:3–4. For information regarding Mormon missionary activity in Mexico see Tullis, *Mormons in Mexico,* pp. 3–8, quote on p. 4; and Embry, *"In His Own Language,"* pp. 14–18.

33. Quoted in Embry, *"In His Own Language,"* p. 27. A Mormon stake is composed of five to ten wards (or branches) and is directed by a stake president and twelve members in a High Council. These men administer various programs for assistance and religious instruction.

34. Domitila Rivera de Martínez, oral history interview with Gordon Irving, 1975, Typescript, pp. 1–6, JMOHP.

35. A Mormon bishop is a leader in the local geographical division (known as a ward). There is no specific training required to be "called" for this position. Bishops usually serve about five years and are responsible for, among other duties, hearing members' confessions, compiling administrative reports, and administering financial and other assistance to the needy of the ward.

36. Domitila Rivera de Martínez, oral history interview with Gordon Irving, 1975, Typescript, pp. 1–6, JMOHP.

37. Betty Ventura, "La Historia de la Rama Mexicana" (The History of the Lucero Ward), Salt Lake City, Utah, 1972, unpublished manuscript, p. 152.

38. Ibid., p. 154.

39. An LDS mission can be defined as a geographic administrative district. In this case the mission was created to serve geographic and language needs. The primary function of the institution was to convert and minister to local Hispanics in Spanish. For more information regarding the early days of this mission see Ventura, "La Historia de la Rama Mexicana," pp. 1–4.

40. Embry, *"In His Own Language,"* pp.15–16.

41. The administrative body of LDS wards or missions consist of three individuals: a president/bishop and his first and second counselors. The three men are responsible to the administration and spiritual guidance of the congregation.

42. Ventura, "La Historia de la Rama Mexicana," p. 3.

43. The change in designation from mission to branch is an administrative decision based on the number of people attending services. A branch is a smaller unit than a ward.

44. Morgan and Mayer, "The Spanish-Speaking Population of Utah," p. 48.

45. Ventura, "La Historia de la Rama Mexicana," p. 9.

46. For more information regarding Anthony R. Ivins's role in the history of the Rama Mexicana, see Embry, *"In His Own Language,"* p. 36.

47. Rafael Torres, interview, Salt Lake City, Utah, Oct. 15, 1984, HOH, Box 4, Folder 7.

48. R. Andrew Chestnut, *Born Again in Brazil: The Pentecostal Boom and the Pathogens of Poverty,* pp. 123–36, 123.

49. Richard L. Jensen, "Mother Tongue: Use of Non-English Languages in the Church of Jesus Christ of Latter-day Saints in the U.S., 1850–1983," in Davis Bitton and Maureen Ursenbach Beecher, eds., *New Views of Mormon History: A Collection of Essays in Honor of Leonard J. Arrington,* pp. 273–303; see especially pages 274, 276, 281, 296.

50. Embry, *"In His Own Language,"* p. 39.

51. Juan Flores, interview, Midvale, Utah, June 28, 1972, SSPU, Box 2, Folder 11.

52. Eufemio Salazar, oral history interview with Gordon Irving, Salt Lake City, Utah, 1976, Typescript, pp. 1–12, JMOHP. Genealogical information is an important facet of the LDS faith. Information on ancestors is gathered in order to perform a variety of religious ceremonies for the dead.

53. Morgan and Mayer, "The Spanish-Speaking Population of Utah," p. 33.

54. Silas Lobato, interview, Salt Lake City, Utah, Dec. 1, 1984, HOH, Box 3, Folder 3.

55. Sherman, *The Soul of Development,* p. 43.

56. For an examination of the significance of these types of activities in building up an individual's pride and self-esteem, see Chestnut, *Born Again in Brazil,* p. 136.

57. Silas Lobato, interview, HOH. For information regarding the LDS Church's ties to the Boy Scouts, see Armand L. Mauss, *The Angel and the Beehive: The Mormon Struggle with Assimilation,* p. 26.

58. Ventura, "La Historia de la Rama Mexicana," pp. 87–104.

59. Ibid., 105–24. See also Embry, *"In His Own Language,"* pp. 38–39.

60. Embry, *"In His Own Language,"* p. 38.

61. Clotilda Gómez, interview, Salt Lake City, Utah, Nov. 16, 1984, HOH, Box 2, Folder 4. See also Edward H. Mayer, "The Evolution of Culture and Tradition in Utah's Mexican-American Community," *Utah Historical Quarterly* 49 (Spring, 1981): 133–44.

62. Pioneer Stake, Historical Records and Minutes, Manuscript Division, Archives, Historical Department, Church of Jesus Christ of Latter-day Saints, Salt Lake City, Utah. See also Embry, *"In His Own Language,"* p. 37.

63. Clotida Gómez, interview, HOH.

64. Helen Salazar-Benavides, interview, Salt Lake City, Utah, June 4, 1985, HOH, Box 1, Folder 7.

65. Lionel A. Maldonado and David R. Byrne, *The Social Ecology of Chicanos in Utah,* p. 3.

66. Embry, *"In His Own Language,"* p. 44.

67. For a similar argument, see also Matovina, *Tejano Religion and Ethnicity,* p. 4; and Díaz-Stevens and Stevens-Arroyo, *Recognizing the Latino Resurgence in U.S. Religion,* 57.

68. A Catholic diocese is an administrative district headed by a bishop. The Salt Lake Diocese encompasses the entire geographic area of the state of Utah.

69. Jerald H. Merrill, "Fifty Years with a Future: Salt Lake's Guadalupe Mission and Parish," *Utah Historical Quarterly* 40 (Summer, 1972): 242–64, 246. During the 1920s (1921–27) the number of baptisms increased to 110. See Morgan and Mayer, "The Spanish-Speaking Population of Utah," p. 33.

70. Merrill, "Fifty Years with a Future," p. 246.

71. Letter from Father Francis M. Alva to the Salt Lake Diocese, Dec., 1920, SLCDA.

72. Ibid. Our Lady of Guadalupe is the patron saint of Mexico, and devotion to her is widespread among Mexican and Mexican American Catholics. A Catholic mission has a similar function to an LDS mission. Its primary purpose, in this case, was to minister to colonia members in Spanish and help limit the number of converts.

73. Ibid.

74. Merrill, "Fifty Years with a Future," p. 248.

75. Dolan and Hinojosa, eds., *Mexican Americans and the Catholic Church,* p. 59.

76. Letter from Father Leroy Callahan to Monsignor Duane G. Hunt, Sept. 29, 1927, SLCDA.

77. The difference between a Catholic parish and a mission is similar to the difference between a Mormon mission, a branch, and a ward. The Catholic mission is established to minister to the needs of a specific group of people. Later on, as the mission's population expands, it may be given independent status and become a parish in its own right.

78. Merrill, "Fifty Years with a Future," p. 250.

79. Letter from Mary A. Thompson to Monsignor Duane G. Hunt, Oct. 24, 1928, SLCDA.

80. The cathedral of a Catholic diocese or archdiocese serves as a parish and as the administrative center for the area. It usually houses the offices of the bishop or archbishop as well as other administrative personnel.

81. Frances Yánez, interview, Salt Lake City, Utah, May 27, 1971, SSPU, Box 1, Folder 3.

82. Vicente Mayer, *Utah,* p. 46.

83. Merrill, "Fifty Years with a Future," p. 251.

84. María Dolores González-Mayo, interview, Salt Lake City, Utah, Feb. 15, 1985, HOH, Box 3, Folder 9.

85. Bertha Amador Mayer, interview, Bountiful, Utah, June 14, 1972, SSPU, Box 2, Folder 9.

86. Father Reyes Rodríguez, interview, Salt Lake City, Utah, Apr. 24, 1985, HOH, Box 4, Folder 8.

87. For an example of a similar situation among Pentecostals in Central America, see Sherman, *The Soul of Development,* p. 44.

88. María Dolores González-Mayo, interview, HOH.

89. Epifanio González, interview, Salt Lake City, Utah, Jan. 12, 1985, HOH, Box 2, Folder 6.

90. Martin Alden Johnson, "A Comparison of Mormon and Non-Mormon Ethnic Attitudes," Ph.D. diss., Brigham Young University, 1973, pp. 27–29.

CHAPTER 3. "El Diablo Nos Esta Llevando":
Utah's Spanish-Speaking Population and the Great Depression, 1930–40

1. A version of this chapter appeared as "'El Diablo Nos Esta Llevando': Utah Hispanics and the Great Depression" in *Utah Historical Quarterly* 66 (Spring, 1998): 159–77. The literal translation of this statement is "The devil is taking us"; however, Mexicans take this statement to mean "things are going to hell."

2. Dean L. May, *Utah: A People's History*, p. 173–74.

3. Leonard J. Arrington, "Utah, the New Deal and the Depression of the 1930s," Dello G. Dayton Memorial Lecture, Mar. 25, 1982, Weber State College, Ogden, Utah, p. 9. Copy of lecture in author's possession.

4. For information regarding the movement of Spanish-speakers into Utah during the 1920s and 1930s, see William H. González and Padilla, "Monticello," pp. 7–28. For a broader picture of conditions affecting the Hispanics of New Mexico and Colorado during the Great Depression, see Deutsch, *No Separate Refuge.*

5. Elizabeth Broadbent, *The Distribution of Mexican Population in the United States*, pp. 62–68, 113.

6. Vicente Mayer, *Utah*, pp. 58–59.

7. Francisco E. Balderrama and Raymond Rodríguez, *Decade of Betrayal: Mexican Repatriation in the 1930s.* Balderrama and Rodríguez's study provides an effective outline of circumstances encountered by Mexicano workers just before and after the economic collapse. The work focuses primarily upon the Detroit and Los Angeles colonias. With the exception of a brief mention of Idaho beet workers and the Salt Lake City Mexican consulate office, Balderrama and Rodriguez completely ignore the Intermountain region and communities. For a broad overview of conditions faced by Spanish-speakers and other minorities throughout the West during the Great Depression, see Richard White, *"It's Your Misfortune and None of My Own": A New History of the American West*, pp. 463–95.

8. Thomas G. Alexander, "The Economic Consequences of the War: Utah and the Depression of the 1920s," in Dean L. May, ed., *A Dependent Commonwealth: Utah's Economy from Statehood to the Great Depression*, pp. 57–89, 59.

9. Ibid., pp. 67–68.

10. Dean L. May, *Utah: A People's History*, pp. 173–74.

11. Garth L. Mangum and Bruce Blumell, *The Mormons' War on Poverty: A History of LDS Welfare, 1830–1990*, pp. 94–95.

12. For a brief overview of conditions for beet workers in the United States during the 1930s, see Balderrama and Rodríguez, *Decade of Betrayal*, pp. 16–17.

13. Ibid., pp. 24, 75.

14. Ibid., p. 34.

15. Pancha González, interview, Salt Lake City, Utah, Nov. 13, 1987, HOH, Box 2, Folder 8.

16. Cruz Campero García, interview, Salt Lake City, Utah, May 31, 1985, HOH, Box 1, Folder 12.

17. Thomas G. Alexander, "The Economic Consequences of War: Utah and the Depression of the 1920s," in Dean L. May, ed., *A Dependent Commonwealth: Utah's Economy from Statehood to the Great Depression*, pp. 60–61.

18. Dean L. May, *Utah: A People's History*, p. 173.

19. Balderrama and Rodríguez, *Decade of Betrayal*, p. 17.

20. Lynn Robison Bailey, *Old Reliable: A History of Bingham Canyon, Utah,* pp. 161–64.

21. Esperanza and Gavino Aguayo, interview, Salt Lake City, Utah, Feb. 6, 1985, HOH, Box 1, Folder 2.

22. Garcilazo, "Traqueros," pp. 244, 245, 255.

23. Vicente Mayer, *Utah,* pp. 39–41.

24. Alexander, "The Economic Consequences of War," pp. 73, 86.

25. Vicente Mayer, *Utah,* pp. 58–59.

26. María Dolores García, interview, Salt Lake City, Utah, Nov. 2, 1984, HOH, Box 3, Folder 4.

27. José Méndel, interview, Woods Cross City, Utah, Oct. 9, 1970, SSPU, Box 1, Folder 1.

28. See the following: Balderrama and Rodríguez, *Decade of Betrayal,* pp. 39–45; and Juan R. García, *Mexicans in the Midwest,* pp. 83–104.

29. Julia Kirk Blackwelder, *Women of the Depression: Caste and Culture in San Antonio, 1929–1939,* p. 9.

30. Ibid., p. 8.

31. E. Ferol Benavides, "The Saints among the Saints: A Study of Curanderismo in Utah," *Utah Historical Quarterly* 41 (Autumn, 1973): 371–92, 381, 384.

32. Ibid., p. 387.

33. John Florez, interview, Salt Lake City, Utah, May 10, 1984, Box 1, Folder 9. See also "People of Color" series, *Salt Lake Tribune,* Apr. 3, 1994, pp. A13–A14.

34. Balderrama and Rodríguez, *Decade of Betrayal,* p. 40.

35. Clotilda (Tilly) Ontiveros-Gómez, interview, Salt Lake City, Utah, Nov. 12, 1984, HOH, Box 2, Folder 3.

36. Balderrama and Rodríguez, *Decade of Betrayal,* pp. 43–45; White, *"It's Your Misfortune and None of My Own,"* p. 466.

37. María Dolores García, interview, HOH.

38. Alex Hurtado, interview with author, Ogden, Utah, July 28, 1995.

39. White, *"It's Your Misfortune and None of My Own,"* p. 473.

40. Ibid., p. 474; Balderrama and Rodríguez, *Decade of Betrayal,* pp. 80–90, 218–19.

41. Juanita Jiménez, interview, Salt Lake City, Utah, June 22, 1985, HOH, Box 2, Folder 12.

42. Pancha González, interview, HOH.

43. Roberto Nieves, interviews, Salt Lake City, Utah, Nov. 30, 1972, and Mar. 14, 1973, SSPU, Box 3, Folder 12, and interview, Apr. 19, 1985, HOH, Box 4, Folder 2.

44. Manuel García, Jr., interview, Salt Lake City, Utah, Jan. 9, 1985, HOH, Box 2, Folder 1.

45. Bertha Amador-Mayer, interview, Bountiful, Utah, June 14, 1972, SSPU, Box 2, Folder 9.

46. Jesús Avila, interview, Lark, Utah, May 6, 1973, SSPU, Box 4, Folder 14.

47. Balderrama and Rodríguez, *Decade of Betrayal,* p. 39.

48. Merrill, "Fifty Years with a Future," pp. 251–54.

49. María Dolores González-Mayo, interview, Salt Lake City, Utah, Mar. 1, 1985, HOH, Box 3, Folder 9.

50. Father Reyes Rodríguez, interview, Salt Lake City, Utah, Mar. 1, 1985, HOH, Box 4, Folder 8.

51. Chestnut, *Born Again in Brazil,* p. 24. Authors writing on the conversion experience in Latin America have tended to exclude Mormons from those whom they classify as *creyentes.* See, for example, Annis, *God and Production in a Guatemalan Town,* p. 78. It is not my objective in this work to argue for the inclusion or exclusion of Mormons from the "Protestant" groups ac-

tive in Latin America. Rather, it is my intent to examine and note the impact of connections to the Mormon "ethnic network" and how those ties have shaped the Hispanic experience in northern Utah.

52. Mangum and Blumell, *The Mormons' War on Poverty,* p. 94.

53. Ibid., p. 97.

54. Record #LR-5089-2, Mexican Branch Minutes, Church Archives, Historical Department, Church of Jesus Christ of Latter-day Saints, Salt Lake City, Utah.

55. Mangum and Blumell, *The Mormons' War on Poverty,* pp. 97–99, 108.

56. The Relief Society of the LDS Church is a charitable organization staffed exclusively by women. Their task is to distribute assistance to the needy, as well as to refer destitute members to bishops for further aid.

57. Mangum and Blumell, *The Mormons' War on Poverty,* p. 101.

58. Ventura, "La Historia de La Rama Mexicana," p. 99.

59. Records of Member Collection, 1836–1970, Call Number 375/8, Reel #3847, Church of Jesus Christ of Latter-day Saints, Historical Department, Church Archives, Salt Lake City, Utah. Other scholars have noted the importance of these economic benefits and ties (among Mormons and other religious groups). See Armand L. Mauss, "God of Gods: Some Social Consequences of Belief in God among Mormons," in William R. Garrett, ed., *Social Consequences of Religious Belief,* pp. 44–65; and Muratorio, "Protestantism, Ethnicity, and Class in Chimborazo," pp. 506–34.

60. Company history of Manuel's Fine Food, Incorporated, unpublished manuscript, 1, copy in author's possession.

61. Chestnut, *Born Again in Brazil,* p. 106. For a brief discussion on how holding various church positions affects individuals, see p. 136 of Chestnut's work.

62. Mangum and Blumell, *The Mormons' War on Poverty,* pp. 112–13.

63. Ibid., pp. 112–30.

64. Ibid., pp. 131–47.

65. Ibid., p. 105.

66. María Dolores García, interview, HOH.

67. Ruth Torres, interview with author, Salt Lake City, Utah, Feb. 19, 1996.

68. Embry, *"In His Own Language,"* p. 38.

CHAPTER 4. "There Was Much Work To Do":
Utah Hispanics and World War II, 1940–45

1. Wayne K. Hinton, "The Economics of Ambivalence: Utah's Depression Experience," *Utah Historical Quarterly* 54 (Summer, 1986): 268–85.

2. Ibid., pp. 284–85.

3. White, *'It's Your Misfortune and None of My Own,'* p. 473. For a more complete examination of in-state expenditures and per capita rankings of Utah for various New Deal programs, see Arrington, "Utah, the New Deal and the Depression of the 1930s," p. 27. Copy of lecture in author's possession.

4. Arrington, "Utah, the New Deal and the Depression of the 1930s," pp. 24–25.

5. White, *'It's Your Misfortune and None of My Own,'* pp. 497–98. For specific information regarding the various military and industrial installations established in Utah before and during the war, see: Thomas G. Alexander, "Utah's War Industry during World War II: A Hu-

man Impact Analysis," *Utah Historical Quarterly* 51 (Winter, 1983): 72–92; Eugene E. Campbell, "The M- Factors in Tooele's History," *Utah Historical Quarterly* 51 (Summer, 1983): 272–88; Leonard J. Arrington, Thomas G. Alexander, and Eugene A. Erb, Jr., "Utah's Biggest Business: Ogden Air Materiel Area at Hill Air Force Base, 1938–1965," *Utah Historical Quarterly* 33 (Winter, 1965): 9–33; Leonard J. Arrington and Thomas G. Alexander, "Supply Hub of the West: Defense Depot Ogden, 1941–1964," *Utah Historical Quarterly* 32 (Spring, 1964): 99–121; Leonard J. Arrington and Thomas G. Alexander, "Sentinels on the Desert: The Dugway Proving Ground, 1942–1963 and Deseret Chemical Depot, 1942–1965," *Utah Historical Quarterly* 32 (Winter, 1964): 32–43; Leonard J. Arrington and Archer L. Durham, "Anchors Aweigh in Utah: The U.S. Naval Supply Depot at Clearfield, 1942–1962," *Utah Historical Quarterly* 31 (Spring, 1963): 109–26; Thomas G. Alexander and Leonard J. Arrington, "Utah's Small Arms Ammunition Plant during World War II," *Pacific Historical Review* 34 (May, 1965): 185–96; James B. Allen, "Crisis on the Home Front: The Federal Government and Utah's Defense Housing in World War II," *Pacific Historical Review* 38 (Nov., 1969): 407–28.

6. John E. Christiansen, "The Impact of World War II," in Richard D. Poll, Thomas G. Alexander, Eugene E. Campbell, and David E. Miller, eds., *Utah's History,* pp. 497–514.

7. William H. González and Padilla, "Monticello," pp. 9–27, 11.

8. Deutsch, *No Separate Refuge.*

9. Vicente Mayer, *Utah,* pp. 36–39. While Deutsch's study effectively examines daily life, working conditions, and gender relations among manitos of the Southwest, her work completely ignores the presence of the Utah portion of this network.

10. William H. González and Padilla, "Monticello," p. 11.

11. William C. Blair, "An Ethnological Survey of Mexicans and Puerto Ricans in Bingham Canyon, Utah," Master's thesis, University of Utah, 1948.

12. Gamboa, *Mexican Labor and World War II,* p. 20.

13. Ibid., pp. 51–67.

14. Vicente Mayer, *Utah,* p. 63.

15. Dr. Orlando A. Rivera, interview, Salt Lake City, Utah, June 11, 1985, HOH, Box 4, Folder 4. For an overview of the history of Hispanics in Colorado, see Vincent C. De Baca, ed., *La Gente: Hispano History and Life in Colorado.* For information on conditions during the years of the Great Depression, see José Aguayo's essay "Los Betabeleros (The Beet Workers)," pp. 105–20, and "Mexican Migrant Workers in Depression-era Colorado," by Tanya W. Kulkosky, pp. 121–34.

16. Dr. Orlando A. Rivera, taped interview with the Utah Arts Council, 1992.

17. White, *"It's Your Misfortune and None of My Own,"* p. 505.

18. Christiansen, "The Impact of World War II," pp. 498–504.

19. Valentín Arámbula, interview, Sunnyside, Utah, Feb. 5, 1972, SSPU, Box 2, Folder 10.

20. Richard C. Roberts, "Railroad Depots in Ogden: Microcosm of a Community," *Utah Historical Quarterly* 53 (Winter, 1985): 74–99.

21. Vicente Mayer, *Utah,* pp. 58–59.

22. John Florez, interview, Salt Lake City, Utah, May 10, 1984, HOH, Box 1, Folder 9.

23. Richard C. Roberts, "Railroad Depots in Ogden," pp. 96–97.

24. Alex Hurtado, interview with author, Ogden, Utah, July 28, 1995.

25. Polk City Directory, Ogden, Utah, 1944.

26. Dan Maldonado, interview, Salt Lake City, Utah, Feb. 27, 1985, HOH, Box 3, Folders 5 and 6.

27. Deutsch, *No Separate Refuge,* pp. 150–62. For information on the role of Utah women

in the wartime economy, see Antonette Chambers Noble, "Utah's Defense Industries Workers in World War II," *Utah Historical Quarterly* 59 (Fall, 1991): 363–79, and her "Utah's Rosies: Women in the Utah War Industries during World War II," *Utah Historical Quarterly* 59 (Spring, 1991): 123–45. While both of these articles provide important overviews of the contributions of women to the home front's economic output, they fail to mention the role of Hispanic women in Utah's economy during the war years.

28. Rose Ortíz, interview, Salt Lake City, Utah, Dec. 30, 1984, HOH, Box 4, Folder 2.

29. Clotilda Gómez, interview, Salt Lake City, Utah, Feb. 27, 1987, HOH, Box 2, Folder 4.

30. Letter from Father James E. Collins to Bishop Duane G. Hunt, Jan. 1, 1944, SLCDA.

31. Merrill, "Fifty Years with a Future," pp. 242–64, 254–55. For more information on the Rama Mexicana, see Document LR 5089-2, Historical Records and Minutes, Mexican Branch, Pioneer Stake, Historical Department, Church Archives, The Church of Jesus Christ of Latter-day Saints, Salt Lake City, Utah. From here on LDS Church collections will be designated as LDSCA.

32. Eduardo Balderas, oral history, interviews with Gordon Irving, Salt Lake City, Utah, 1973, Call # MS 200 104, p. 75, LDSCA.

33. Samuel Victor Miera, oral history, interviews with Gordon Irving, Salt Lake City, Utah, 1975–76, Call # MS 200 175, pp. 63–64, LDSCA.

34. Blair, "An Ethnological Survey of Mexicans and Puerto Ricans in Bingham Canyon, Utah," p. 86.

35. Ibid., p. 89.

36. Ibid., pp. 90–92.

37. Rúben Gómez, interview, Salt Lake City, Utah, Oct. 30, 1984, HOH, Box 2, Folder 4.

38. Chris Wilson, *The Myth of Santa Fe: Creating a Modern Regional Tradition,* p. 155.

39. Francisco Solorio, interview, Salt Lake City, Utah, Dec. 19, 1970, SSPU, Box 1, Folder 6.

40. Dr. Orlando A. Rivera, interview, HOH.

41. Blair, "An Ethnological Survey of Mexicans and Puerto Ricans in Bingham Canyon, Utah," pp. 43–46, 81–92.

42. *Salt Lake Tribune* editorials and articles on Cinco de Mayo and Sept. 16 celebrations, 1942–45. For a discussion on American propaganda and Hispanics during World War II, see Mauricio Mazón, *The Zoot-Suit Riots: The Psychology of Symbolic Annihilation,* p. 25.

43. In addition to Mazón, a detailed discussion on relations between Anglos and Spanish speakers in the United States during the war years is found in several works, including the following: Montejano, *Anglos and Mexicans in the Making of Texas,* pp. 264–74; and Gamboa, *Mexican Labor and World War II.*

44. Dr. Orlando A. Rivera, interview, HOH.

45. Mazón, *The Zoot-Suit Riots,* pp. xi–9.

46. Dan Maldonado, interviews, HOH.

47. Ventura, "La Historia de la Rama Mexicana," n.pag.

48. Clotilda and Rúben Gómez, interview, Salt Lake City, Utah, Nov. 23, 1984, HOH, Box 2, Folder 4.

49. Epifanio Gonzalez, interview, Salt Lake City, Utah, Jan. 12, 1985, HOH, Box 2, Folder 6.

50. Noble, "Utah's Rosies," p. 145.

51. Epifanio Gonzalez, interview, HOH.

CHAPTER 5. "Second-Rate Citizens":
Utah Hispanics during the Postwar Years, 1946–67

1. White, *"It's Your Misfortune and None of My Own,"* pp. 513–14.

2. Ibid., p. 515. For information regarding the economic impact of military spending upon Salt Lake County, see Linda Sillitoe, *A History of Salt Lake County,* p. 211.

3. James L. Clayton, "Contemporary Economic Development," in Richard D. Poll, Thomas G. Alexander, Eugene E. Campbell, and David E. Miller, eds., *Utah's History,* pp. 531–44, 535.

4. Clotilda and Rúben Gómez, interview, Salt Lake City, Utah, Feb. 27, 1985, HOH, Box 2, Folder 4.

5. Carl Allsup, *The American G.I. Forum: Origins and Evolution,* p. xiv.

6. Sillitoe, *A History of Salt Lake County,* p. 205.

7. Joseph E. Allen, "A Sociological Study of Mexican Assimilation in Salt Lake City," p. 12.

8. Ibid., p. 4.

9. Ibid., pp. 33, 51–52.

10. Ibid., p. 51.

11. United States Department of Commerce, Bureau of the Census, *Census of Population 1950, Characteristics of the Population,* Part 44, Table 1, p. 57.

12. Ibid., p. 19. See also Joseph E. Allen, "A Sociological Study of Mexican Assimilation in Salt Lake City," pp. 67–69.

13. Joseph E. Allen, "A Sociological Study of Mexican Assimilation in Salt Lake City," pp. 68, 82.

14. Ibid., pp. 40–45, 76–79.

15. Ibid., pp. 99–100.

16. Annual Financial Report of Our Lady of Guadalupe Parish for fiscal year 1946, SLCDA.

17. Joseph E. Allen, "A Sociological Study of Mexican Assimilation in Salt Lake City," pp. 46–49. For information on the total number of members at the Rama, see Record of Members Collection, 1836–1970, Reel 3847, Call # 375-8, LDSCA.

18. Ibid., pp. 35–36.

19. Ibid., pp. 38, 61–66. Sánchez has noted this change in dating and marriage partner selection pattern in his work *Becoming Mexican American,* pp. 141, 143.

20. Doris Meyer, *Speaking for Themselves: Neomexicano Cultural Identity and the Spanish Language Press, 1880–1920,* p. 35.

21. Edward H. Mayer, "The Evolution of Culture and Tradition in Utah's Mexican American Community," pp. 133–44.

22. Joseph E. Allen, "A Sociological Study of Mexican Assimilation in Salt Lake City," p. 45.

23. Edward H. Mayer, "The Evolution of Culture and Tradition," pp. 137–39.

24. Helen Mickelsen Crampton, "Acculturation of the Mexican American in Salt Lake County, Utah," Ph.D. diss., University of Utah, 1967.

25. Ibid., pp. 44–45, 62–64.

26. Joseph E. Allen, "A Sociological Study of Mexican Assimilation in Salt Lake City," p. 116.

27. Mario T. García, *The Making of a Mexican American Mayor: Raymond L. Telles of El Paso,* p. 3.

28. United States Department of Commerce, Bureau of the Census, *Census of Population, 1950, Characteristics of the Population,* Part 44, Table 1, p. 68.

29. United States Department of Commerce, Bureau of the Census, *1960 Census Tract for Salt Lake City, Utah,* p. 3.

30. United States Department of Commerce, Bureau of the Census, *Census of Population, 1960, Characteristics of the Population,* Part 46, Table 89, p. 135.

31. *Census of Population, 1950, Characteristics of the Population,* Part 44, Table 10, pp. 19, 38, 42, 45. The median incomes were as follows: Salt Lake City $3,204; Bingham Canyon $3,000; Salt Lake County $3,255; and Weber County $3,214.

32. United States Department of Commerce, Bureau of the Census, *1960 Census Tract for Salt Lake City, Utah,* P1, pp. 13–22, and *1960 Census Tract for Ogden, Utah,* P1, pp. 13–16.

33. White, *"It's Your Misfortune and None of My Own,"* p. 514. See also *Census of the Population, 1950,* Part 44, Table 5, p. 9.

34. Clayton, "Contemporary Economic Development," pp. 534–35.

35. Vicente Mayer, *Utah,* p. 66.

36. Norbert Martínez, interviews, Midvale, Utah, Mar. 13 and 27, 1985, HOH, Box 3, Folder 7.

37. John Dale Ensign II, "Two Unions in the Utah Copper Industry: The Effect of Ideology Upon Their Dealings With Management," pp. 86–87.

38. Norbert Martínez, interviews, HOH.

39. Ann Nelson, "The Spanish-Speaking Migrant Laborer in Utah, 1950–1965," in Vicente Mayer, ed., *Working Papers toward a History of the Spanish-Speaking Peoples of Utah,* p. 68. See also Richard O. Ulibarri, "Utah's Unassimilated Minorities," in Richard D. Poll, Thomas G. Alexander, Eugene E. Campbell, and David E. Miller, eds., *Utah's History,* pp. 629–50.

40. Nelson, "The Spanish-Speaking Migrant Laborer in Utah," p. 89.

41. Ibid., pp. 78, 65, 89, 105–106, 93, 98. For more-in-depth information on conditions faced by seasonal workers in the Intermountain West, see Richard Baker, *Los Dos Mundos: Rural Mexican Americans, Another America.*

42. Nelson, "The Spanish-Speaking Migrant Laborer in Utah," pp. 104–105.

43. Stanley H. Henderson, "Social and Academic Problems of Spanish-Speaking Students in Davis County, Central Junior High," Master's thesis, University of Utah, 1958, pp. 1, 48, 103–106, 73–75, 50.

44. Orlando A. Rivera, "A Descriptive Study of Students of Spanish-Speaking Descent at West High School," Master's thesis, University of Utah, 1959, pp. 52, 64–70.

45. Dean O. Stevens, "A Status Study of a Group of Mexican-American Children in Layton Elementary School," Master's thesis, University of Utah, 1962, pp. 1, 4–6, 94–96.

46. Ibid., p. 40. For more information on Hispanic children in Texas schools during the 1950s, see: Everett Ross Clinchy, Jr., "Equality of Opportunity for Latin Americans in Texas: A Study of Economic, Social, and Educational Discrimination against Latin Americans in Texas and Efforts of the State Government on Their Behalf," Ph.D. diss., Columbia University, 1954; Guadalupe San Miguel, Jr., *"Let Them All Take Heed": Mexican Americans and the Campaign for Educational Equality in Texas, 1910–1981;* and Thomas P. Carter, *Mexican Americans in School: A History of Educational Neglect.*

47. John Florez, interview, Salt Lake City, Utah, May 10, 1984, HOH, Box 1, Folder 9. See also Lili Wright, "People of Color" series, *Salt Lake Tribune,* Apr. 3, 1994, pp. A13–A14.

48. Robert "Archie" Archuleta, interviews, Salt Lake City, Utah, May 28 and Sept. 14, 1985, HOH, Box 1, Folders 4 and 5.

49. Bailey, *Old Reliable,* pp. 167–78.

50. Sillitoe, *A History of Salt Lake County,* pp. 212–13.

51. United States Department of Commerce, Bureau of the Census, *1960* Census *Tract for Salt Lake City, Utah,* P1, pp. 13, 22, and *1960 Census Tract of Ogden, Utah,* P1, pp.13–16.

52. Epifanio Gonzalez, interview, Salt Lake City, Utah, Jan. 12, 1985, HOH, Box 2, Folder 6.

53. Esperanza and Gavino Aguayo, interview, Salt Lake City, Utah, Feb. 6, 1985, HOH, Box 1, Folder 2. See also Rivera, "A Descriptive Study of Students of Spanish-Speaking Descent at West High School," pp. 37, 47.

54. Vicente Mayer, *Utah,* p. 66.

55. *America Unida Newspaper,* Salt Lake City, Utah, Mar. 20, 1989, p. 3.

56. *Let's Help Build a New Mexican Civic Center,* fund-raising pamphlet, Centro Cívico Mexicano, Salt Lake City, Utah, 1968, copy in author's possession.

57. Centro Cívico Mexicano, events programs for Cinco de Mayo and Sept. 16, 1956–62.

58. Felix F. Gutiérrez and Jorge Reina Schement, *Spanish Language Radio in the Southwestern United States,* p. 3.

59. Tomás Perez, interviews, Salt Lake City, Utah, Dec. 4 and 21, 1984, HOH, Box 4, Folder 3.

60. Centro Cívico Mexicano, by-laws, 1959, pp. 6–7.

61. Judge Andrew Valdez, interview with author, Mar. 8, 1995.

62. Centro Cívico Mexicano event programs for Cinco de Mayo and Sept. 16th celebrations, 1960, 1961.

63. *America Unida Newspaper,* Mar. 20, 1989, p. 3.

64. For information on the dearth of recreational facilities on the west side of Salt Lake City during the 1950s, see Sillitoe, *A History of Salt Lake County,* pp. 210–11.

65. Tomás Pérez, interviews, HOH.

66. José Timoteo López, *La Historia de la Sociedad Proteccion Mutua de Trabajadores Unidos,* pp. 27–28.

67. Allsup, *The American G.I Forum,* pp. 16, 33.

68. Dr. Hector P. García, M.D., "Your Chairman's Message," 1951, Hector P. García Collection, Document 141.1, Texas A&M University—Corpus Christi, Mary and Jeff Bell Library, Department of Special Collections and Archives. From here on this collection is designated as HPGC.

69. Letters from Molly C. Gálvan to Dr. Hector P. García, Aug. 21, 1954, and Feb. 22, 1955, unprocessed documents. Letter from Molly C. Gálvan to Ed Idar, Jr., Dec. 20, 1954, unprocessed document, HPGC.

70. Letter from Molly C. Gálvan to Dr. Hector P.García, Sept. 18, 1955, unprocessed document, HPGC.

71. Letter from Congressman H. A. Dixon to Molly C. Gálvan, July 30, 1955, Document 65.47, HPGC.

72. Letter from Larry Jaramillo to Dr. Hector P. García, unprocessed document; "Report of Forum Happenings in Utah," *Forum News Bulletin,* Oct., 1955, unprocessed document, HPGC.

73. Letter from Larry Jaramillo to Dr. Hector P. García, Oct. 7, 1955, unprocessed document, HPGC.

74. Letter from Molly C. Gálvan to Dr. Hector P. García, Sept. 18, 1955, unprocessed document; *Forum News Bulletin,* Oct. 1956, p. 6, HPGC.

75. Letter from Molly C. Gálvan to Dr. Hector P. García, Oct. 18, 1955, unprocessed document; letter from Molly C. Gálvan to FBI office in Salt Lake City, Utah, Sept. 17, 1955, unprocessed document, HPGC.

76. Letters from Molly C. Gálvan to Dr. Hector P. García, Mar. 10, 1956, and Mar. 12, 1956, unprocessed documents; letter from Dr. Hector P. García to Father Marceau, Mar. 19, 1956, unprocessed document, HPGC.

77. For more information regarding the AGIF during the McCarthy era, see Allsup, *The American G.I Forum,* pp. 61–62.

78. Molly C. Gálvan, *Ogden Forum Bulletin,* Dec., 1955, HPGC.

79. Merrill, "Fifty Years with a Future," pp. 242–64, 254–56.

80. Mooney, *Salt of the Earth,* p. 231.

81. Gilberto Hinojosa, "Antecedents to the Twentieth Century" and "The Immigrant Church, 1910–1940," in Dolan and Hinojosa, eds., *Mexican Americans and the Catholic Church,* pp. 7 and 63, respectively; Díaz-Stevens and Stevens-Arroyo, *Recognizing the Latino Resurgence in U.S. Religion,* p 110.

82. Mooney, *Salt of the Earth,* pp. 260–61.

83. Gilberto Hinojosa, "The Mexican American Church, 1930–1965," in Dolan and Hinojosa, eds., *Mexican Americans and the Catholic Church,* pp. 107, 116. For more information on the role of *cursillos* and similar programs in the Catholic Church, see also Anthony M. Stevens-Arroyo, "The Emergence of a Social Identity among Latino Catholics," and Edmundo Rodríguez, S.J., "The Hispanic Community and Church Movements: Schools of Leadership," both of which are in Dolan and Figueroa Deck, S.J., eds., *Hispanic Catholic Culture in the U.S.,* pp. 100 and 215–22, respectively; and Díaz-Stevens and Stevens-Arroyo, *Recognizing the Latino Resurgence in U.S. Religion,* pp. 116–48.

84. Record of Members Collection, 1836–1970, Reel 3847, Call # 375-8, LDSCA.

85. Ventura, "La Historia de la Rama Mexicana," p. 77.

86. Robert H. Burton, interview with William G. Hartley, Aug. 8, 1972, pp. 21–23, LDSCA.

87. Cumorah is the hill where, Mormons believe, Church founder Joseph Smith found the golden plates he eventually translated and which are the basis for the Book of Mormon.

88. Embry, *"In His Own Language,"* pp. 41, 7. See also Samuel Victor Miera, interview with Gordon Irving, Midvale, Utah, 1975–76, pp. 50–56, LDSCA.

89. Judge Andrew Valdez, interview.

90. Robert H. Burton, interview, pp. 6–7, LDSCA.

91. Samuel Victor Miera, interview, pp. 56–64, LDSCA. In his recent work *The Angel and the Beehive* (see pp. 77, 85, 92–95) Armand L. Mauss argues that during the 1960s the LDS Church's leadership decided to bolster a spirit of "separateness" from other Christian denominations. As a result, the church instituted several practices (including the family home evenings on Monday nights) designed to "separate" Mormons from others outside the faith.

CHAPTER 6. "The Advocacy Battle for Our People":
Hispanic Activism in Northern Utah, 1968–86

1. White, *"It's Your Misfortune and None of My Own,"* pp. 513–19.

2. Clayton, "Contemporary Economic Development," pp. 531–44.

3. Ibid., p. 536.

4. "Superintendent Bell Cites Dropouts in Utah Minorities," *Salt Lake Tribune,* Sept. 27, 1969, p. 25.

5. Dr. Orlando A. Rivera, "Why a Chicano Movement?," in *The Spanish-Speaking American Challenge: A Report on the Brigham Young University Chicano Conference,* pp. 82–86, MS # 5006-d, Folder 7, LDSCA.

6. SOCIO Articles of Incorporation, Mar. 21, 1968, SOCIO Collection, Box 1, Folder 2, Accession 1142, University of Utah, Marriott Library, Manuscript Division. From here on this collection will be designated as SOCIOC.

7. "Salt Lake Spanish To Form New Group," *Salt Lake Tribune,* Dec. 9, 1967, p. A15.

8. Robert "Archie" Archuleta, interview, Salt Lake City, Utah, June 4, 1985, HOH, Box 1, Folder 4.

9. "SOCIO Chapter Development," Box 2, Folder 26, SOCIOC.

10. United States Department of Commerce, Bureau of the Census, *Census of Population, 1960, Characteristics of the Population,* Part 46, Table 89, p. 135, and *1960 Census Tract for Salt Lake City, Utah,* p. 3.

11. United States Department of Commerce, Bureau of the Census, *1970 Census of Population, Educational Attainment,* Volume 2, Part 5B, Appendix C, p. 6.

12. United States Department of Commerce, Bureau of the Census, *1970 Census of Population, Characteristics of the Population,* Volume 1, Part 46, Table 48, p. 111. Some of Utah's colonia leaders argued that this estimate missed between 7,000 and 17,000 of the state's Hispanic population. See Lionel A. Maldonado and David R. Byrne, *The Social Ecology of Chicanos in Utah,* pp. 3–4.

13. United States Department of Commerce, Bureau of the Census, *1970 Census of Population, Characteristics of the Population,* Volume 1, Part 46, Table 58, p. 131, and Table 133, p. 246.

14. Ibid., Table 112, p. 207.

15. Ibid., Table 48, p. 113.

16. Ibid., Table 54, p. 123.

17. Ibid. See also Joseph E. Allen, "A Sociological Study of Mexican Assimilation in Salt Lake City," pp. 51–52; and United States Department of Commerce, Bureau of the Census, *Census of Population, 1950, Characteristics of the Population,* Part 44, Table 1, p. 57.

18. United States Department of Commerce, Bureau of the Census, *1970 Census of Population, Characteristics of the Population,* Volume 1, Part 46, Table 54, p. 123.

19. Maldonado and Byrne, *The Social Ecology of Chicanos in Utah,* p. 8.

20. Joseph E. Allen, "A Sociological Study of Mexican Assimilation in Salt Lake City," pp. 67–69.

21. United States Department of Commerce, Bureau of the Census, *1970 Census of Population, Characteristics of the Population,* Volume 1, Part 46, p. 109, and Table 51, p. 117.

22. Ibid.

23. Ibid., Table 175, pp. 427, 431.

24. Ibid., Table 175, pp. 433, 435.

25. Ibid., Table 176, pp. 437, 439–41.

26. Ibid., Table 57, pp. 129, 130.

27. Ibid., Table 58, p. 131.

28. Padilla, *Latino Ethnic Consciousness,* pp. 3, 7–13.

29. Ibid., p. 11.

30. Jay P. Dolan and Gilberto Hinojosa, "Introduction," in Dolan and Hinojosa, *Mexican Americans and the Catholic Church,* pp. 1–8.

31. Díaz-Stevens and Stevens-Arroyo, *Recognizing the Latino Resurgence in U.S. Religion,* pp. 125, 117, 144.

32. SOCIO Articles of Incorporation, Mar. 21, 1968, Box 1, Folder 2, SOCIOC.

33. For an examination of the impact of diversity regarding a political issue among Hispanics, see David G. Gutiérrez, *Walls and Mirrors.*

34. Padilla, *Latino Ethnic Consciousness,* p. 6.

35. Ignacio M. García, *Chicanismo: The Forging of a Militant Ethos among Mexican Americans.* García examines both the interclass and intergenerational ties and divisions within the Chicano movement; see pp. 15, 73, 75, 114.

36. United States Department of Commerce, Bureau of the Census, *1970 Census of Population, Characteristics of the Population,* Volume 1, Part 46, Table 48, p. 111.

37. See Quintard Taylor, *The Forging of a Black Community: Seattle's Central District from 1870 through the Civil Rights Era;* and Robert A. Goldberg, "Racial Change on the Southern Periphery: The Case of San Antonio, Texas, 1960–1965," *Journal of Southern History* 69 (Aug., 1983): 349–74.

38. Mártin Sánchez Jankowski, "'Where Have All the Nationalists Gone?': Change and Persistence in Radical Political Attitudes among Chicanos, 1976–1986," in David Montejano, ed., *Chicano Politics and Society in the Late Twentieth Century,* pp. 201–33.

39. Samuel Victor Miera, interview with Gordon Irving, 1975–76, p. 233, MS 200 175, LDSCA.

40. Orlando A. Rivera, "Mormonism and the Chicano," in F. Lamond Tullis, Arthur Henry King, Spencer J. Palmer, and Douglas F. Tobler, eds., *Mormonism: A Faith for All Cultures,* pp. 115–25.

41. Ibid., 116.

42. Ibid., 124.

43. "Mexican Center Groundbreaking Rite December 1," *Deseret News,* Nov. 25, 1968, p. 8A. See also Ignacio M. García, *Chicanismo,* 22.

44. Dr. Orlando A. Rivera, interview, Salt Lake City, Utah, Nov. 27, 1973, SSPU, Box 3, Folder 4; Robert "Archie" Archuleta, interview, Salt Lake City, Utah, May 28, 1985, HOH, Box 1, Folder 4.

45. Susan Herbst, *Politics at the Margin: Historical Studies of Public Expression Outside the Mainstream,* pp. 22, 23.

46. Ibid., pp. 23, 29, 164.

47. Herbst's work describes the difference between "direct" and "backchannel" access to power and influence. SOCIO's leaders were not at the pinnacles of power and status in their respective organizations, but they did fill posts in institutions that could help improve the civil rights and struggle for equal treatment of Utah's Hispanic population. See Ibid., pp. 29, 164, 181.

48. Merrill, "Fifty Years with a Future," pp. 242–64, 254–56.

49. Embry, *"In His Own Language,"* pp. 13–34, 59–66.

50. *Salt Lake Tribune,* Nov. 20, 1969, p. D1.

51. Roberto Nieves, interviews, Salt Lake City, Utah, Mar. 14, 1973, SSPU, Box 4, Folder 2, and HOH, Box 4, Folder 1.

52. "Spanish Utahns Set Goals," *Salt Lake Tribune,* Feb. 18, 1968, p. C5.

53. Dr. Orlando A. Rivera, interview, Salt Lake City, Utah, SSPU, Box 3, Folder 5.

54. Dr. Orlando A. Rivera, "Why a Chicano Movement?," in *The Spanish-Speaking American Challenge: A Report on the Brigham Young University Chicano Conference,* p. 83, MS # 5006-d, Folder 7, LDSCA.

55. Brent McGregor, "Access to Employment and Education," in *The Spanish-Speaking American Challenge: A Report on the 1974 Brigham Young University Chicano Conference*, pp. 96–97.

56. "Advisory Group Works for Minority Employment," *Salt Lake Tribune*, Nov. 19, 1968, p. 25.

57. "Employment Service Follows Own Tenets," *Deseret News*, Mar. 31, 1969, pp. B1, B4.

58. "Job Program for Minorities," *Deseret News*, Sept. 2, 1970, p. A20.

59. "Salt Lake Minorities Embittered by Area's 'Built-in' Racism," *Salt Lake Tribune*, Sept. 21, 1970, pp. 17, 27.

60. "Group Gains City Study of Officer Height Cut," *Salt Lake Tribune*, Mar. 18, 1971, p. C6.

61. "Salt Lake Businessmen Pledge Jobs for Minorities," *Salt Lake Tribune*, Jan. 6, 1970, p. 21.

62. "Seven Step Plan Would Aid Minorities," *Deseret News*, June 8, 1971, p. A9.

63. "City's Effort to Hire Minority Groups Stirs Controversy," *Salt Lake Tribune*, Dec. 2, 1973, p. F7.

64. "Weber Chicanos Helping Selves," *Salt Lake Tribune*, Feb. 9, 1970, p. 14.

65. "City's Effort," *Salt Lake Tribune*, Dec. 2, 1973, p. F7.

66. "Recommendations to the Utah State Association of Civil Service Commissioners on the Problems and Hiring Practices of Minorities under the Merit Commission Laws," May 28, 1971, Box 18, Folder 15, SOCIOC.

67. Notes from meetings between SOCIO representatives and Gov. Calvin M. Rampton, Box 2, Folder 20, SOCIOC.

68. In her work *Politics at the Margin* (p. 16) Susan Herbst defines "outsiders" or "marginal groups" as "groups and . . . ideas that are either ignored or de-legitimated by mainstream leaders and institutions."

69. "Rampton Names Chicano Liaison," *Salt Lake Tribune*, May 15, 1973, p. B6; "Minorities-Slow Pace," *Deseret News*, June 24, 1974, p. B1.

70. For information on the development of minority business enterprise in the United States and the importance of economic "self-help" among minorities, see Juliet K. Walker, *The History of Black Business in America: Capitalism, Race, Entrepreneurship*.

71. "Free Enterprise Frowns on 'Latin Intrusion,'" *Salt Lake Tribune*, May 3, 1970, pp. F1, F3.

72. Promotional pamphlet, Guadalupe Center, Salt Lake City, Utah, 1974, copy in author's possession.

73. "La Morena Café May Reopen at Its Old Location," *Salt Lake Tribune*, Apr. 8, 1987, p. B1.

74. Merrill, "Fifty Years with a Future," p. 262.

75. Promotional pamphlet, Guadalupe Center, 1974.

76. United States Department of Commerce, Bureau of the Census, *1977 Survey of Minority Owned Business Enterprises: Spanish Origin*, Table 2, p. 60, Table 3, p. 67, Table 4, p. 112, and Table 5, p. 142.

77. Executive Order by Gov. Scott M. Matheson, Feb. 23, 1977, Box 1, Folder 6, SOCIOC.

78. Schedule D, Supporting Contract Information for Department of Transportation Program, Box 20, Folders 1–8, SOCIOC.

79. Bilingual Secretarial Program, Monthly Report, Budget Summary for 1979–80 and letters from First Security Bank and Kennecott Mineral Company, Box 1, Folders 9, SOCIOC.

80. Minority Women Employment Program, Statement of Purpose, Box 114, Folder 1, SOCIOC.

81. Chicano Development and Cohesion Program, Box 3, Folder 10, pp. 1–4, SOCIOC.

82. "Barriers to Employment Breaking Down, SOCIO Hears," *Salt Lake Tribune*, Sept. 30, 1973, p. B1.

83. "Barriers to Employment," *Salt Lake Tribune*, Sept. 30, 1973, p. B1. This body consisted of eleven members representing the viewpoints of various Hispanic groups to provide the governor with "a broader perspective" of community concerns; see "Rampton Okays Chicano Advisory Unit," *Salt Lake Tribune*, June 26, 1973, p. 17.

84. Chicano Development and Cohesion Program, Box 3, Folder 10, p. 4, SOCIOC.

85. For an examination of the problems caused by changes in organizational incentive structure, see Benjamin Márquez, *LULAC: The Evolution of a Mexican American Political Organization*, pp. 5–6.

86. Chicano Development and Cohesion Program, Box 3, Folder 10, pp. 5–6, SOCIOC.

87. Supporting Contract Information, Box 3, Folders 1–8, SOCIOC.

88. Roberto "Archie" Archuleta, José E. Martínez, and Dr. Orlando A. Rivera, *Institute for Human Resource Development, 1974–1994*, pamphlet, Institute for Human Resource Development, pp. 1-4, copy in author's possession. See also Centro de La Familia, *Annual Report, 1992–1993*, pp. 6, 10.

89. "Schools Must Add Bilingual Teachers, Chicanos Say," *Salt Lake Tribune*, Aug. 22, 1971, pp. B1, B2.

90. "SOCIO Airs School Needs," *Deseret News*, Jan. 14, 1970, pp. B1, B5.

91. "Salt Lake Schools Panel Pledges to Meet More Needs of Minority Students," *Salt Lake Tribune*, June 10, 1970, p. 32.

92. "Chicanos Present Demands," *Deseret News*, Dec. 2, 1971, pp. B1, B8.

93. "Chicanos Fear Lessened Role from Granite School Revamp," *Deseret News*, Dec. 15, 1976, p. F5; "SOCIO History," Box 2, Folder 25, p. 2, SOCIOC.

94. "Chicano Needs Cry Out for Educational Program Extension," *Salt Lake Tribune*, Sept. 10, 1972, p. B3.

95. Maldonado and Byrne, *The Social Ecology of Chicanos in Utah*, pp. 14–16, 24.

96. Ibid., pp. 25–30, 35–41.

97. Frederick S. Buchanan and Raymond G. Briscoe, "Public Schools as a Vehicle for Social Accommodation in Utah: The Strangers within Our Gates," in Charles S. Knowlton, ed., *Social Accommodation: American West Center Occasional Papers*, pp. 115–16, 120.

98. Maldonado and Byrne, *The Social Ecology of Chicanos in Utah*, pp. 33–34.

99. "Chicanos, Supporters Demand Action for Better Education at Board Meet," *Salt Lake Tribune*, May 16, 1979, p. B1.

100. David Bowen Luke, "Academic and Social Differences between Mexican and Non-Mexican Students at Layton Senior High School," Master's thesis, University of Utah, pp. 30, 47.

101. Rose Gurule, interview, Ogden, Utah, July 19, 1972, SSPU, Box 3, Folder 4.

102. "Dedication and Self-Help—They're Winning," *Deseret News*, May 18, 1976, p. B2; Mooney, *Salt of the Earth*, pp. 232–34.

103. "Mexican Racism Charged in U. Entrance Policies," *Deseret News*, Aug. 15, 1969, p. B3.

104. "Study Urges More Minority Students at U of U," *Salt Lake Tribune,* June 17, 1970, p. 25.

105. Memorandum from Lewis M. Rogers to Frank McKean, Oct. 14, 1969, pp. 3, 4. See also "Historical Perspectives," Box 1, Folder 33, SOCIOC.

106. Dr. Clark S. Knowlton, "Minority Group Education and the University: Cultural Benefit Proposal," May 12, 1969, p. 7.

107. Memorandum from Lewis M. Rogers to Frank McKean, Oct. 14, 1969, pp. 3, 4.

108. "U. Attempts to Prepare Minorities for College," *Salt Lake Tribune,* July 3, 1970, p. 28. See also Steven Sandoval Martínez, "An Evaluation of Various Admission Procedures and the 1970 Ford Foundation Program in Relation to Mexican American and American Indian Students at the University of Utah," Master's thesis, University of Utah, 1971. This author does not approve of all aspects of this program. In the author's view, the Ford Foundation students often took courses in which professors were "very lax in their expectations and grading," see especially pp. 38–41.

109. Judge Andrew Valdez, interview with author, Mar. 8, 1995.

110. John Florez worked for the National Urban Coalitions between 1969 and 1974. He returned to Utah in 1974 and accepted a position at the University of Utah. Upon his return he became actively involved with SOCIO and provided the group with access to the university bureaucracy and the state's Republican Party apparatus.

111. Dr. Alfonso R. Trujillo, "Proposal: Request to the Department of Health, Education and Welfare for the Development of Chicano Studies Program at the College of Eastern Utah," unpublished material, Price, Utah, 1969. See also "The Spanish and Mexican Americans of Carbon County, Utah," *La Luz,* Apr., 1974, p. 16.

112. "Statewide Youth Organization Arouses Interest in Utah," *Peldanos,* April/May, 1975, pp. 1, 4.

113. Carlos Muñoz, Jr., *Youth, Identity and Power: The Chicano Movement,* p. 1. In this work Munoz argues that youths were the principal driving force of the Chicano movement. The evidence uncovered regarding SOCIO and *el movimiento* in northern Utah contradicts this assessment. For a different view, see Ignacio M. García, *Chicanismo,* pp. 134–35.

114. Dr. Orlando A. Rivera, interview, Salt Lake City, Utah, Nov. 27, 1973, SSPU, Box 3, Folder 5.

115. "Utah's Brown Power Movement Heading for Militant Action," *Salt Lake Tribune,* Nov. 20, 1969, p. D1.

116. Richard A. Garcia, *Rise of the Mexican American Middle Class,* pp. 6–7, 306–22. See also Ignacio M. García, *Chicanismo,* p. 6.

117. "'Explosion of Justice' Cry Fills Salt Palace as Chicano Activist Speaks," *Salt Lake Tribune,* Apr. 1, 1972, p. B1. See also "'You Have a Racist Institution' Gonzalez Tells Students," *Daily Utah Chronicle* (the student newspaper of the University of Utah), Dec. 2, 1972, p. 1.

118. "A Message from Orlando," *Peldanos,* April/May, 1975, p. 2. See also "Chicanos Must Find Identity, Explains Illinois Instructor," *Daily Utah Chronicle,* Dec. 4, 1970, p. 1.

119. See the following articles from the *Daily Utah Chronicle:* "Chicanos Help Themselves, Others," Jan. 17, 1972, p. 6; "Center Provides Chicanos a 'Home Away from Home,'" Jan. 17, 1972, p. 4; "U Chicano Student Association Act as Liaison for U, Community," Feb. 10, 1983, p. 1; "Chicano Student Association Works for Success at U," May 24, 1983, p. 6.

120. Mike Meléndez, interviews, Salt Lake City, Utah, June 3 and 15, 1972, SSPU, Box 1, Folder 13, and Box 2, Folder 7.

121. "Group Helps Chicanos Adjust to Life at U," *Daily Utah Chronicle,* Nov. 1, 1983, pp.

1, 5. For a discussion of the impact the conservative tide had in the 1980s on Hispanic student organizations, see Munoz, *Youth, Identity and Power,* pp. 175–78.

122. Maldonado and Byrne, *The Social Ecology of Chicanos in Utah,* pp. 54–55.

123. Archuleta, Martínez, and Rivera, *Institute for Human Resource Development,* pamphlet, p. 3.

124. *Esperanza Para Manana:* A Community Based Alternative for Hispanic Juvenile Delinquent Youth," Proposal, Box 106, Folder 6, SOCIOC, pp. 1, 4–8.

125. *Casa de Orgullo,* Proposal, Box 106, Folder 6, SOCIOC, pp. 3–5.

126. Archuleta, Martinez, and Rivera, *Institute for Human Resource Development,* pamphlet, pp. 8–11.

127. Mexican American Community Corrections Support Program, Proposal, July, 1974, Box 20, Folder 3, SOCIOC.

128. "In Utah: Mexican and Spanish Americans Show What Unity Can Do," *La Luz,* Apr., 1974, pp. 6, 7, 12.

129. "Ranch for Youths Founded on 810 Acres Near Tooele," *Salt Lake Tribune,* June 28, 1969, p. 29.

130. Letter from Afton Forsgren, Chairman, Board of Directors, Utah Housing Coalition, Nov. 7, 1973, Box 107, Folder 19, SOCIOC.

131. Promotional pamphlet, Guadalupe Center, 1974.

132. Mooney, *Salt of the Earth,* pp. 416–17, 421.

133. Ibid., pp. 393, 418–21 .

134. "Hispanos in Utah Have Interesting History," *La Luz,* Apr., 1974, p. 4.

135. United States Department of Commerce, Bureau of the Census, *1980 Census of Population, Detailed Population Characteristics, Utah,* Part 46, Table 194, p. 7.

136. Maldonado and Byrne, *The Social Ecology of Chicanos in Utah,* p. 6. For the 1980 census, blue-collar workers include those designated as working in precision production, operator, fabricator, and laborer positions.

137. United States Department of Commerce, Bureau of the Census, *1980 Census of Population, Detailed Population Characteristics, Utah,* Part 46, Table 203, pp. 30–31. Hispanic men graduated at a slightly higher rate than did young women (50.3 percent versus 48.0 percent).

138. Ibid. A higher percentage of Spanish-surnamed men than women (in the fifteen and older group) graduated from college (6.7 percent versus 4.3 percent). A higher percentage of Spanish-surnamed men than women (in the twenty-five and older group) graduated from college (10.0 percent versus 5.7 percent).

139. SOCIO Conference brochure, Nov. 8 and 9, 1985, Marriott Hotel, 75 South West Temple, Salt Lake City, Utah, Box 1, Folder 12, SOCIOC.

140. Robert A. Goldberg, *Grassroots Resistance: Social Movements in Twentieth Century America,* pp. 230–31.

141. Ibid.; pp. 9–10. Susan Herbst makes a similar argument in her work *Politics at the Margin,* especially on pp. 29 and 164. Herbst describes the use of "backchannels" by individuals at the "margin" of politics and how these ties permit the "outsider's" agenda to come to influential people's attention. The leaders of SOCIO were connected to, but not in, leadership positions in some of the most important organizations in the state of Utah.

142. Material incentives are monetary in nature. Solidary benefits are social and derive from association, such as camaraderie or prestige. Purposive rewards are predominantly psychological and are gained by advocating a particular cause or ideological belief. See Márquez, *LULAC,* p. 5.

143. Dr. Orlando A. Rivera, interview, HOH.

144. Márquez, *LULAC,* pp. 6–7.

145. Ibid., p. 8.

146. Robert Nieves, interview, Salt Lake City, Utah, Apr. 19, 1985, HOH, Box 4, Folder 1.

147. David Montejano, "Introduction," in Montejano, *Chicano Politics and Society in the Late Twentieth Century,* p. xxvii.

148. Márquez, *LULAC,* p. 8.

149. Dr. Orlando A. Rivera, interview, HOH.

150. Ignacio M. García, *Chicanismo,* p. 142.

151. Ibid., pp. 9, 11–13.

152. Mauss, *The Angel and the Beehive,* p. 77.

153. For more information on the expansion of the LDS Church among Spanish speakers, see Tullis, *Mormons in Mexico,* pp. 201–11.

154. "As LDS Church Nears Ten Million Mark, How Does It Grow?," *Salt Lake Tribune,* Apr. 5, 1997, p. B1. See also: "La Iglesia Mormona Presenta un Crecimiento: La Mayoria de los Miembros Son Extranjeros," *La Prensa Spanish Newspaper,* Mar. 1–15, 1996, p. 9; United States Department of Commerce, Bureau of the Census, *1990 Census of Population, Social and Economic Characteristics,* Table 48, p. 63; Utah Governor's Office of Hispanic Affairs, *Fiscal Year 1995 Annual Report,* pp. 3–4.

CHAPTER 7. The Mainstreamed and the Polarized:
Hispanics in Northern Utah, 1987–99

1. Ignacio M. García, *Chicanismo,* p. 133.

2. Ibid., p. 139.

3. Díaz-Stevens and Stevens-Arroyo, *Recognizing the Latino Resurgence in U.S. Religion,* p. 179.

4. "Panel Discusses History of Chicano Movement," *Daily Utah Chronicle,* May 7, 1997, pp. 1, 5.

5. Richard Griswold del Castillo, "Latinos and the New Immigration: Mainstreaming and Polarization," in Thomas Gelsinon, ed., *Renato Rosaldo Lecture Series Monograph, Volume 10,* pp. 1–31; see pp. 6 –7.

6. Ignacio M. García, *Chicanismo,* p. 142.

7. "Bureau To Aid Illegal Aliens," *Deseret News,* Apr. 27, 1987, p. B3. For information regarding the impact of recently enacted Illegal Immigration Reform and Immigrant Responsibility Act of 1996 in Utah, see: "'We Want To Be Legal': Immigrants Line Up To Stay in U.S," *Salt Lake Tribune,* Mar. 31, 1997, pp. A1, A6. In Mártin Sánchez Jankowsky's essay "'Where Have All the Nationalists Gone': Change and Persistence in Radical Political Attitudes among Chicanos, 1976–1986," in Montejano's *Chicano Politics and Society in the Late Twentieth Century* (pp. 201–33, see especially pages 220–26), the author notes that, among the individuals in the population under study, those who have achieved some economic mobility are more likely to have discarded radical politics and joined the Democratic or Republican Party.

8. Griswold del Castillo, "Latinos and the New Immigration," p. 31.

9. United States Department of Commerce, Bureau of the Census, *1990 Census of Population, General Population Characteristics,* Table 3, p. 7.

10. Ibid., Table 5, pp. 9–11, and Table 6, pp. 12–25.

11. United States Department of Commerce, Bureau of the Census, *1980 Census of Population, Detailed Population Characteristics,* Part 46, Table 219, pp. 115–24. See also *1990 Census of Population, Social and Economic Characteristics,* Table 5, pp. 65–66.

12. Ibid., Table 96, p. 111.

13. Governor's Office of Planning and Budget, *Economic Report to the Governor,* Jan., 1996, pp. 12–13.

14. "Shift Seen in Federal Spending," *Salt Lake Tribune,* Aug. 26, 1998, p. A1.

15. "Migrants in Utah Are Leaving Nomadic Life and Putting Down Roots," *Salt Lake Tribune,* Dec. 29, 1996, pp. A1, A6–A7.

16. "Growing in Numbers and Influence, Utah Latinos Are Making a Change and Making a Difference," *Salt Lake Tribune,* May 26, 1996, pp. A1, A14–A15.

17. "Migrants in Utah," *Salt Lake Tribune,* Dec. 29, 1996, pp. A1, A6–A7.

18. "'We Want To Be Legal': Immigrants Line Up To Stay in U.S," *Salt Lake Tribune,* Mar. 31, 1997, pp. A1, A6.

19. "Park City Mayoral Candidates Have Time To Apologize to Town's Latinos," *Salt Lake Tribune,* Oct. 9, 1997, p. C4. See also: "Latinos, Anglos Connect in Park City," *Salt Lake Tribune,* May 7, 1997, p. D6; "Priest Warns Against Bigotry in Park City," Oct. 8, 1997, p. D1.

20. "Wendover's Aliens: A Big Scale Bust Rounds Up a Lot of Criticism, Too," *Utah Magazine,* June 22, 1986, p. 6. See also: "Migrants Struggle for Daily Bread," *Salt Lake Tribune,* Nov. 3, 1991, p. A14; Jorge Iber, "Nevada's Neon Jesus: The Catholic Church and Hispanic Casino Workers in Wendover, Utah, 1980–1993," paper presented at Utah State Historical Society Meeting, Price, Utah, July, 1995.

21. Father Reyes Rodríguez, interview with author, Salt Lake City, Utah, Oct. 16, 1993.

22. Dale Stewart, interview with author, Wendover, Nevada, Nov. 6, 1993.

23. Father Reyes Rodriguez, interview with author, Salt Lake City, Utah, Oct. 16, 1993.

24. Yolanda Durán, interview with author, Wendover, Nevada, Nov. 6, 1993.

25. "Migrants in Utah," *Salt Lake Tribune,* Dec. 29, 1996, pp. A1, A6–A7.

26. United States Department of Commerce, Bureau of the Census, *1990 Census of Population, Social and Economic Characteristics,* Table 8, p. 21, and Table 12, p. 26. Disparities regarding unemployment were even more pronounced in Salt Lake (8.9 percent versus 4.6 percent) and Weber Counties (10.4 versus 5.5 percent).

27. Ibid., Table 50, pp. 65–66, Table 5, pp. 9–11, Table 19, p. 47, and Table 54, pp. 88–97. Another possible explanation for this increase in the number of unskilled workers in this population may be the overall youthfulness of the Hispanic populace in comparison to whites. Spanish-speakers in this group tend to be much younger than whites (by almost five years) and have had less time on the job to acquire the skills and training necessary to move into higher level, higher paying positions.

28. Griswold del Castillo, "Latinos and the New Immigration," p. 2.

29. United States Department of Commerce, Bureau of the Census, *1980 Census of Population, Detailed Population Characteristics, Utah,* Part 46, Table 241, pp. 308–12. See also *1990 Census of Population, Social and Economic Characteristics,* Table 53, p. 68.

30. Ibid., *1990 Census of Population, Social and Economic Characteristics,* Table 54, p. 69.

31. Ibid., *1990 Census of Population, Social and Economic Characteristics,* Table 8, p. 21, and Table 12, p. 26. See also "Hispanics Ask Bangerter To Take Action: Request Reforms in Employment, Education, Health and Immigration," *Deseret News,* May 19, 1986, p. 2B.

32. State Office of Hispanic Affairs, *Fiscal Year 1995 Annual Report,* Apr., 1996, pp. 3–4, and *Fiscal Year 1996 Annual Report,* p. 5.

33. At a recent panel discussion, University of Utah sociologist Armando Solórzano estimated that Hispanic students accounted for 87 percent of Utah's school dropouts. Solórzano
claims that this disparity had increased dramatically since the start of the 1990s. In 1993 Hispanic boys left school at 2.5 times the rate for whites, and by 1996 this ratio had increased to 3.3
times. See Solorzano, "The Quest for Educational Equality," unpublished manuscript, 1997,
pp. 21–22.

34. United States Department of Commerce, Bureau of the Census, *1990 Census of Population, Social and Economic Characteristics,* Table 47, p. 62. The 9.1 percent figure includes only
those men and women with four or more years of college training. If the number of Hispanics
in Utah with community college degrees is included, this percentage increases to 14.9 percent.

35. "Ex-U Head: Affirmative Action Needed; Ex-U Head Says," *Salt Lake Tribune,* June 14,
1997, p. D1.

36. "Chicano Scholarship Celebrates 20th Anniversary: A Legacy Continued," *Mundo
Hispano,* Mar. 30, 1995, p. B6. See also State Office of Hispanic Affairs, *Fiscal Year 1995 Annual
Report,* pp. 6–7, and *Fiscal Year 1996 Annual Report,* pp. 10–11.

37. Utah Commission on Criminal and Juvenile Justice, *Detention Study Committee Report,* Dec. 1, 1993, p. ii.

38. State Office of Hispanic Affairs, *Fiscal Year 1995 Annual Report,* pp. 6–7. This infor-
mation is based on criminal activity statistics provided by the various police departments in the
Salt Lake Valley: Murray City, Midvale, Salt Lake City, Sandy City, South Salt Lake City, West
Valley City, and West Jordan police departments and the Salt Lake County sheriff's office.

39. "A Few Words on the 'Gang Problem,'" *Intermountain Hispanic Magazine,* Apr./May,
1994, p. 23.

40. Utah Commission on Criminal and Juvenile Justice, *Strategic Plan of the Advisory
Committee on Disproportionate Minority Confinement: Including Preliminary Recommendations
to the Utah Board of Juvenile Justice,* Jan., 1995, pp. 6, 7.

41. Pat L. Aguilar, letter to membership of Image de Utah, "1994–1995 Accomplishment
Report," copy in author's possession. For a recent listing of Hispanic organizations in the state,
see State Office of Hispanic Affairs and Governor's Hispanic Advisory Council, *State of Utah
Directory of Hispanic Organizations and Publications,* revised Jan. 6, 1995, pp. 2–3. See also Utah
Hispanic Women's Association, *U.H.W.A. News,* Volume 1, Issue 1, Winter, 1995, Ogden, Utah.

42. Brochure published by Impact Business Consultants, Inc. See also Utah Hispanic
Chamber of Commerce, Corporate Proposal, undated and unpublished material, Salt Lake
City, Utah, copies in author's possession.

43. "Hispanics Said To Be Essential Fuel to Utah's Economic Growth," *The Hispanic Register,* Nov./Dec., 1996, p. 19.

44. United States Department of Commerce, Bureau of the Census, *1992 Economic Census, Survey of Minority-Owned Business Enterprises: Hispanics,* June 1996, pp. 20, 26, 32, 51, 54,
74–75, 87, 99, 105.

45. "Emerging Latin Culture Making Its Mark on Salt Lake: Utah's Image as 'The Pretty
White State' Changing; Latin Community Continues To Grow," *Daily Utah Chronicle,* Jan. 3,
1994, pp. 8–9. See also *Paginas Amarillas Hispanas* (Hispanic Yellow Pages), Edition 10, Oct.,
1996. The growth of the Hispanic market had led to the expansion of the Spanish-language media in the Salt Lake City area. A recent list produced by the Utah State Office of Ethnic Affairs
lists four newspapers—*La Prensa, Mundo Hispano, Mundo Latino,* and *Venceremos*—that serve
the needs of Hispanics in this area. In addition, by 1998 Utah's capital city boasted two Spanish-

language radio stations as well as local outlets for the programming of both Telemundo (Channel 48) and Univision (Channel 66).

46. "Police Raid Turns Businessman's American Dream into Nightmare," *Salt Lake Tribune,* May 18, 1997, p. B1.

47. The Institute for Human Resource Development, Migrant Head Start Program, Fiscal Year 1993/1994, Continuing Appropriation Grant, # 90, CM 0144-03, p. 2. For other information on migrants and undocumented aliens in Utah (during the 1970s) see Sam Martínez, "The Undocumented Alien: Impact on Utah," Box 129, Folder 7, SOCIOC.

48. Utah State Office of Education, Utah Migrant Education, *Annual Summer Evaluation Report,* Summer, 1994. In 1994 a total of 2,468 migrant students received services from the following Utah school districts: Alpine, Box Elder, Cache, Davis, Iron, Jordan, Fillmore, Delta, Nebo, North Sanpete, and Ogden, pp. ix–9.

49. "Debate Stirs Over Facilities for Migrant Workers," *Salt Lake Tribune,* Aug. 8, 1986, p. B1.

50. Utah Department of Health, Office of Surveillance and Analysis, Division of Community Health Services, *Utah's Healthy People 2000: Health Status Indicators by Race and Ethnicity,* May, 1993, pp. 1–19.

51. "Weaning Women from Welfare," *Private Eye Weekly,* May 1, 1997, pp. 12–15.

52. "Some Cultures More Ready than Others To Embrace Mormonism," *Salt Lake Tribune,* Apr. 5, 1997, p. B2.

53. United States Department of Commerce, Bureau of the Census, *1990 Census of Population, Social and Economic Characteristics,* Table 48, p. 63.

54. State Office of Hispanic Affairs, *Fiscal Year 1995 Annual Report,* pp. 3–4.

55. Letter from Jessie L. Embry, assistant director of the Charles Redd Center for Western Studies at Brigham Young University, to Jorge Iber, Apr. 28, 1997, copy of letter in author's possession.

56. Embry, *"In His Own Language,"* p. 94.

57. Ibid., pp. 94, 46, 123.

58. Mooney, *Salt of the Earth,* pp. 418–21. For a recent listing of masses offered in Spanish throughout the diocese (which covers the entire state), see *Intermountain Hispanic Magazine,* Sept./Oct. 1993, p. 9.

59. Sillitoe, *A History of Salt Lake County,* pp. 271–73.

60. *Short History of Guadalupe Center,* brochure, Guadalupe Center, Salt Lake City, Utah, May, 1996, pp. 1–2.

61. Ibid., p. 3. Figures for this program continued to grow during the 1990s. For the 1995–96 school year, the total expenditures for these programs equaled $944,935. See *Guadalupe Schools, Year-End Newsletter—1996,* Guadalupe Center, Salt Lake City, Utah, May, 1996.

62. Jessie L. Embry, "Cultural Diversity in the Intermountain West: Ethnic Members of the Mormon Church in Utah," unpublished manuscript, p. 9. Embry estimates that Utah's population is 72.0 percent Mormon and 3.8 percent Catholic, with all other denominations totaling less than 1.0 percent each.

63. "Cinco de Mayo Began with a Battle: Now It's Leaving Them in Stitches; Holiday is a Banner Day for Comedians," *Salt Lake Tribune,* May 5, 1997, p. D1.

64. For an example of the types of activities among other national groups in Utah, see "Club Infantil de la Colonia Colombiana," *La Prensa Spanish Newspaper,* Mar. 1–15, 1996, p. 12.

65. Dr. Jeffrey Garcilazo, letter to the editor, *Daily Utah Chronicle,* May 25, 1995, p. 7.

66. Latino Educational Association Committee, letter to the editor, *Daily Utah Chronicle,* May 18, 1994, p. 8.

67. Dr. Jeffrey Garcilazo, letter to the editor, *Daily Utah Chronicle,* May 25, 1995, p. 7; "Equality Basis of Chicano Movement," *Daily Utah Chronicle,* May 20, 1994, p. 1.

68. *Hispano/Latino Newsletter,* Weber State University, Autumn Quarter, 1996, p. 4.

69. Brochure for the UCLR's 1996 Hispanic Unity and Youth Leadership Training Conference, Celebracion Centenial, 200 Years of History, 100 Years of Contribution.

70. UCLR's board of directors includes a representative from the state's Office of Hispanic Affairs, the Catholic Diocese, and both major political parties, providing the organization with "routine access to government officials" and an opportunity to "influence the direction of decisions." See Goldberg, *Grassroots Resistance,* pp. 9–10.

71. "Panel Discusses History of Chicano Movement," *Daily Utah Chronicle,* May 7, 1997, pp. 1, 5.

72. "Of the Wendover Immigration Raid," *The Event Newspaper,* June, 1986, p. 8.

73. "Wendover's Aliens: A Big Scale Bust Rounds Up a Lot of Criticism, Too," *Utah Magazine,* June 22, 1986, pp. 4–6.

74. "Hispanics Considering Rights Suit as a Result of Wendover Arrests," *Deseret News,* Apr. 11, 1986, p. B15.

75. "Latino Activist: Provo Cops Overstep Bounds When They Ask Immigration Questions," *Salt Lake Tribune,* Mar. 6, 1994, p. B2.

76. "Traditional Dogma Converting Utah Latinos to GOP," *Salt Lake Tribune,* Apr. 8, 1995, p. A1. See also "Latinos Se Preguntan Cual Fue el Motivo de la Consfiscacion de Drogas en Salt Lake," (Latinos Ask Themselves about the Motive for the Confiscation of Drugs in Salt Lake), *La Prensa Spanish Newspaper,* Mar. 14, 1995, pp. 1, 7.

77. "Provo Cops Overstep Bounds," *Salt Lake Tribune,* Mar. 6, 1994, p. B2.

78. "Utah Police May Receive INS Powers; Opponents Fear Officers Will Target Minorities," *Salt Lake Tribune,* July 5, 1997, p. D1; "Officers To Receive Limited INS Powers," *Salt Lake Tribune,* July 18, 1997, p. B2; "S.L. Police as INS Agents: Is This a Good Idea; Police as INS Agents: Is This Good," *Salt Lake Tribune,* Oct. 13, 1997, p. B1.

79. "Hispanic-American Festival Comes to Franklin Quest Field," *Salt Lake Tribune,* Aug. 30, 1996, pp. F1, F5.

80. "Latino Fest Draws Crowds, Not Critics," *Salt Lake Tribune,* Aug. 31, 1996, pp. B1, B11.

81. Sommers, "Inventing Latinismo," pp. 33–53; Michael Jones-Correa and David L. Leal, "Becoming 'Hispanic': Secondary Panethnic Identification among Latin American–Origin Populations in the United States," *Hispanic Journal of Behavioral Sciences* 18 (May, 1996): 214–54.

82. State Office of Hispanic Affairs, *Fiscal Year 1995 Annual Report,* p. 33.

Conclusion: "A Place in the American Mosaic"

1. Saragoza, "Recent Chicano Historiography," pp. 1–77.

2. "Utah's People of Color: The East-West Wall Hasn't Fallen in Racially Divided S.L. Valley," *Salt Lake Tribune,* Mar. 20, 1994, pp. A1, A4. In a census brief (of the 1990 federal census) the Governor's Office of Planning and Budget revealed that Hispanics accounted for approximately one-half of the population of the border town of Wendover (in Tooele County). See

Governor's Office of Planning and Budget, *1990 Census Brief: Minorities of Utah, Second in a Series of 1990 Census Analysis,* pp. 10, 14.

3. See the following articles in local newspapers and magazines for an overview of this trend: "A Difference of Style: While State Representative Patrice Argent Works To Form Coalitions, Representative Loretta Baca Is Bursting Balloons," *Private Eye Weekly,* Mar. 6, 1997, p. 8, 13; "Beating the Odds: Hard Work Has Put Minority-Owned Businesses on Path to Success," *Salt Lake Tribune,* Oct. 20, 1996, pp. E1, E2; "Maximo R. Guerra: YLD Profile," *Utah Bar Journal* 9 (Apr., 1996): 28–29; Zions Bank, *1994 Community Reinvestment Act Statement,* Zions Bank, Salt Lake City, Utah, 1994, copy in author's possession. For more information on the development of Hispanic-owned business firms in northern Utah, see Jorge Iber, "A Report on Hispanic Owned Businesses in Northern Utah," unpublished manuscript, 1997; and United States Department of Commerce, Bureau of the Census, *1992 Economic Census, Survey of Minority-Owned Business Enterprises: Hispanics,* June, 1996, pp. 20, 26, 32, 51, 54, 74, 75, 87, 99, 105.

4. For one view on the drug problem on Salt Lake City's west side, see Henry Quintana and Ben Fulton, "The Drug Dealing Life," *Private Eye Weekly,* Jan. 9, 1997, pp. 9–11, 13. For one view on the limitation of Chicano studies programs at the University of Utah, see Marco Leavitt, "Why Can't U Keep Its Latina(o) Faculty?," *Venceremos* 3 (Fall, 1995): 3.

5. Vargas, *Proletarians of the North,* p. 209.

BIBLIOGRAPHY

BOOKS

Acuña, Rodolfo. *Occupied America: A History of Chicanos.* New York: Harper and Row, 1988.
———. *Occupied America: The Chicano's Struggle Toward Liberation.* San Francisco: Canfield Press, 1972.
Alexander, Thomas G., and James B. Allen. *Mormons and Gentiles: A History of Salt Lake City.* Boulder: Pruett Publishing Company, 1984.
Allsup, Carl. *The American G.I. Forum: Origins and Evolution.* Austin: Center for Mexican American Studies, University of Texas, 1982.
Almaguer, Tomás. *Racial Fault Lines: The Historical Origins of White Supremacy in California.* Berkeley: University of California Press, 1994.
Alonso, Armando. *Tejano Legacy: Rancheros and Settlers in South Texas, 1734–1900.* Albuquerque: University of New Mexico Press, 1998.
Anderson, Karen. *Wartime Women: Sex Roles, Family Relations and the Status of Women During World War II.* Westport, Conn.: Greenwood Press, 1981.
Annis, Sheldon. *God and Production in a Guatemalan Town.* Austin: University of Texas Press, 1990.
Arrington, Leonard J. *Beet Sugar in the West: A History of the Utah-Idaho Sugar Company, 1891–1966.* Seattle: University of Washington Press, 1966.
———. *Great Basin Kingdom: An Economic History of Latter-day Saints, 1830– 1900.* Lincoln: University of Nebraska Press, 1958.
———. *The Richest Hole on Earth: A History of Bingham Copper Mine.* Logan: Utah State University Press, 1963.
Bailey, Lynn Robison. *Old Reliable: A History of Bingham Canyon, Utah.* Tucson: Westernlore Press, 1988.
Baker, Richard. *Los Dos Mundos: Rural Mexican Americans, Another America.* Logan: Utah State University Press, 1995.
Balderrama, Francisco E. *In Defense of La Raza: The Los Angeles Mexican Consulate and the Mexican Community, 1929–1936.* Tucson: University of Arizona Press, 1982.
Balderrama, Francisco E., and Raymond Rodríguez. *Decade of Betrayal: Mexican Repatriation in the 1930s.* Albuquerque: University of New Mexico Press, 1995.
Barrera, Mario. *Beyond Aztlan: Ethnic Autonomy in Comparative Perspective.* New York: Praeger, 1988.
———. *Race and Class in the Southwest: A Theory of Racial Inequality.* Notre Dame: University of Notre Dame Press, 1979.

Bean, Frank D., and Marta Tienda. *The Hispanic Population of the United States.* New York: Russell Sage Foundation, 1987.

Benjamin, Lois. *The Black Elite: Facing the Color Line in the Twilight of the Twentieth Century.* Chicago: Nelson-Hall Publishers, 1991.

Bitton, Davis, and Maureen Ursenbach Beecher, eds. *New Views of Mormon History: A Collection of Essays in Honor of Leonard J. Arrington.* Salt Lake City: University of Utah Press, 1987.

Blackwelder, Julia Kirk. *Women of the Depression: Caste and Culture in San Antonio, 1929–1939.* College Station: Texas A&M University Press, 1998.

Blea, Irene Isabel. *Researching Chicano Communities: Social-Historical, Physical, Psychological, and Spiritual Space.* Westport, Conn.: Praeger, 1995.

Bodnar, John E. *The Transplanted: A History of Immigrants in Urban America.* Bloomington: Indiana University Press, 1985.

Boswell, Thomas D. *The Cuban American Experience: Culture, Image, and Perspectives.* Totowa, N. J.: Rowan and Allanhald, 1981.

Brekenridge, R. Douglas, and Francisco O. García-Tetro. *Iglesia Presbiteriana: A History of Presbyterians and Mexican Americans in the Southwest.* San Antonio: Trinity University Press, 1974.

Broadbent, Elizabeth. *The Distribution of Mexican Population in the United States.* San Francisco: R and E Research Associates, 1972.

Byrne, David R., Lionel A. Maldonado, and Orlando A. Rivera. *Chicanos in Utah.* Salt Lake City: Utah State Board of Education, 1976.

Camarillo, Albert. *Chicanos in a Changing Society: From Mexican Pueblos to American Barrios in Santa Barbara and Southern California, 1848–1930.* Cambridge: Harvard University Press, 1979.

Carter, Thomas P. *Mexican Americans in School: A History of Educational Neglect.* New York: College Entrance Examination Board, 1970.

Chávez, John R. *The Lost Land: The Chicano Image of the Southwest.* Albuquerque: University of New Mexico Press, 1984.

Chávez, Linda. *Out of the Barrio: Toward a New Politics of Hispanic Assimilation.* New York: Basic Books, 1991.

Chestnut, R. Andrew. *Born Again in Brazil: The Pentecostal Boom and the Pathogens of Poverty.* New Brunswick, N. J.: Rutgers University Press, 1997.

Cohen, Lizbeth. *Making a New Deal: Industrial Workers in Chicago, 1919–1939.* New York: Cambridge University Press, 1990.

Cronon, William, George Miles, and Jay Gitlin, eds. *Under an Open Sky: Rethinking America's Western Past.* New York: W. W. Norton and Company, 1992.

Daniel, Cletus E. *Chicano Workers and the Politics of Fairness: The FEPC in the Southwest, 1941–1945.* Austin: University of Texas Press, 1991.

De Baca, Vincent C., ed. *La Gente: Hispano History and Life in Colorado.* Denver: Colorado Historical Society, 1998.

De la Garza, Rodolfo O., Louis DeSipio, F. Chris García, John A. García, and Angelo Falcón. *Latino Voices: Mexican, Puerto Rican, and Cuban Perspectives on American Politics.* Boulder: Westview Press, 1998.

De León, Arnoldo. *Ethnicity in the Sunbelt: A History of Mexican Americans in Houston.* Houston: Mexican American Studies Program, University of Houston, 1989.

———. *Memorias: A West Texas Life.* Lubbock: Texas Tech University Press, 1991.

————. *Tejanos and the Numbers Game: A Socio Historical Interpretation from the Federal Census, 1850–1900.* Albuquerque: University of New Mexico Press, 1989.

————. *They Called Them Greasers: Anglo Attitudes toward Mexicans in Texas, 1821–1900.* Austin: University of Texas Press, 1983.

Deutsch, Sarah. *No Separate Refuge: Culture, Class, and Gender on an Anglo Hispanic Frontier, 1880–1940.* New York: Oxford University Press, 1987.

Díaz-Stevens, Ana María, and Anthony M. Stevens-Arroyo. *Recognizing the Latino Resurgence in U. S. Religion: The Emmaus Paradigm.* Boulder: Westview Press, 1998.

Dolan, Jay P., and Allan Figueroa Deck, S. J., eds. *Hispanic Catholic Culture in the U. S.: Issues and Concerns.* Notre Dame: University of Notre Dame Press, 1994.

Dolan, Jay P., and Gilberto Hinojosa, eds. *Mexican Americans and the Catholic Church, 1900–1965.* Notre Dame: University of Notre Dame Press, 1994.

Dolan, Jay P., and Jaime R. Vidal, eds. *Puerto Rican and Cuban Catholics in the U. S., 1900–1965.* Notre Dame: University of Notre Dame Press, 1994.

Edsforth, Ronald William. *Class Conflict and Cultural Consensus: The Making of a Mass Consumer Society in Flint, Michigan.* New Brunswick, N. J.: Rutgers University Press, 1987.

Embry, Jessie L. *Black Saints in a White Church: Contemporary African American Mormons.* Salt Lake City: Signature Books, 1991.

————. *In His Own Language: Mormon Spanish-Speaking Congregations in the United States.* Salt Lake City: Signature Books, 1997.

Fox, Geoffrey. *Hispanic Nation: Culture, Politics and the Construction of Identity.* Secaucus, N. J.: Carol Publishing Group, 1996.

Gamboa, Erasmo. *Mexican Labor and World War II: Braceros in the Pacific Northwest, 1942–1947.* Austin: University of Texas Press, 1990.

García, Ignacio M. *Chicanismo: The Forging of a Militant Ethos Among Mexican Americans.* Tucson: University of Arizona Press, 1997.

García, Juan R. *Mexicans in the Midwest, 1900–1932.* Tucson: University of Arizona Press, 1996.

García, Maria Cristina. *Havana USA: Cuban Exiles and Cuban Americans in South Florida, 1959–1994.* Berkeley: University of California Press, 1996.

García, Mario T. *Desert Immigrants: The Mexicans of El Paso, 1880–1920.* New Haven: Yale University Press, 1981.

————. *Memories of Chicano History: The Life and Narrative of Bert Corona.* Berkeley: University of California Press, 1994.

————. *Mexican Americans: Leadership, Ideology, and Identity, 1930–1960.* New Haven: Yale University Press, 1989.

————. *The Making of a Mexican American Mayor: Raymond L. Telles of El Paso.* El Paso: Texas Western Press, 1998.

Garcia, Richard A. *Rise of the Mexican American Middle Class: San Antonio, 1929–1941.* College Station: Texas A&M University Press, 1991.

Garrard-Burnett, Virginia, and David Stoll, eds. *Rethinking Protestantism in Latin America.* Philadelphia: Temple University Press, 1993.

Garrett, William R., ed. *Social Consequences of Religious Belief.* New York: Paragon House, 1989.

Gelsinon, Thomas, ed. *Renato Rosaldo Lecture Series Monograph, Volume 10.* Tucson: University of Arizona Press, 1992–93.

Goldberg, Robert A. *Grassroots Resistance: Social Movements in Twentieth Century America.* Belmont, Calif.: Wadsworth Publishing Company, 1991.

Gómez, Arthur R. *Quest for the Golden Circle: The Four Corners and the Metropolitan West, 1945–1970.* Albuquerque: University of New Mexico Press, 1994.

Griswold del Castillo, Richard. *La Familia: Chicano Families in the Urban Southwest, 1848 to the Present.* Notre Dame: University of Notre Dame Press, 1984.

———. *The Los Angeles Barrio, 1850–1890: A Social History.* Berkeley: University of California Press, 1979.

Guerin-Gonzalez, Camille. *Mexican Workers, American Dreams: Immigration, Repatriation, and California Farm Labor, 1900–1939.* New Brunswick, N. J.: Rutgers University Press, 1994.

Gutiérrez, David G. *Walls and Mirrors: Mexican Americans, Mexican Immigrants and the Politics of Ethnicity.* Berkeley: University of California Press, 1995.

———. ed. *Between Two Worlds: Mexican Immigrants in the United States.* Wilmington, Del.: Jaguar Books on Latin America, Scholarly Resources, Inc., 1996.

Gutiérrez, Félix F., and Jorge Reina Schement. *Spanish Language Radio in the Southwestern United States.* Austin: Center for Mexican American Studies, University of Texas, 1979.

Gutiérrez, Ramón A. *When Jesus Came, the Corn Mothers Went Away: Marriage, Sexuality, and Power in New Mexico, 1500–1846.* Stanford, Calif.: Stanford University Press, 1991.

Haas, Lisbeth. *Conquest and Historical Identities in California, 1769–1936.* Berkeley: University of California Press, 1995.

Hallum, Anne Motley. *Beyond Missionaries: Toward an Understanding of the Protestant Movement in Central America.* Lanham, Md.: Rowan and Littlefield, 1996.

Harrison, Rebecca C. *Houston Hispanic Entrepreneurs: Profile and Needs Assessment.* New York: Garland Publishers, 1995.

Herbst, Susan. *Politics at the Margin: Historical Studies of Public Expression Outside the Mainstream.* New York: Cambridge University Press, 1994.

Hernandez, José Amaro. *Mutual Aid for Survival: The Case of the Mexican American.* Malabar, Fla.: Krieger, 1983.

Herrera, Agrícol Lozano. *Historia Del Mormonismo en Mexico.* Mexico City: Editorial Zarahemla, S. A., 1983.

Hill, Patricia Everidge. *Dallas: The Making of a Modern City.* Austin: University of Texas Press, 1996.

Hinojosa, Gilberto Miguel. *A Borderlands Town in Transition: Laredo, 1755–1870.* College Station: Texas A&M University Press, 1983.

Hoffman, Abraham. *Unwanted Mexican Americans in the Great Depression: Repatriation Pressures, 1929–1939.* Tucson: University of Arizona Press, 1974.

Holland, Clifton L. *The Religious Dimension in Hispanic Los Angeles: A Protestant Case Study.* South Pasadena: William Carey Library, 1974.

Johnson, G. Wesley, Jr. *Phoenix in the Twentieth Century: Essays in Community History.* Norman: University of Oklahoma Press, 1993.

Keefe, Susan E., and Amado M. Padilla. *Chicano Ethnicity.* Albuquerque: University of New Mexico Press, 1987.

Kelen, Leslie G. *The Other Utahns: A Photographic Portfolio.* Salt Lake City: University of Utah Press, 1988.

Knowlton, Charles S., ed. *Social Accommodation: American West Center Occasional Papers.* Salt Lake City: American West Center, 1975.

Lieberson, Stanley. *A Piece of the Pie: Blacks and White Immigrants Since 1880.* Berkeley: University of California Press, 1980.

Light, Ivan H. *Ethnic Enterprise in America: Business and Welfare among Chinese, Japanese and Blacks*. Berkeley: University of California Press, 1972.

———. *Immigration and Entrepreneurship: Culture, Capital, and Ethnic Networks*. New Brunswick, N. J.: Transaction Publishers, 1993.

Limerick, Patricia Nelson. *Legacy of Conquest: The Unbroken Past of the American West*. New York: W. W. Norton and Company, 1987.

Loewen, James W. *The Mississippi Chinese: Between Black and White*. Cambridge: Harvard University Press, 1971.

López, José Timoteo. *La Historia de La Sociedad Proteccion Mutua de Trabajadores Unidos*. New York: Comet Press Books, 1958.

Maldonado, Lionel A., and David R. Byrne. *The Social Ecology of Chicanos in Utah*. Iowa City: University of Iowa, 1978.

Mangum, Garth L., and Bruce Blumell. *The Mormons' War on Poverty: A History of LDS Welfare, 1830–1990*. Salt Lake City: University of Utah Press, 1993.

Marquez, Benjamin. *LULAC: The Evolution of a Mexican American Political Organization*. Austin: University of Texas Press, 1993.

Martin, Marty E., and R. Scott Appleby, eds. *Accounting for Fundamentalisms: The Dynamic Character of Movements, Volume 4*. Chicago: University of Chicago Press, 1994.

Martínez, Oscar J. *Border Boom Town: Ciudad Juarez Since 1848*. Austin: University of Texas Press, 1978.

Matovina, Timothy M. *Tejano Religion and Ethnicity: San Antonio, 1821–1860*. Austin: University of Texas Press, 1995.

Mauss, Armand L. *The Angel and the Beehive: The Mormon Struggle with Assimilation*. Urbana: University of Illinois Press, 1994.

May, Dean L. *Three Frontiers: Family, Land, and Society in the American West, 1850–1900*. New York: Cambridge University Press, 1994.

———. *Utah: A People's History*. Salt Lake City: University of Utah Press, 1987.

May, Dean L., ed. *A Dependent Commonwealth: Utah's Economy from Statehood to the Great Depression*. Provo: Brigham Young University Press, 1974.

Mayer, Vicente. *Utah: A Hispanic History*. Salt Lake City: American West Center, University of Utah Printing Service, 1975.

Mayer, Vicente, ed. *Working Papers toward a History of the Spanish-Speaking Peoples of Utah*. Salt Lake City: American West Center, Mexican American Documentation Project, University of Utah, 1973.

Mazón, Mauricio. *The Zoot-Suit Riots: The Psychology of Symbolic Annihilation*. Austin: University of Texas Press, 1984.

McNitt, Frank. *The Indian Traders*. Norman: University of Oklahoma Press, 1962.

Meier, Matt S., and Feliciano Ribera. *Mexican Americans/American Mexicans: From Conquistadors to Chicanos*. New York: Hill and Wang, 1993.

Menchaca, Martha. *The Mexican Outsiders: A Community History of Marginalization and Discrimination in California*. Austin: University of Texas Press, 1995.

Meyer, Doris. *Speaking for Themselves: Neomexicano Cultural Identity and the Spanish-Language Press, 1880–1920*. Albuquerque: University of New Mexico Press, 1996.

Milner, Clyde A., II, ed. *A New Significance: Re-Envisioning the History of the American West*. New York: Oxford University Press, 1996.

Miranda, M. L. *A History of Hispanics in Southern Nevada*. Reno: University of Nevada Press, 1997.

Montejano, David. *Anglos and Mexicans in the Making of Texas, 1836–1986.* Austin: University of Texas Press, 1987.

———, ed. *Chicano Politics and Society in the Late Twentieth Century.* Austin: University of Texas Press, 1999.

Mooney, Bernice M. *Salt of the Earth: The History of the Catholic Church in Utah, 1776–1987.* Salt Lake City: Catholic Diocese of Salt Lake City, 1992.

———. *Salt of the Earth: The History of the Catholic Diocese of Salt Lake City.* Salt Lake City: Litho Graphics, 1987.

Moore, Joan, and Raquel Pinderhughes. *In the Barrios: Latinos and the Underclass Debate.* New York: Russell Sage Foundation, 1993.

Morris, Aldon D. *The Origins of the Civil Rights Movement: Black Communities Organizing for Change.* New York: Free Press, 1984.

Muñoz, Carlos, Jr. *Youth, Identity and Power: The Chicano Movement.* New York: Verso, 1989.

Owsley, Beatrice Rodríguez. *The Hispanic American Entrepreneur: An Oral History of the American Dream.* New York: Twayne Publishers, 1992.

Padilla, Félix M. *Latino Ethnic Consciousness: The Case of Mexican Americans and Puerto Ricans in Chicago.* Notre Dame: University of Notre Dame Press, 1985.

Peña, Manuel H. *The Texas-Mexican Conjunto: History of a Working Class Music.* Austin: University of Texas Press, 1985.

Pérez-Firmat, Gustavo. *Life on the Hyphen: The Cuban American Way.* Austin: University of Texas Press, 1994.

Poll, Richard D., Thomas G. Alexander, Eugene E. Campbell, and David E. Miller, eds. *Utah's History.* Logan: Utah State University Press, 1989.

Portes, Alejandro, and Rubén G. Rumbaut. *Immigrant America: A Portrait.* Berkeley: University of California Press, 1996.

Portes, Alejandro, and Robert L. Bach. *Latin Journey: A Longitudinal Study of Cuban and Mexican Immigrants in the United States.* Berkeley: University of California Press, 1985.

Powell, Alan Kent. *Utah Remembers World War II.* Logan: Utah State University Press, 1991.

Reyes, David, and Tom Waldman. *Land of a Thousand Dances: Chicano Rock 'n' Roll in Southern California.* Albuquerque: University of New Mexico Press, 1998.

Romo, Ricardo. *History of a Barrio: East Los Angeles.* Austin: University of Texas Press, 1983.

Rosenbaum, Robert J. *Mexicano Resistance in the Southwest: "The Sacred Right of Self Preservation."* Austin: University of Texas Press, 1981.

Ruiz, Vicki L., and Susan Tiano, eds. *Women on the U. S.-Mexico Border: Responses to Change.* Boston: Allen & Unwin, 1987.

Sánchez, George J. *Becoming Mexican American: Ethnicity, Culture, and Identity in Chicano Los Angeles, 1900–1945.* New York: Oxford University Press, 1993.

San Miguel, Guadalupe, Jr. *"Let Them All Take Heed:" Mexican Americans and the Campaign for Educational Equality in Texas, 1910–1981.* Austin: University of Texas Press, 1987.

Sheridan, Thomas E. *Del Rancho al Barrio: The Mexican Legacy of Tucson.* Tucson: The Mexican Heritage Project, Arizona Heritage Center, 1983.

———. *Los Tucsonenses: The Mexican Community of Tucson, 1854–1941.* Tucson: University of Arizona Press, 1986.

Sherman, Amy L. *The Soul of Development: Biblical Christianity and Economic Transformation in Guatemala.* New York: Oxford University Press, 1997.

Sillitoe, Linda. *A History of Salt Lake County.* Salt Lake City: Utah State Historical Society and Salt Lake County Commission, 1996.

Smith, Michael M. *The Mexicans in Oklahoma.* Norman: University of Oklahoma Press, 1980.

The Spanish-Speaking American Challenge: A Report on the 1974 Brigham Young University Chicano Conference. Provo: Brigham Young University Publications, 1975.

Stavans, Ilan. *The Hispanic Condition: Reflections on Culture & Identity in America.* New York: HarperPerennial, 1995.

Takaki, Ronald. *A Different Mirror: A History of Multicultural America.* New York: Little, Brown and Company, 1993.

Taylor, Quintard. *The Forging of a Black Community: Seattle's Central District from 1870 through the Civil Rights Era.* Seattle: University of Washington Press, 1994.

Tullis, F. Lamond. *Mormons in Mexico: The Dynamics of Faith and Culture.* Logan: Utah State University Press, 1993.

Tullis, F. Lamond, Arthur Henry King, Spencer J. Palmer, and Douglas F. Tobler, eds. *Mormonism: A Faith for All Cultures.* Provo: Brigham Young University Press, 1978.

Vargas, Zaragosa. *Proletarians of the North: A History of Mexican Industrial Workers in Detroit and the Midwest, 1917–1933.* Berkeley: University of California Press, 1993.

Waldinger, Roger, Howard Aldrich, Robin Ward, and Associates, eds. *Ethnic Entrepreneurs: Immigrant Business in Industrial Societies.* Newbury Park, Calif.: Sage Publications, 1990.

Walker, Juliet K. *The History of Black Business in America: Capitalism, Race, Entrepreneurship.* New York: Twayne Publishers, 1998.

Weber, David J. *Foreigners in Their Native Land: Historical Roots of Mexican Americans.* Albuquerque: University of New Mexico Press, 1973.

White, Richard. *"It's Your Misfortune and None of My Own": A New History of the American West.* Norman: University of Oklahoma Press, 1991.

Whitten, Norman E., ed. *Cultural Transformations and Ethnicity in Modern Ecuador.* Urbana: University of Illinois Press, 1981.

Wilson, Chris. *The Myth of Santa Fe: Creating a Modern Regional Tradition.* Albuquerque: University of New Mexico Press, 1997.

DOCTORAL DISSERTATIONS, MASTER'S THESES, LECTURES, AND
UNPUBLISHED MANUSCRIPTS AND LECTURES

Allen, Joseph E. "A Sociological Study of Mexican Assimilation in Salt Lake City." Master's thesis, University of Utah, 1947.

Arrington, Leonard J. "Utah, the New Deal and the Depression of the 1930s." Dello G. Dayton Memorial Lecture, March 25, 1982, Weber State College, Ogden, Utah.

Blair, William C. "An Ethnological Survey of Mexicans and Puerto Ricans in Bingham Canyon, Utah." Master's thesis, University of Utah, 1948.

Chambers, Antonette. "Utah's Rosies: Women in the Utah War Industries during World War II." Master's thesis, University of Utah, 1987.

Clinchy, Everett Ross, Jr. "Equality of Opportunity for Latin Americans in Texas: A Study of Economic, Social, and Educational Discrimination against Latin Americans in Texas and Efforts of the State Government on Their Behalf." Ph.D. diss., Columbia University, 1954.

"Company History of Manuel's Fine Foods, Incorporated." Unpublished manuscript. Copy in author's possession.

Crampton, Helen Mickelsen. "Acculturation of the Mexican American in Salt Lake County, Utah." Ph.D. diss., University of Utah, 1967.

Embry, Jessie L. "Cultural Diversity in the Intermountain West: Ethnic Members of the Mormon Church in Utah." Unpublished manuscript. Copy in author's possession.

Ensign, John Dale, II. "Two Unions in the Utah Copper Industry: The Effect of Ideology upon Their Dealings with Management." Master's thesis, University of Utah, 1957.

Garcilazo, Jeffrey Marcos. "Traqueros: Mexican Railroad Workers in the United States, 1870 to 1930." Ph.D. diss., University of California, Santa Barbara, 1995.

Godbold, Barbara Louise. "An Examination of the Maintenance of Ethnic Identity in the Small Urban Community." Ph.D. diss., Rutgers, the State University of New Jersey, 1983.

Henderson, Stanley H. "Social and Academic Problems of Spanish-Speaking Students in Davis County, Central Junior High." Master's thesis, University of Utah, 1958.

Iber, Jorge. "Nevada's Neon Jesus: The Catholic Church and Hispanic Casino Workers in Wendover, Utah, 1980–1993." Paper presented at Utah State Historical Society Meeting, Price, Utah, July, 1995. Unpublished manuscript. Copy in author's possession.

———. "A Report on Hispanic Owned Businesses in Northern Utah." Unpublished manuscript, 1997. Copy in author's possession.

Johnson, Martin Alden. "A Comparison of Mormon and Non-Mormon Ethnic Attitudes." Ph.D. diss., Brigham Young University, 1973.

Knight, Robert D. "A Study of the Role of the Episcopal Diocese of Los Angeles in Meeting the Psychosocial Needs of Hispanics." Master's thesis, University of California, Long Beach, 1989.

Luke, David Bowen. "Academic and Social Differences between Mexican and Non-Mexican Students at Layton Senior High School." Master's thesis, University of Utah, 1971.

Martínez, Steven Sandoval. "An Evaluation of Various Admission Procedures and the 1970 Ford Foundation Program in Relation to Mexican-American and American Indian Students at the University of Utah." Master's thesis, University of Utah, 1971.

Rivera, Orlando A. "A Descriptive Study of Students of Spanish-Speaking Descent at West High School." Master's thesis, University of Utah, 1959.

Saenz, Hulberto. "Perceptions toward School of Mexican American Secondary School Leavers and Remainers in Utah Public Schools." Ph.D. diss., University of Southern California, 1990.

Schermocker, Ruth. "A Study of Various Events in the Life of Juan Valente Trinidad de San Rafael Torrez Alvarez." Salt Lake City, Utah. Unpublished manuscript. Copy in author's possession.

Solórzano, Armando. "The Quest for Educational Equality: Mexican Americans and Hispanics in Utah." Unpublished manuscript, 1997. Copy in author's possession.

Stevens, Deon O. "A Status Study of a Group of Mexican-American Children in Layton Elementary School." Master's thesis, University of Utah, 1962.

Ventura, Betty. "La Historia de la Rama Mexicana" (The History of the Lucero Ward). Salt Lake City, Utah, 1972. Unpublished manuscript. Copy in author's possession.

Zone-Andrews, Enrique. "Suggested Competencies for the Hispanic Protestant Church Leader of the Future." Ph.D. diss., Pepperdine University, 1996.

JOURNALS AND EDITED COLLECTIONS

Adams, Eleanor B. "Fray Francisco Atanasio Dominguez and Fray Silvestre Velez de Escalante." *Utah Historical Quarterly* 44 (Winter, 1976): 40–58.

Alexander, Thomas G. "The Burgeoning of Utah's Economy, 1910–1918." In *A Dependent Commonwealth: Utah's Economy from Statehood to the Great Depression*, edited by Dean L. May. Provo: Brigham Young University Press, 1974.

———. "The Economic Consequences of War: Utah and the Depression of the 1920s." In *A Dependent Commonwealth: Utah's Economy from Statehood to the Great Depression*, edited by Dean L. May. Provo: Brigham Young University Press, 1974.

———. "Stewardship and Enterprise: The LDS Church and the Wasatch Oasis Environment, 1847–1930." *Western Historical Quarterly* 12 (Autumn, 1994): 341–66.

———. "Utah War Industry during World War II: A Human Impact Analysis." *Utah Historical Quarterly* 51 (Winter, 1983): 72–92.

Alexander, Thomas G., and Leonard J. Arrington. "Utah's Small Arms Ammunition Plant during World War II." *Pacific Historical Review* 34 (May, 1965): 185–96.

Allen, James B. "The Changing Impact of Mining on the Economy of Twentieth Century Utah." *Utah Historical Quarterly* 38 (Summer, 1970): 240–55.

———. "Crisis on the Home Front: The Federal Government and Utah's Defense Housing in World War II." *Pacific Historical Review* 38 (November, 1969): 407–28.

Almaguer, Tomás. "Toward the Study of Chicano Colonialism." *Aztlan* 2 (Spring, 1971): 8–21.

Arrington, Leonard J. "The Commercialization of Utah's Economy: Trends and Developments from Statehood to 1910." In *A Dependent Commonwealth: Utah's Economy from Statehood to the Great Depression*, edited by Dean L. May. Provo: Brigham Young University, 1974.

———. "Utah's Pioneer Beet Sugar Plant: The Lehi Factory of the Utah Sugar Company." *Utah Historical Quarterly* 34 (Spring, 1966): 95–120.

Arrington, Leonard J., and Thomas G. Alexander. "Sentinels on the Desert: The Dugway Proving Ground, 1942–1963 and Deseret Chemical Depot, 1942– 1965." *Utah Historical Quarterly* 32 (Winter, 1964): 32–43.

———. "Supply Hub of the West: Defense Depot Ogden, 1941–1964." *Utah Historical Quarterly* 32 (Spring, 1964): 99–121.

Arrington, Leonard J., Thomas G. Alexander, and Eugene A. Erb, Jr. "Utah's Biggest Business: Ogden Air Materiel Area at Hill Air Force Base, 1938–1965." *Utah Historical Quarterly* 33 (Winter, 1965): 9–33.

Arrington, Leonard J., and Archer L. Durham. "Anchors Aweigh in Utah: The U. S. Naval Supply Depot at Clearfield, 1942–1962." *Utah Historical Quarterly* 31 (Spring, 1963): 109–26.

Arrington, Leonard J., and Ralph W. Hansen. "Mormon Economic Organization: A Sheaf of Illustrative Documents." *Utah Historical Quarterly* 28 (January, 1960): 40–55.

Auerbach, Herbert., ed. "Father Escalante's Journal with Related Documents and Maps." *Utah Historical Quarterly* 11 (January–October, 1943): 27–113.

Bastian, Jean-Pierre. "The Metamorphosis of Latin American Protestant Groups: A Sociohistorical Perspective." *Latin American Research Review* 28 (1993): 33–61.

Benavides, E. Ferol. "The Saints among the Saints: A Study of Curanderismo in Utah." *Utah Historical Quarterly* 41 (Autumn, 1973): 373–92.

Buchanan, Frederick S., and Raymond G. Briscoe. "Public Schools as a Vehicle for Social Accommodation in Utah: The Strangers within Our Gates." In *Social Accommodation: American West Center Occasional Papers*, edited by Charles S. Knowlton. Salt Lake City: American West Center, 1975.

Campbell, Eugene E. "The M-Factors in Tooele's History." *Utah Historical Quarterly* 51 (Summer, 1983): 272–88.

Christiansen, John E. "The Impact of World War II." In *Utah's History*, edited by Richard D.

Poll, Thomas G. Alexander, Eugene E. Campbell, and David E. Miller. Logan: Utah State University Press, 1989.

Clayton, James L. "Contemporary Economic Development." In *Utah's History,* edited by Richard D. Poll, Thomas G. Alexander, Eugene E. Campbell, and David E. Miller. Logan: Utah State University Press, 1989.

————. "An Unhallowed Gathering: The Impact of Defense Spending on Utah's Population Growth, 1940–1964." *Utah Historical Quarterly* 34 (Summer, 1966): 227–42.

Coronado, Greg. "Spanish-Speaking Organizations in Utah." In *Working Papers toward a History of Spanish-Speaking Peoples of Utah,* edited by Vicente Mayer. Salt Lake City: American West Center, Mexican American Documentation Project, University of Utah, 1973.

Crowin, Arthur M. "Mexican American History: An Assessment." *Pacific Historical Review* 42 (August, 1973): 269–308.

Dwyer, Robert J. "Catholic Education in Utah: 1875–1975." *Utah Historical Quarterly* 43 (Fall, 1975): 362–78.

Engh, Michael E., S. J. "'A Multiplicity of Faiths': Religion's Impact on Los Angeles and the Urban West, 1890–1940." *Western Historical Quarterly* 27 (Winter, 1997): 463–92.

García, Mario T. "Americanization and the Mexican Immigrant." *Journal of Ethnic Studies* 6 (Summer, 1978): 19–34.

————. "On Mexican Immigration in the U. S. and Chicano History." *Journal of Ethnic Studies* 7 (Spring, 1979): 80–88.

Garcia, Richard A. "The Chicano Movement and the Mexican Community, 1972–1978: An Interpretive Essay." *Socialist Review* 8 (July–October, 1978): 117–36.

Goldberg, Robert A. "Racial Change on the Southern Periphery: The Case of San Antonio, Texas, 1960–1965." *Journal of Southern History* 69 (August, 1983): 349–74.

González, Gilbert G. "Labor and Community: The Camps of Mexican Citrus Pickers in Southern California." *Western Historical Quarterly* 22 (August, 1991): 298–312.

González, William H., and Genaro M. Padilla. "Monticello, the Hispanic Cultural Gateway to Utah." *Utah Historical Quarterly* 52 (Winter, 1984): 7–28.

Griswold del Castillo, Richard. "Latinos and the New Immigration: Mainstreaming and Polarization." In *Renato Rosaldo Lecture Series Monograph, Volume 10,* edited by Thomas Gelsinon. Tucson: University of Arizona Press, 1992–93.

Gutiérrez, David G. "'Significant to Whom?': Mexican Americans and the History of the American West." *Western Historical Quarterly* 24 (November, 1993): 519–39.

Gutiérrez, Ramón A. "Unraveling America's Hispanic Past." *Aztlan* 17 (Spring, 1986): 79–101.

Hafen, Thomas K. "City of Saints, City of Sinners: The Development of Salt Lake City as a Tourist Attraction, 1869–1900." *Western Historical Quarterly* 28 (Autumn, 1997): 343–78.

Hayes-Bautista, David E., and Jorge Chapa. "Latino Terminology: Conceptual Basis of Standardized Terminology." *American Journal of Public Health* 77 (January, 1987): 61–68.

Heinerman, Joseph. "The Mormon Meetinghouse: Reflections of Pioneer Religious and Social Life in Salt Lake City." *Utah Historical Quarterly* 50 (Fall, 1982): 340–53.

Hershberg, Theodore. "Toward the Historical Study of Ethnicity." *Journal of Ethnic Studies* 1 (Spring, 1973): 1–5.

Hinton, Wayne K. "The Economics of Ambivalence: Utah's Depression Experience." *Utah Historical Quarterly* 54 (Summer, 1986): 268–85.

Hurtado, Aida, and Carlos H. Arce. "Mexicans, Chicanos, Mexican Americans, or Pochos . . . Que Somos? The Impact of Language on Ethnic Labeling." *Aztlan* 17 (Spring, 1986): 103–30.

Iber, Jorge. "'El Diablo Nos Esta Llevando': Utah Hispanics and the Great Depression." *Utah Historical Quarterly* 66 (Spring, 1998):159–77.

Jackson, W. Turrentine. "British Impact on the Utah Mining Industry." *Utah Historical Quarterly* 31 (Fall, 1963): 347–75.

Jacobs, G. Clell. "The Phantom Pathfinder: Juan Maria Antonio de Rivera and His Expedition." *Utah Historical Quarterly* 60 (Summer, 1992): 200–223.

Jensen, Richard L. "Mother Tongue: Use of Non-English Languages in the Church of Jesus Christ of Latter-day Saints in the U. S., 1850–1983." In *New Views of Mormon History: A Collection of Essays in Honor of Leonard J. Arrington,* edited by Davis Bitton and Maureen Ursenbach Beecher. Salt Lake City: University of Utah Press, 1987.

Jones-Correa, Michael, and David L. Leal. "Becoming 'Hispanic': Secondary Panethnic Identification among Latin American–Origin Populations in the United States." *Hispanic Journal of Behavioral Sciences* 18 (May, 1996): 214–54.

Márquez, Benjamin. "The Politics of Race and Class: The League of United Latin American Citizens in the Post World War II Period." *Social Science Quarterly* 68 (March, 1987): 84–101.

Mauss, Armand L. "God of Gods: Some Social Consequences of Belief in God among the Mormons." In *Social Consequences of Religious Belief,* edited by William R. Garrett. New York: Paragon House, 1989.

Mayer, Edward H. "The Evolution of Culture and Tradition in Utah's Mexican American Community." *Utah Historical Quarterly* 49 (Spring, 1981): 133–44.

McGolin, John Bernard, S. J. "Two Early Reports Concerning Roman Catholicism in Utah, 1876–1881." *Utah Historical Quarterly* 29 (October, 1961): 332–44.

Melville, Margarita B. "Hispanics: Race, Class, or Ethnicity?" *Journal of Ethnic Studies* 16 (Spring, 1988): 67–83.

Merrill, Jerald H. "Fifty Years with a Future: Salt Lake's Guadalupe Mission and Parish." *Utah Historical Quarterly* 40 (Spring, 1972): 242–64.

Morgan, Paul, and Vicente Mayer. "The Spanish-Speaking Population of Utah: From 1900 to 1935." In *Working Papers toward a History of the Spanish-Speaking Peoples of Utah,* edited by Vicente Mayer. Salt Lake City: American West Center, Mexican American Documentation Project, University of Utah, 1973.

Muratorio, Blanca. "Protestantism, Ethnicity, and Class in Chimborazo." In *Cultural Transformations and Ethnicity in Modern Ecuador,* edited by Norman E. Whitten. Urbana: University of Illinois Press, 1981.

Murguía, Edward. "On Latino/Hispanic Identity." *Latino Studies Journal* 2 (September, 1991): 8–18.

Nelson, Ann. "The Spanish-Speaking Migrant Laborer in Utah, 1950–1965." In *Working Papers toward a History of the Spanish-Speaking Peoples of Utah,* edited by Vicente Mayer. Salt Lake City: American West Center, Mexican American Documentation Project, University of Utah, 1973.

Noble, Antonette Chambers. "Utah's Defense Industries and Workers in World War II." *Utah Historical Quarterly* 59 (Fall, 1991): 365–79.

———. "Utah's Rosies: Women in the Utah War Industries during World War II." *Utah Historical Quarterly* 59 (Spring, 1991): 123–45.

Norget, Kristin. "The Politics of Liberation: The Popular Church, Indigenous Theology, and Grassroots Mobilization in Oaxaca, Mexico." *Latin American Perspectives* 24 (September, 1997): 96–127.

Okihiro, Gary Y. "Oral History and Writing of Ethnic History: A Reconnaissance into Method and Theory." *Oral History Review* 9 (1981): 27–46.

Palmer, William R. "The Early Sheep Industry in Southern Utah." *Utah Historical Quarterly* 42 (Spring, 1974): 178–88.

Papanikolas, Helen Z. "Immigrants, Minorities, and the Great War." *Utah Historical Quarterly* 58 (Fall, 1990): 351–70.

———. "Life and Labor among the Immigrants of Bingham Canyon." *Utah Historical Quarterly* 33 (Fall, 1965): 289–315.

———. "Utah's Coal Lands: A Vital Example of How America Became a Great Nation." *Utah Historical Quarterly* 43 (Spring, 1975): 104–24.

Peck, Gunther. "Padrones and Protest: 'Old' Radicals and 'New' Immigrants in Bingham, Utah, 1905–1912." *Western Historical Quarterly* 24 (May, 1993): 157–78.

Quinn, T. A. "Out of the Depression's Depths: Henry H. Blood's First Year as Governor." *Utah Historical Quarterly* 54 (Summer, 1986): 216–39.

Rivera, Orlando A. "Mormonism and the Chicano." In *Mormonism: A Faith for All Culture,* edited by F. Lamond Tullis, Arthur Henry King, Spencer J. Palmer, and Douglas F. Tobler. Provo: Brigham Young University Press, 1978.

Roberts, Bryan R. "Protestant Groups and Coping with Urban Life in Guatemala City." *American Journal of Sociology* 73 (May, 1968): 753–67.

Roberts, Richard C. "Railroad Depots in Ogden: Microcosm of a Community." *Utah Historical Quarterly* 53 (Winter, 1985): 74–99.

Rodríguez, Joseph A. "Becoming Latinos: Mexican Americans, Chicanos, and the Spanish Myth in the Urban Southwest." *Western Historical Quarterly* 29 (Summer 1998): 166–85.

Rubio-Goldsmith, Raquel. "Oral History: Considerations and Problems for Its Use in the History of Mexicanas in the United States." In *Women on the U. S.- Mexico Border: Responses to Change,* edited by Vicki L. Ruiz and Susan Tiano. Boston: Allen & Unwin, 1987.

Sadler, Richard W. "The Impact of Mining on Salt Lake City." *Utah Historical Quarterly* 47 (Summer, 1979): 236–53.

Saragoza, Alex M. "Recent Chicano Historiography: An Interpretive Essay." *Aztlan* 19 (Spring, 1988–90): 1–77.

Schmalz, Charles L. "Sugar Beets in the Cache Valley: An Amalgamation of Agriculture and Industry." *Utah Historical Quarterly* 57 (Fall, 1989): 370–88.

Simon, Daniel T. "Mexican Repatriation in East Chicago, Indiana." *Journal of Ethnic Studies* 2 (Summer, 1974): 11–23.

Sommers, Laurie Kay. "Inventing Latinismo: The Creation of 'Hispanic' Panethnicity in the United States." *Journal of American Folklore* 104 (November, 1991): 33–53.

Stoffel, Jerome. "The Hesitant Beginnings of the Catholic Church in Utah." *Utah Historical Quarterly* 36 (Winter, 1968): 41–62.

Stoll, David. "'Jesus Is Lord of Guatemala': Evangelical Reform in a Death-Squad State." In *Accounting for Fundamentalisms: The Dynamic Character of Movements, Volume 4,* edited by Marty E. Martin and Scott Appleby. Chicago: University of Chicago Press, 1994.

Taylor, Quintard. "African Americans and Japanese in Seattle." *Western Historical Quarterly* 22 (November, 1991): 401–30.

Treviño, Fernando M. "Standardized Terminology for Hispanic Populations." *American Journal of Public Health* 77 (January, 1987): 69–72.

Ulibarri, Richard O. "Utah's Ethnic Minorities: A Survey." *Utah Historical Quarterly* 40 (Summer, 1972): 210–32.

———. "Utah's Unassimilated Minorities." In *Utah's History*, edited by Richard D. Poll, Thomas G. Alexander, Eugene E. Campbell, and David E. Miller. Logan: Utah State University Press, 1989.

Valle, Maria Eva. "The Quest for Ethnic Solidarity and a New Public Identity among Chicanos and Latinos." *Latino Studies Journal* 2 (September, 1991): 72–83.

Walker, Don D. "The Carlisles: Cattle Barons of the Upper Basin." *Utah Historical Quarterly* 32 (Summer, 1964): 268–84.

Weber, Francis J. "Father Lawrence Scanlan's Report on Catholicism in Utah, 1880." *Utah Historical Quarterly* 34 (Fall, 1966): 283–89.

Yankauer, Alfred. "Hispanic/Latino—What's in a Name?" *American Journal of Public Health* 77 (January, 1987): 15–17.

Archival Sources

Church of Jesus Christ of Latter-day Saints Oral History Program. Archives, History Department, Church of Jesus Christ of Latter-day Saints, Salt Lake City, Utah.

Ethnic Studies Collection, Chicano Studies Collection, University of California, Berkeley.

García, Dr. Hector P. Papers. Texas A&M University, Corpus Christi, Mary and Jeff Bell Library, Department of Special Collections and Archives, Corpus Christi, Texas.

Hispanic Oral Histories. Accession 1369, University of Utah, Marriott Library, Manuscript Division, Salt Lake City, Utah.

Mexican Branch Minutes. Record LR 5089-2, Historical Department, Church Archives, Church of Jesus Christ of Latter-day Saints, Salt Lake City, Utah.

Mexican Branch, Pioneer Stake Historical Records and Minutes. Manuscript Division, Historical Department, Archives, Church of Jesus Christ of Latter-day Saints, Salt Lake City, Utah.

Moyle, James, Oral History Program. Historical Department, Church Archives, Church of Jesus Christ of Latter-day Saints, Salt Lake City, Utah.

Paul Schuster Taylor Papers. BANC/MSS 84/38, Series 3, Carton 11, Folders 24–28, The Bancroft Library, University of California, Berkeley.

Record of Members Collection, 1836–1970. Call Number 375/8, Reel 3847, Church of Jesus Christ of Latter-day Saints, Historical Department, Church Archives, Salt Lake City, Utah.

Salt Lake Catholic Diocese Archives, Salt Lake City, Utah.

Spanish-Speaking Organization for Community, Integrity, and Opportunity (SOCIO) Collection. Accession 1142, University of Utah, Marriott Library, Manuscript Division, Salt Lake City, Utah.

Spanish-Speaking Peoples of Utah. MS 96, University of Utah, Marriott Library, Manuscript Division, Salt Lake City, Utah.

Utah Copper Company, Employee Identification Cards, 1909–19. Accession 1440, University of Utah, Marriott Library, Manuscript Division, Salt Lake City, Utah.

Federal Government Publications

United States Department of Commerce, Bureau of the Census. *Fourteenth Census of the United States, 1920, Volume II, Population General Report and Analytical Tables.* Washington, D. C.: Government Printing Office.

————. *Census of Population, 1950, Characteristics of the Population*, Part 44.

————. *Census of Population, 1960, Characteristics of the Population*, Part 46.

————. *1960 Census Tract for Ogden, Utah.*

————. *1960 Census Tract for Salt Lake City, Utah.*

————. *1970 Census of Population, Characteristics of the Population*, Volume 1, Part 46.

————. *1970 Census of Population, Educational Attainment*, Volume 2, Part 5B.

————. *1977 Survey of Minority Owned Business Enterprises: Spanish Origin.*

————. *1980 Census of Population, Detailed Population Characteristics, Utah*, Part 46.

————. *1990 Census of Population, General Population Characteristics.*

————. *1990 Census of Population, Social and Economic Characteristics, Utah.*

————. *1990 General Population Characteristics, Utah Hispanics.*

————. *1992 Economic Census, Survey of Minority-Owned Business Enterprises: Hispanics.*

UTAH GOVERNMENT PUBLICATIONS

Governor's Office of Planning and Budget. *Economic Report to the Governor.* Salt Lake City, Utah, January, 1996.

————. *1990 Census Brief: Minorities of Utah, Second in a Series of 1990 Census Analysis.* Salt Lake City, Utah, April, 1991.

State Office of Hispanic Affairs. *Fiscal Year 1995 Annual Report.* Salt Lake City, Utah, October, 1995.

State Office of Hispanic Affairs. *Fiscal Year 1996 Annual Report.* Salt Lake City, Utah, October, 1996.

State Office of Hispanic Affairs. *Fiscal Year 1997 Annual Report.* Salt Lake City, Utah, 1997.

State Office of Hispanic Affairs and Governor's Hispanic Advisory Council. *State of Utah Directory of Hispanic Organizations and Publications.* Salt Lake City, Utah, January, 1995.

Utah Bureau of Immigration, Labor and Statistics. *First Report, 1911–1912.* Salt Lake City, Utah, 1913.

Utah Commission on Criminal and Juvenile Justice. *Detention Study Committee Report.* Salt Lake City, Utah, 1993.

————. *Strategic Plan of the Advisory Committee on Disproportionate Minority Confinement: Including Preliminary Recommendations to the Utah Board of Juvenile Justice.* Salt Lake City, Utah, 1993.

Utah Department of Health, Office of Surveillance and Analysis, Division of Community Health Services. *Utah's Healthy People 2000: Health Status Indicators by Race and Ethnicity.* Salt Lake City, Utah, May, 1993.

Utah Governor's Hispanic Advisory Council. *The Conditions of Hispanics in the State of Utah.* Salt Lake City, Utah, September, 1992.

Utah State Office of Education, Utah Migrant Education. *Annual Summer Evaluation Report.* Salt Lake City, Utah, Summer, 1994.

INDEX